HELP YOUR KIDS WITH
computer
science

HELP YOUR KIDS WITH
COMPUTER
SCIENCE

A UNIQUE VISUAL STEP-BY-STEP GUIDE TO COMPUTERS, CODING, AND COMMUNICATION

DK LONDON
Senior Editor Steven Carton
Senior Art Editor Sunita Gahir
US Editor Kayla Dugger
Jacket Editor Claire Gell
Jacket Design Development Manager Sophia MTT
Producer, Pre-production Jacqueline Street
Senior Producer Anna Vallarino
Managing Editor Lisa Gillespie
Managing Art Editor Owen Peyton Jones
Publisher Andrew Macintyre
Associate Publishing Director Liz Wheeler
Art Director Karen Self
Design Director Phil Ormerod
Publishing Director Jonathan Metcalf

DK DELHI
Senior Editor Suefa Lee
Senior Art Editor Shreya Anand
Editorial team Vatsal Verma, Aadithyan Mohan
Art Editor Sachin Singh
Assistant Art Editors Baibhav Parida, Rohit Bhardwaj
Jacket Designer Juhi Sheth
Jackets Editorial Coordinator Priyanka Sharma
Senior DTP Designer Neeraj Bhatia
DTP Designers Bimlesh Tiwary, Rakesh Kumar
Managing Jackets Editor Saloni Singh
Pre-production Manager Balwant Singh
Production Manager Pankaj Sharma
Managing Editor Kingshuk Ghoshal
Managing Art Editor Govind Mittal

First American Edition, 2018
Published in the United States by DK Publishing
345 Hudson Street, New York, New York 10014

A catalog record for this book is available from the Library of Congress.
ISBN 978-1-4654-7360-8

Printed and bound in China

A WORLD OF IDEAS:
SEE ALL THERE IS TO KNOW

www.dk.com

CONSULTANTS

HELEN CALDWELL
Helen Caldwell is a Senior Lecturer at the University of Northampton, where she is curriculum lead for primary computing and program lead for the Postgraduate Certificate in Primary Computing. A member of the Computing in ITT Expert Group, Helen currently sits on the Association for Information Technology in Teacher Education (ITTE) National Executive Committee. She has been a lead author on several computing books and massive online open courses (MOOCs), including "Lessons in Teaching Computing" and "Teaching Computing Unplugged," published by Sage.

DR. TAMMY RANDALL PIRMANN
Dr. Tammy Pirmann is a computer science professor at Temple University. She is an award-winning educator recognized for her focus on equity in computer science education and for promoting guided inquiry in secondary computer education. She was the co-chair of the Computer Science Teachers Association's Standards Committee and an advisor on the K12 CS Framework.

DR. ALEKS KROTOSKI
Dr. Aleks Krotoski is an award-winning international broadcaster, author, and academic. She has a PhD in the social psychology of relationships in online communities. She has written and presented numerous TV, radio, and podcast programs on technology and social science, including *The Digital Human* and *The Virtual Revolution* with the BBC, and the Tech Weekly podcast with *The Guardian*.

CONTRIBUTORS

DR. CLAIRE QUIGLEY
Dr. Claire Quigley studied Computing Science at Glasgow University, where she obtained a BSc and PhD. She has worked in the Computer Laboratory at Cambridge University and at Glasgow Science Centre. She is currently STEM Coordinator for Glasgow's libraries, and lectures part time at the Royal Conservatoire of Scotland, working with BEd Music students. She has been involved in running CoderDojo Scotland since its initial session in 2012.

PATRICIA FOSTER
Patricia Foster is a professional software developer. She received her Bachelor's degree from Carleton University and worked in computer security for the Government of Canada. She is also a staff writer for *beanz*, an award-winning magazine about kids, code, and computer science.

Foreword

Digital technology is all around us, giving us access to information, communication, and entertainment that would have seemed unimaginable to people 100 years ago. Computer science is the study of how this technology works, from the microchips at the heart of devices to the code that controls them. Studying computer science gives young people the tools to understand today's technology and puts them in a position to create the machines, apps, websites, and services of the future. Rather than being restricted by what others create, computer science gives students the ability to turn their own ideas into reality.

The technology of the future will benefit from having a diverse array of people develop and shape it, and the creators of that technology will need to be able to work with others, communicate effectively, and also have some great ideas.

The skills developed in understanding computer science are useful even to those not intending to specialize in it. Some of the main lessons of computer science, such as breaking complex problems down into sections and seeing patterns in them, are skills that are useful in any career. Understanding the core concepts of how computers work is fast becoming a necessity for many careers, even if they are not directly related to making technology.

As computers continue to play an increasing role in the modern world, we must also think about the way we use them. Social networking has revolutionized the way we communicate with each other, but it's worth being aware of the potential problems that we can face—from too much screentime, to social media bubbles, and even to being victims of cyberbullying. This book also tackles issues that the Internet age has ushered in, from the digital divide, to net neutrality, to diversity and inclusion in the digital world.

Computer science might appear daunting to many parents, particularly if their child is a "digital native" who is very comfortable using the Internet and digital devices. This book aims to demystify the subject and help parents share their child's journey through the digital world.

Science fiction writer and futurist Arthur C. Clarke once stated that "any sufficiently advanced technology is indistinguishable from magic." This book will hopefully help parents and kids realize that computer science is the sort of magic that anyone and everyone can learn.

Contents

Foreword   6
How to use this book   10

1 Getting started

Computers are everywhere   14
Computing for you   16
Computing with others   18
Search engines   20
Cybersecurity   22
Fixing common problems   24

2 What is computer science?

Computer science   28
Computing before computers   30
Computing since the 1940s   32
Inside a computer   34
Peripheral devices   36
The computer chip   38
How modern computers compute   40
Processing and memory   42
Operating systems   44

3 Hardware

What is hardware?   48
Desktop computers and laptops   50
Smartphones and tablets   52
Build your own computers   54
Wearable computers   56
Connected appliances   58
Digital toys   60
Gaming consoles   62
Hidden computers   64

4 Computational thinking

What is computational thinking?   68
Decomposition   70
Abstraction   72
Patterns   74
Algorithms   76

5 Data

Bits and digitization   80
Binary code   82
ASCII and Unicode   84
Logic gates   86
Databases   88
Encoding images   90
Encoding audio and video   92
Encryption   94

6 Programming techniques

Early programming methods   98
Analog programming   100
Applying algorithms   102
Boolean logic   104
Storing and retrieving data   106
Program structures   108
Translation   110
Assemblers, interpreters, and compilers   112
Software errors   114

7 Programming languages

What do programming languages do?   118
Types of programming language   120
Language breakthroughs   122
Application programming interface   124
C and C++   126
Java   128
Python   130

Ruby 132
JavaScript 134
Scratch 136
Kodu 138
Future languages 140

8 Networks

What is a network? 144
Types of network 146
Connections 148
The Internet and the World Wide Web 150
Cloud computing 152
Streaming 154
Malware 156
The deep web 158

9 Website and app construction

HTML 162
Cascading Style Sheets 164
Using JavaScript 166
Developing and designing 168
Planning ahead 170
Testing 172
Maintenance and support 174

10 Digital behaviors

Online and digital identities 178
Maintaining balance 180
Being a digital citizen 182
Communicating online 184
Staying safe online 186
Cyberbullying 188
Hacking and privacy 190

11 Social media

What is social media? 194
Social media platforms 196
Sharing content 198
Social media apps 200
Using social networks 202
Gaming and social networks 204
Social media bubbles 206

12 Digital issues

Digital literacy 210
Net neutrality 212
Digital divide 214
Global development 216
Equality and computer science 218
Computer science and disabilities 220

13 The future of computers

Predicting the future 224
The Internet of Things 226
Virtual reality 228
Cryptocurrencies 230
Global connectivity 232
Biological interfaces 234
Artificial intelligence 236
Thinking outside the chip 238
Careers 240

Useful links 244
Glossary 248
Index 252
Acknowledgments 256

How to use this book

The world of computer science is an exciting one, with hardware and software developing at an amazing pace. As a result, it can be easy to be left behind. This book aims to clearly explain the key concepts in computer science, as well as the issues arising from using computers.

Who is this book for?

This book can be read separately by parents or young readers, but it's also designed to be read together. The book is aimed at readers at all levels of familiarity with the topic, from people who have little to no understanding of computer science to those studying it at school or college. The "Getting started" chapter is specifically designed to help readers with no previous computer knowledge to understand basic computer functions, such as how to find files, send emails, or use a web browser. The "Digital behaviors," "Social media," and "Digital issues" chapters focus on the way in which people use computers and the potential dangers and opportunities they present; this may be of particular interest to parents and teachers worried about things such as social media or cyberbullying.

How the book works

Divided into different sections, this book guides readers through the world of computer science—its origins and history, how hardware and software work, what constitutes good digital behavior, and what the future might hold. The book defines the concept and builds on it step by step. Diagrams and illustrations help to flesh out the concepts, and labels and annotations help to point out specific points of interest.

Tips and hints

Throughout the book, you'll find colored boxes offering extra information and useful, practical advice and tips.

Purple **IN DEPTH** boxes go further into a topic, giving tips or noteworthy information on it.

Orange boxes are **TOP TECH**. They explain some of the latest developments within computing.

TOP TECH
Trending tools

More than 600 million tweets are posted every day. By analyzing them as they happen, Twitter is able to identify and highlight trends in what is being discussed. People are often alerted to an event when it first starts trending on Twitter. Similarly, the Google Trends tool gives users access to data on Google searches. It's possible to see graphs of how often people across the world searched for a particular topic or top 10 lists of popular searches in different categories. Both tools give users a picture of how people in their own vicinity and other countries are reacting to events.

IN DEPTH
Steganography

Steganography involves sending secret messages by hiding the fact that there is a message. This is like messages written in invisible ink. Information can be hidden in a digital image by using a program that changes only one bit of each binary number that represents the colors of the pixels. The same program can also extract a hidden message.

LINGO
Communication protocols

When two devices communicate, a protocol dictates whose turn it is to send data, what kind of data is being sent, and how this data is formatted.
Protocol: A set of rules that governs the transmission of data between devices.
HTTP (Hypertext Transfer Protocol): Used for visiting webpages.
HTTPS (Hypertext Transfer Protocol Secure): A secure HTTP.
DHCP (Dynamic Host Configuration Protocol): All computers use this to obtain their IP address from a router.

Yellow color boxes explain **LINGO**: terms that might not be clear to most readers.

BIOGRAPHY boxes are green and give background on the lives and ideas of important people in computer science.

BIOGRAPHY
Ada Lovelace

English mathematician Ada Lovelace (1815–1852) created the world's first computer program when she wrote the earliest algorithm to be processed on English scientist Charles Babbage's (1791–1871) Analytical Engine machine in 1844. She was the first to see that computers could do so much more than basic number-crunching and calculations.

REAL WORLD
First integrated circuit

The first integrated circuit was created in 1958 by American electrical engineer Jack Kilby (1923–2005). Before Kilby's invention, machines used vacuum tubes, which were bulky and unreliable. Kilby's IC was based on tiny transistors, and all the parts were made on the one piece of material: the integrated chip was born.

BLUE boxes explain how an idea in the computer science world worked, or works, in the **REAL WORLD**.

Code boxes

Though there are no exercises in this book, some pages feature snippets of computer code. These are clearly marked out in gray and blue boxes. These feature on every entry in the "Programming languages" chapter, through a simple "Hello, World!" program. A "Hello, World!" program is the simplest way to demonstrate the syntax of a programming language and is usually the first working program that someone unfamiliar with a new programming language attempts.

```c
#include <stdio.h>
int main()
{
    int i;
    for (i = 0; i < 5; i++){
        printf("Hello, World!");
    }
    return 0;
}
```

Getting
started

Computers are everywhere

Some people feel computers are too complex for them to use without special skills and knowledge. However, they interact with computers all the time without necessarily realizing it.

SEE ALSO	
Computing for you	16–17 ❯
Inside a computer	34–35 ❯
Peripheral devices	36–37 ❯
The computer chip	38–39 ❯
What is hardware?	48–49 ❯
Smartphones and tablets	52–53 ❯

Look closely

Computers are almost everywhere, not just in the conventional setup that includes a monitor, keyboard, and mouse. They are also found in everyday devices such as cell phones, elevators, televisions, and cars. From watching movies to playing games and even making dinner, computers can be used to do almost anything.

▷ **Household devices**
Many household devices contain computers. Selecting a program on a microwave, for example, actually runs a small program on the computer embedded in the device.

Pressing the buttons on a microwave's control panel runs code on its internal microprocessor.

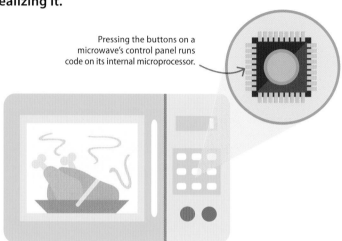

Hardware and software

The physical parts of a computer are called hardware. These include things we can see, such as the monitor and computer tower, as well as things we can't see, such as the motherboard and microprocessor inside the computer tower. Things like programs, the operating system, and firmware (a type of program that is embedded into the microprocessor) are called software. They allow users to access the capabilities of the hardware.

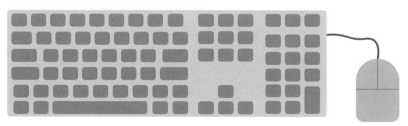

△ **Input devices**
There are a lot of ways to input information and interact with software running on a computer. The most common ways to do this are by using a keyboard, mouse, or touchscreen.

Looking for files

Searching for files on a computer is similar to finding them in a real-world filing cabinet. The file system on a computer is usually accessed using a window containing small icons of folders or documents. A folder can be opened to display the files inside by touching with a finger on a touchscreen or double-clicking with a mouse or touchpad.

△ **Searching for files**
The best way to look for a file is to find the magnifying glass icon. Then, click on it and type the filename or keywords in the search bar.

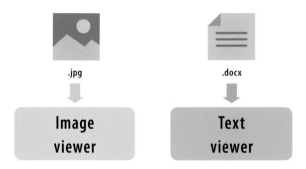

△ **Opening files**
A filename usually includes a period followed by some letters. This is the file extension, which identifies the type of file and tells the computer what kind of program it should use to open it.

△ **In the bin**
Deleting a file by mistake is quite common. Deleted files usually go into the recycle bin or trash can, and can be restored by opening the bin or can and taking the file out.

Moving data

There are various ways to transfer data between computers. Emails can be used to attach pictures, documents, and other files to a message. There are also systems, such as Google Drive or Dropbox, that allow people to upload large files and folders to the cloud. These can be shared with others through a link to the uploaded file, which can then be downloaded or even edited online.

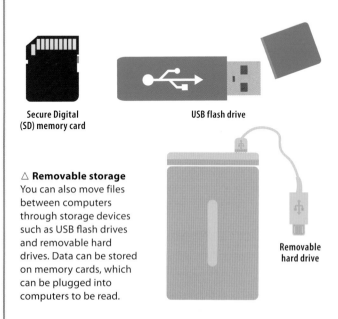

Secure Digital (SD) memory card

USB flash drive

Removable hard drive

△ **Removable storage**
You can also move files between computers through storage devices such as USB flash drives and removable hard drives. Data can be stored on memory cards, which can be plugged into computers to be read.

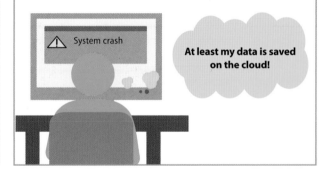

Computing for you

SEE ALSO

❮ **14–15** Computers are everywhere

Operating systems　　　　**44–45** ❯

Desktop computers and laptops　**50–51** ❯

Software is programs that allow people to use a computer's hardware. Most computers come with preinstalled software, but additional pieces of software are also widely available.

System software

System software allows user applications to run on the computer's hardware. The operating system (OS)—which controls the computer's basic functions—is the most common example. It makes the computer work by displaying information on the screen and getting user input from the keyboard, touchscreen, or mouse. For computer security, it's important to install any updates that become available for the OS.

▽ **Different operating systems**
There are many operating systems available. Microsoft Windows and Linux are the most commonly used ones. Apple machines use a specific operating system, called macOS.

Windows　　　**Linux**　　　**macOS**

Application software

Application software is designed to complete specific tasks on a computer. Some of these are paid, as either a onetime purchase or a monthly subscription. Others may be free to download and use. A lot of free software is also open source, which enables users to see and modify the application's code.

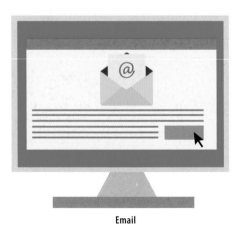

Email　　　　　　　　　　Banking

△ **Different platforms**
Application software is available for different types of device. Those used for cell phones and tablets are usually known as apps. Apps can perform a variety of tasks, such as sending emails, social networking, and even banking.

IN DEPTH

Icons

Small symbols representing applications or functions on a computer are called icons. They make it easier for people to use their computer. Many functions are symbolized by similar icons across different operating systems—for instance, a floppy disk denoting the save option or a magnifying glass symbolizing the search option.

Save　　　　　　　　　　Volume

Settings　　　　　　　　Trash

Types of application software

Modern application software comes in a variety of forms. Some popular types include software for email, word processing, spreadsheets, databases, presentations, desktop publishing, media editing, and graphics creation. Applications are sometimes combined into suites, or sets of interconnected and related programs. Many applications allow users to track changes to documents made by themselves or colleagues.

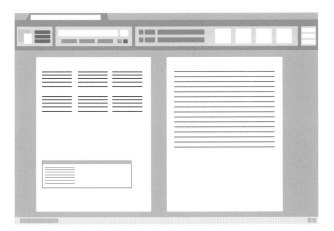

△ **Words**

Word processors are one of the most widely used applications. They can be used to create many styles of document, from a simple letter or business contract to a complex report or even a whole book. A very simple version of a word processor is called a text editor, but this is solely for text and can't handle images.

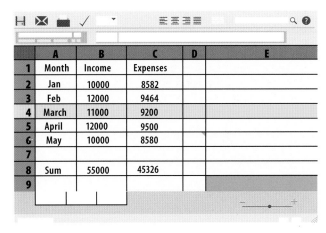

△ **Numbers**

Spreadsheets allow users to work with numbers and other data, applying mathematical and statistical formulas. They can be used for simple tasks, such as basic accounts, and also for complex analyses of data.

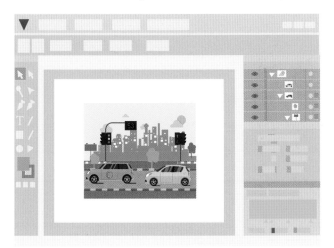

△ **Images**

With the spread of digital cameras, many people use computers to organize and edit pictures. Photo editing applications allow users to modify their pictures— for instance, by altering the lighting and color.

△ **Videos**

Video applications allow users to adjust and improve lighting and color, and add special effects. They can also edit video clips, combine clips into longer videos, and add titles and transitions—such as crossfades—between scenes.

Computing with others

Computers are not just used in isolation. They also allow people to collaborate with colleagues, keep in touch with friends and family, and connect with the world at large.

SEE ALSO	
❮ 16–17 Computing for you	
What is social media?	194–195 ❯
Social media apps	200–201 ❯
Using social networks	202–203 ❯

Video calling

There are several applications available that allow users to make video calls. These calls include the video as well as the sound of the callers. Most of these applications don't charge users, but it's good to check. It's also possible to have group calls with several callers in different locations. Sound-only calls are another option for people who prefer not to be seen, or if the video service is slow or jerky.

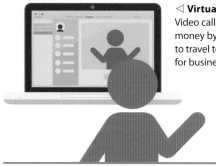

◁ **Virtual travel**
Video calls can save time and money by reducing the need to travel to another location for business meetings.

Shared calendars

Online calendars, such as ones provided by Google and Microsoft, are a useful feature for work. They make it easier to set up meetings by showing details of other people's schedules. These calendars can also be used by families to plan events or by groups of friends to arrange a date and time to meet up.

It's possible to set a shared calendar to show when a user is busy.

◁ **Time management**
Anyone trying to plan a meeting can simply view each person's schedule to figure out the best possible day and time.

Slides

Presentation software allows users to make digital slideshows, including slide transitions and background themes, to accompany their work presentations. The slideshow can be shown by attaching the user's laptop to the screen or projector. Alternatively, the file can be transferred to a dedicated computer via a USB drive or accessed online from a cloud storage service.

◁ **Visual aids**
Digital slides can act as a prompt during a presentation and help in displaying visual information, such as graphs.

Making websites

It's not necessary to know how to code to create a website. Many specialty websites allow users to make a site with a graphical editor, similar to a word processor. Some fee-based sites also include these graphical editors. These sites enable users to build more involved websites with extra features, such as online stores.

◁ **Blogging**
Blogs are online journals where people write about events or topics that interest them. Other people on the web can read and comment on the articles.

Social networking

Social networking sites and applications have become increasingly popular in recent years. Facebook is typically used by people to connect with friends and family. It's also possible to restrict access to posts at different levels—for instance, they can be seen by only friends of the user. Twitter is more public, and people often "follow" people they don't know. Instagram is similar to Twitter but is based on images.

> "**Technology** and **social media** have brought **power** back to the **people**."
> **Mark McKinnon (b. 1955), American political advisor and reform advocate**

▽ **Apps**
The word "app" is short for "application." It's usually used to describe a program that runs on a smartphone. Apps can be used for all sorts of things, such as maps, counting the number of steps walked, and taking photos with special effects.

Filter effects can be added to photos using image-editing apps.

Apps can be used to order a taxi to a user's current location.

Information on a runner's heart rate from a fitness tracker can be seen on a health-based app.

File compression

Compression programs, also called zip programs, reduce the size of a file in a reversible way. This allows them to be emailed and then uncompressed by the receiver. They can also be used to compress a folder of files, which can be particularly useful when emailing several photos.

▽ **Reversing the process**
The same programs that compress files can also be used to uncompress them. Many computers come complete with compression software, which is also available online.

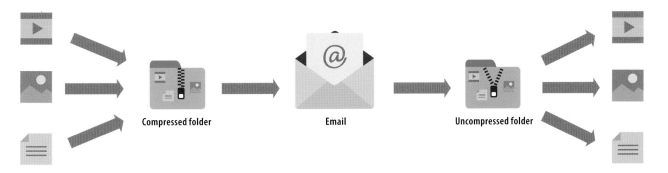

Compressed folder   Email   Uncompressed folder

Search engines

Search engines are integral parts of the online experience. They help people efficiently filter the vast world of the Internet to find what they're looking for.

SEE ALSO	
The Internet and the World Wide Web	150–151 ❯
Social media platforms	196–197 ❯

What are search engines?

A search engine is a program that looks through the World Wide Web for webpages containing particular words or phrases. In the early days of the web, there were so few sites that search engines weren't really necessary. As the number of websites increased, there was a need to be able to efficiently search the web. The number of search engines competing to do this job peaked in the late 1990s.

▷ **Early search engines**
Archie, launched in 1990, was the first web content search engine. It was followed by others, including Excite, Infoseek, Inktomi, AltaVista, and Yahoo!. Google appeared only in 1998, but quickly overtook all other sites by using new and more effective ways of searching the web.

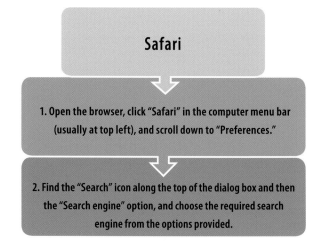

Setting a default search engine

Search engines are not all the same, and some users might prefer one over the rest. The method for setting a default search engine varies slightly for each browser and can change with browser updates. The best way to find out how to do this is to use a search engine to search for "set default search engine" along with a specific browsing program. The graphic below shows how to set a default search engine in two of the most popular browsers.

Google Chrome

1. Open the browser, press the three vertical dots next to the address bar, and then scroll down to "Settings."

2. Go to "Search engine" and choose the required search engine from the list.

Safari

1. Open the browser, click "Safari" in the computer menu bar (usually at top left), and scroll down to "Preferences."

2. Find the "Search" icon along the top of the dialog box and then the "Search engine" option, and choose the required search engine from the options provided.

Effective searching

With over a billion websites in existence, finding the right one can be very difficult. For a more focused search, it is useful to think about the words used to search. The words typed into a search engine are called search terms. The more specific a search query is, the more likely it is that the search engine will find the right website.

"shoe," "boots," "footwear," "fashion," "style," "value"

Better searching

Quotation marks (" "): Putting a phrase in quotation marks returns only those pages where that specific phrase appears.

Plus sign (+): A plus symbol between two search terms returns pages where both of the terms appear. Searching for "cats + ships" will return pages that mention both cats and ships.

Minus sign (-): A minus symbol between two search terms returns pages where only the first term appears. Searching for "islands - tropical" returns pages about nontropical islands.

Asterisk (*): An asterisk is a wildcard that can match a variety of words. Putting an asterisk in a phrase searches for that phrase containing any word in place of the asterisk. Searching for "comput*" returns results for computer, computation, computes, and so on.

◁ **Keywords**

People creating websites often add keywords to them. Keywords make it easier for search engines to find the website. For instance, a webpage for shoes might add "shoes" and "boots" as keywords to its website.

Comparison websites

These websites undertake multiple related searches to collect the results in an easily comparable format. Instead of looking at several websites and filling in a variety of online forms, users can just use one comparison website. Website owners often allow comparison websites to access their data for a charge. It's also possible for the website to get the data by a systematic process called crawling, where a web robot or crawler gathers information from different websites.

▷ **What's the secret?**

The exact methods used by search engines to work out which websites to return at the top of search results are kept secret. Getting websites to appear farther up the rank of results is now a big business for many Search Engine Optimization (SEO) companies.

Cybersecurity

Cybersecurity is an issue that's often in the news. Exactly what is it though? And how can computer users protect themselves and their data?

SEE ALSO	
Malware	156–157 ❭
Staying safe online	186–187 ❭
Hacking and privacy	190–191 ❭

What is cybersecurity?

Cybersecurity is the protection of computers and data from attacks by malicious individuals on the Internet. Attacks can include stealing data, such as a person's banking details, or infecting computers with viruses that lock users out of their machine. In organizations where physical systems are controlled by computers, it's even possible for cyberattacks to cause physical damage to equipment.

Hackers can steal all kinds of data if they gain access to a computer.

▷ **User behavior**
Effective security depends on user behavior, as well as technical safeguards. Social engineering, where hackers use psychological tricks and insights to deceive people and gain access to computer systems, is a very successful technique.

Hacked computers

Once a hacker gains access to a computer, there are many ways to harm its owner, their family, or colleagues. Computers contain a lot of information its owner would not want others to have. Data such as passwords, documents, emails, and photographs can all be copied and used for criminal purposes.

White hat
These hackers use their skills to help people. They obtain permission to hack into systems to identify weaknesses for the owners.

Gray hat
These hackers hack into systems without permission, which is a crime, but subsequently tell the system owners about any flaws they find.

Black hat
Black hat hackers hack into systems without permission in order to steal data or cause disruption to the system's operation and its owners.

LINGO
Hacking methods

Brute-force attack: Trying all possible password values to find one that works.

Distributed Denial of Service (DDoS): Overloading a website with fake traffic so that it becomes unavailable.

Keylogger: A program that secretly records every key pressed by a user.

Phishing: Impersonating a website via email to get users to reveal login details.

Social engineering: Manipulating someone to gain access to their data.

Virus: A malicious program that spreads to other computers by replication.

◁ **Types of hacker**
Hackers are often described in terms of hat colors. This comes from cowboy films, where heroes wore white hats and villains wore black.

Stealing data

Data is valuable, particularly personal information or financial data. There are a number of methods hackers can use to compromise devices in order to steal data. Many of these can be done remotely or sometime prior to someone using the device.

The user would normally connect to the Internet directly.

Wi-Fi hotspot

Device connecting to Wi-Fi

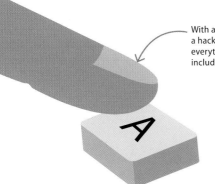

With a keystroke logger, a hacker can read everything typed, including any passwords.

The mirroring device looks and acts just like the regular hotspot, but the hacker can see everything people connected to it do online.

Wi-Fi mirror

△ Keyloggers

Keystroke loggers, or keyloggers, are programs that silently store every key pressed on the computer they're installed on. They are often used to steal users' passwords and bank details. Both software and hardware keystroke loggers exist.

△ Wi-Fi mirror

Hackers can use Wi-Fi mirroring devices that mimic public Wi-Fi hotspots. Instead of connecting directly to the hotspot, unsuspecting users connect to the mirror device, and as they browse online, the hacker can see what they do.

Staying safe from scammers

Scammers try to gain access to people's money via email. It's wise not to click on any links or open any attachments in emails from strangers. In phishing attacks, the scammers try to imitate an email from a bank or other organization in order to get people to give up details such as PIN numbers or passwords. Banks and other legitimate organizations will never ask for security details via email in this way.

Hackers can even target social media accounts.

◁ Social media

Hackers can compromise social media accounts. Changing the password for that site will usually fix this. However, contacting the site's support team will be necessary if a hacker changes a user's password.

Hazards and good practices

While the presence of malware may make the Internet seem very dangerous, there are simple ways of making your information safer. Installing or activating firewall and antivirus software to scan network traffic for suspicious packets is a good first step. Downloading and installing a password manager means passwords for multiple sites can be stored and operated using only one master password.

1. Use secure sites for making online payments
2. Clear browser cache
3. Update computer software
4. Use trusted Wi-Fi connections
5. Download files only from trusted sources
6. Log out of a session once you have finished

Fixing common problems

SEE ALSO	
Peripheral devices	36–37 〉
Connections	148–149 〉
Staying safe online	186–187 〉

Computer glitches are common, and most can be fixed easily and quickly. This is known as troubleshooting. Advice can be found online or from local computer stores or technicians.

Difficulty logging in

Problems with logging in to a computer can be caused by having pressed the caps lock key or accidentally trying to log in to another user's account. Forgotten logins can be fixed by using the administrator account to reset the login or by using a password reset disk.

▷ **Locked out**
Dealing with a forgotten password can be tricky. If the solutions above don't work, seeking advice from a local computer technician is the best plan.

Simple problems

A very common issue is the computer freezing or failing to respond to a mouse or keyboard input. This can usually be fixed by shutting down the machine by pressing the power button for several seconds and then restarting it again. Avoid simply unplugging it from the outlet, as this can make matters worse.

"… there is a **solution** to every **problem**. It may take you a while, but eventually you're going to **find it**."
Tony Cárdenas (b. 1963), American politician

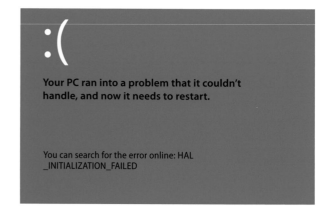

△ **Task Manager**
If a particular program isn't responding, hold down the ctrl, alt, and delete keys on a computer running Windows or command, option, and esc keys on a Mac.

△ **Blue Screen of Death**
Windows shows the "Blue Screen of Death" when a serious failure occurs. After restarting, the computer should be able to guide users toward a solution.

Printers

Printer problems are often caused by a lack of paper or paper jams. Most printers have warning lights and displays to indicate these issues. Another possible issue is low ink or toner levels. Opening the printer settings in the Control Panel in Windows, or System Preferences on a Mac, will reveal more specific error messages.

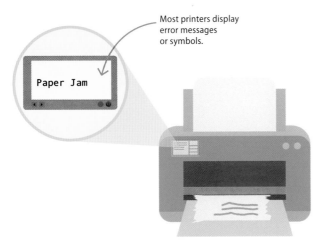

Most printers display error messages or symbols.

Paper Jam

△ **Quality issues**
Bad-quality printing can be caused by badly aligned or clogged printer heads. Printers usually come with software that allows users to diagnose and fix these types of issues.

Sound and webcams

Problems with sound and webcams can be frustrating, particularly for users trying to take part in online meetings. Checking the computer's settings for sound output and input might help to solve the problem. Forgetting that headphones are plugged in can also be the source of missing sound. Some computers and headphones have built-in microphones, but a computer may still need an external microphone to be plugged in.

No sound could be due to the computer being muted or the sound settings not being set up properly.

△ **Webcam connectivity**
People often cover the webcam when not in use to protect against hackers. If so, it's important to remember to uncover it before use.

Wi-Fi and data

Wi-Fi connections can sometimes be temperamental. Check that the computer is actually connecting to the correct Wi-Fi and not a neighboring one with a weaker signal. If there seems to be no signal at all, try switching the router off for a few seconds and then turn it back on. If a Wi-Fi connection seems slow, there are speed-test websites online that can determine the current speed. A slow connection is usually short-lived and mostly due to issues with the Internet provider, possibly affecting many users in a local area.

▷ **Data usage**
Some Internet providers, and many cell phone contracts, limit the amount of data customers can use each month. It therefore is useful to know how much data different online activities use.

1MB

Viewing an email with an attached picture

25MB

Browsing for an hour

150MB

Downloading music for an hour

2GB

Streaming HD videos for an hour

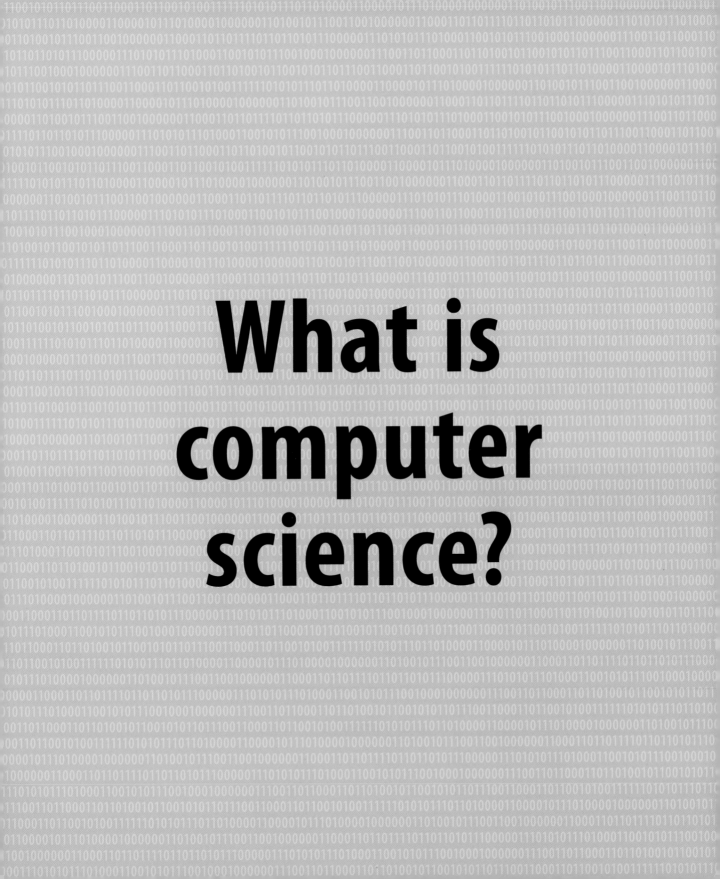

What is computer science?

Computer science

Computers are everywhere, from smartphones to intelligent refrigerators. Technology might seem like magic, but computer science explores the secrets behind it.

SEE ALSO	
What is computational thinking?	**68–69 〉**
Types of programming language	**120–121 〉**
Careers	**240–243 〉**

Getting involved

Most young people today are very comfortable using computers and technology, so it's easy to assume there's no point in studying computing. However, computer science isn't simply about using digital tools; it also involves exploring how these technologies work. Studying computer science can help young people develop skills to solve problems, invent new things, and create new technologies for the future.

▷ **No limits**
People without computing skills are limited to using the websites, apps, and games that are already available. People with computing skills, on the other hand, are in a position to turn their ideas into reality, and to make the things that will shape the future of computers.

The world is digital

The world is becoming increasingly digital. Computers control a lot of the basics of modern life, from paying for things to driving cars, and from hospitals to satellites. Here are just a few of the ways in which computers control aspects of everyday life.

Televisions connected to the Internet give users the ability to stream content in real time.

Global Positioning Systems (GPS) use satellites to show you where you are on Earth.

Most retailers give their customers the option to shop online.

Skills for thinking

Programming is a large part of computer science, but it involves more than simply stringing together a list of commands. Before any code is written, we must think about what we are trying to achieve in a step-by-step manner in order to see and overcome problems. We call this computational thinking, and it can be useful for things that don't involve computers at all.

Programming languages

Some people wonder which programming language to learn in order to get a job. However, the most important skill is learning how to apply computational thinking to a problem, and then produce a solution that can be expressed in code. Once a computer scientist is comfortable solving problems using one programming language, learning others becomes less intimidating. Here are some of the most common programming languages.

C	Ruby
C#	Python
Java	Javascript

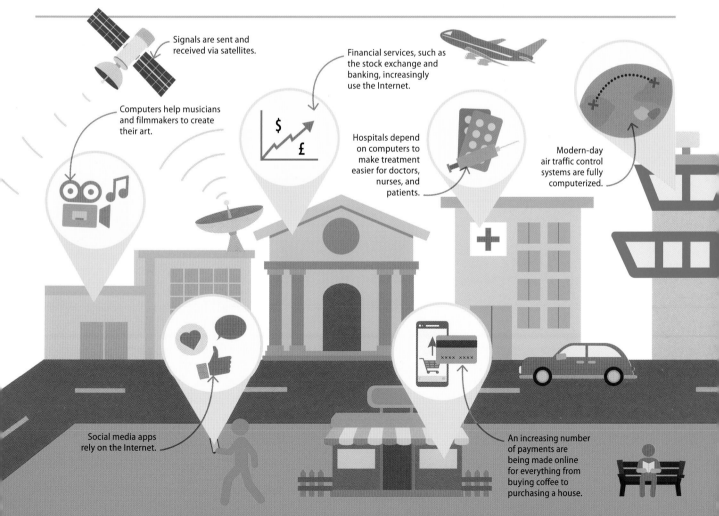

Signals are sent and received via satellites.

Financial services, such as the stock exchange and banking, increasingly use the Internet.

Computers help musicians and filmmakers to create their art.

Hospitals depend on computers to make treatment easier for doctors, nurses, and patients.

Modern-day air traffic control systems are fully computerized.

Social media apps rely on the Internet.

An increasing number of payments are being made online for everything from buying coffee to purchasing a house.

Computing before computers

SEE ALSO	
Desktop computers and laptops	**50–51 ❯**
Algorithms	**76–77 ❯**
Early programming methods	**98–99 ❯**

Most people think of a computer as an electronic device with a screen and a keyboard. However, humans have been using calculating devices for thousands of years.

The earliest computers

The earliest calculations were done using the 10 fingers of the hands, which is why most number systems are based on multiples of 10. The Romans had a method for solving complex calculations using their fingers. This practice gave us the word digit, from the Latin word *digitus*, meaning finger. It is now used to denote any number between 0 and 9.

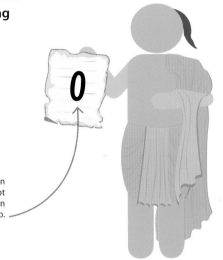

The ancient Indian Bakhshali manuscript contains the first known mention of zero.

▷ **Counting numbers**
Computers use only the digits 0 and 1 to represent numbers using the binary system, which is based on multiples of two. The concept of zero as we know it today originated in India in the 5th century.

Stone structures and counting boards

Early calculating devices were used for determining time. They included ancient Egyptian structures called obelisks, where large columns of stone cast shadows that moved with the Sun. The direction of the shadows helped people roughly determine the time. The earliest counting boards, which used columns of metal or stone disks (but had no wires), appeared in about 2400 BCE in Babylon (modern-day Iraq). Here are two other examples of early calculating aids.

Movable beads strung on wires.

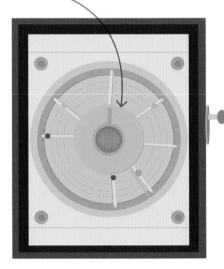

Bronze dial showing constellations of the zodiac.

△ **Abacus**
Building on the invention of the counting board, the abacus used beads on wires to represent units, tens, hundreds, and so on.

△ **Antikythera mechanism**
Found off the coast of the Greek island of Antikythera, this ancient Greek clocklike mechanism has 37 gears and was used to calculate the positions of stars and planets and predict eclipses.

From math to machines

From the 8th to the 14th centuries, a lot of mathematical work that ultimately proved crucial to computing was done in the Islamic world. Scholars translated mathematical texts by ancient Greek and Indian mathematicians into Arabic and built on the knowledge they contained to develop new methods of calculation. Two particularly notable mathematicians were Muhammad ibn Musa al-Khwarizmi (c.780–850), from whose name the word algorithm comes, and Al-Kindi (c.801–873), who developed techniques still used in cryptography today.

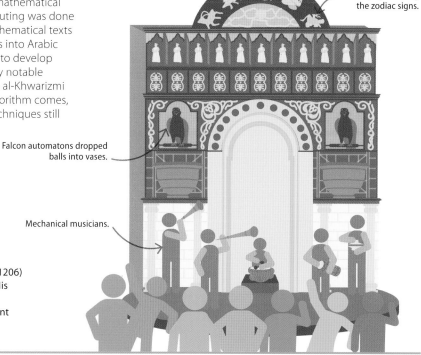

Display showing the zodiac signs.

Falcon automatons dropped balls into vases.

Mechanical musicians.

▷ **Al-Jazari castle water clock**
A 12th-century engineer, Ismail al-Jazari (1136–1206) invented many ingenious mechanical devices. His castle clock was particularly complex and could be programmed to take into account the different lengths of day and night throughout the year.

Napier and Schickard

Scottish mathematician John Napier (1550–1617) created a manually operated calculating device called Napier's bones. A set of square rods carved from bone inscribed with numbers, it made multiplication, division, and finding square roots much easier. Napier based his device on an Arabic method introduced to Europe by the Italian mathematician Fibonacci (1175–1250).

▽ **Schickard's calculating clock**
German astronomer Wilhelm Schickard built a calculating machine by remodeling Napier's bones as cylinders. His clock could add and subtract six-digit numbers.

Calculation results were read through windows in these wooden slats.

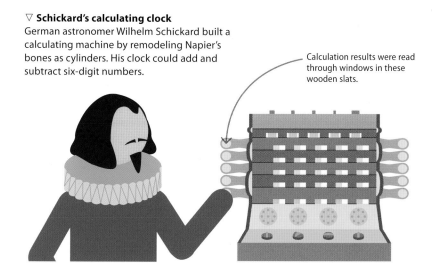

Ada Lovelace

English mathematician Ada Lovelace (1815–1852) created the world's first computer program when she wrote the earliest algorithm to be processed on English scientist Charles Babbage's (1791–1871) Analytical Engine machine in 1844. She was the first to see that computers could do so much more than basic number-crunching and calculations.

Computing since the 1940s

SEE ALSO

❮ 30–31 Computing before computers

Desktop computers and laptops 50–51 ❯

Gaming consoles 62–63 ❯

Computing has advanced dramatically since the 1940s. Starting as an abstract, mathematical pursuit carried out by academics, it's now a part of life for a huge number of people.

WWII and computers

World War II was a catalyst for the development of electronic computing. The German forces used a cryptography machine called Enigma to make their messages secret. English computer scientist Alan Turing led a team that deciphered Enigma by building a computer called Bombe. This computer contained hundreds of moving parts and was a step away from being the forerunner of today's computers.

▽ **Code-breakers during WWII**
Britain gathered together 10,000 of its top mathematicians and engineers at Bletchley Park, where they worked to break Germany's secret codes.

About 75 percent of the Bletchley Park staff were female.

REAL WORLD

Human computers

The word "computer" used to refer to humans who calculated mathematical results using pencil and paper. From the late 19th century to the mid-20th century, human computers were often women, including American mathematician Katherine Johnson. Their work was essential in a number of fields—for example, computing data for early space flights at NASA.

Stored-program computers

Colossus, built in 1943, was a computer that had a fixed function: to break coded messages. The same was true of the ENIAC (Electronic Numerical Integrator and Computer), developed around the same time, which calculated the paths of missiles for the US Army. Changing the program of either of these computers involved rewiring the machine and physically pulling switches. The first practical general-purpose stored-program electronic computer was EDSAC (electronic delay storage automatic calculator), which ran its first program in 1949. It could be reprogrammed with ease and typically worked for 35 hours a week, carrying out calculations that a human would find complex and time-consuming.

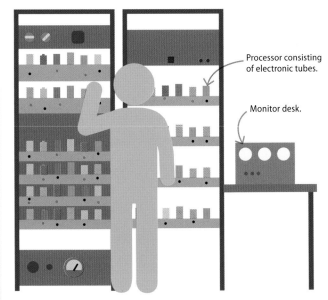

Processor consisting of electronic tubes.

Monitor desk.

△ **EDSAC**
The developers of the ENIAC went on to design and build the EDSAC, the first computer that stored programs and data in the same machine.

Personal computers

Personal computers started appearing in the late 1970s, when several basic models went on sale. One of these machines was made by Apple Computers, a company started by Steve Jobs, Steve Wozniak, and Ronald Wayne in 1976. One year earlier, Bill Gates and Paul Allen had founded Microsoft, developing operating system software that allowed users to interact with various personal computers.

▷ **Apple II**
Personal computers, such as the Apple II, were mainly aimed at small businesses and amateur electronics fans.

◁ **Microsoft Disk Operating System (MS-DOS)**
MS-DOS is the basic operating system developed by Microsoft for personal computers.

MS-DOS's command-line interface.

REAL WORLD

Computer gaming

One factor that greatly popularized home computers and programming was computer gaming. The first commercially available computer game was Pong, a simple table tennis–style game, brought out in 1972. Originally played on machines in arcades, a home console version was released by the company Atari in 1975.

Supercomputers

Most computers work through a problem from start to finish using one processor to do the calculations. The first really powerful supercomputers appeared in the 1990s. They have many individual processors working on lots of tiny parts of a big problem at the same time. These computers are used for tasks such as weather forecasting, designing aircraft engines, and breaking coded messages.

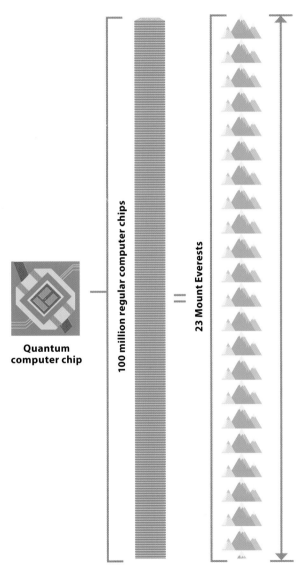

Quantum computer chip

100 million regular computer chips

23 Mount Everests

△ **D-wave quantum chip**
The D-wave quantum supercomputer has the same processing power as 100 million regular computers. If 100 million computer chips were stacked on top of each other, they would be the same height as 23 Mount Everests.

Inside a computer

Under the casing, a computer's hardware is a host of electronic circuitry, components, and connections. As they become ever more powerful, their components need to be smaller, use less power, and generate less heat.

SEE ALSO

❮ 14–15 Computers are everywhere
Peripheral devices　　　　　　36–37 ❯
Processing and memory　　　　42–43 ❯

Components of a computer

The components inside a computer are fairly similar, regardless of the type of computer it is. The parts may look a bit different, but they fulfill the same functions. Understanding what the various parts do and how they work can help users troubleshoot problems or decide whether it is time to upgrade their hardware.

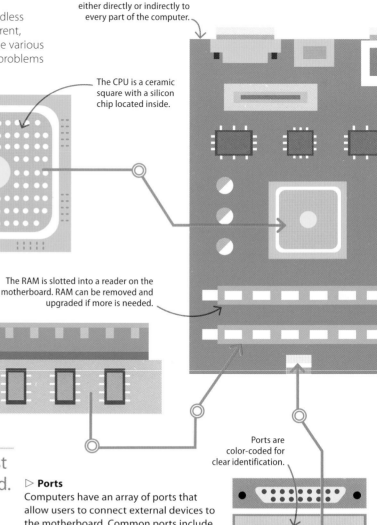

The motherboard connects either directly or indirectly to every part of the computer.

The CPU is a ceramic square with a silicon chip located inside.

The RAM is slotted into a reader on the motherboard. RAM can be removed and upgraded if more is needed.

Ports are color-coded for clear identification.

▷ **Central processing unit**
The central processing unit (CPU), also known as a microprocessor, acts as the brain of the computer. It controls most of the machine's operations and carries out commands. Instructions are sent to the CPU by pressing a key, clicking the mouse, or starting an application or file.

▷ **RAM**
This is the system's short-term memory. Whenever a computer performs calculations, it temporarily stores the data in the random-access memory (RAM) until it is needed. The data on the RAM is cleared when the computer is turned off.

> "... **computers** have become the most **empowering tool** we've ever created. They're tools of **communication**, they're tools of **creativity**, and they can be **shaped** by their **user**."
> **Bill Gates (b. 1955), American co-founder of Microsoft**

▷ **Ports**
Computers have an array of ports that allow users to connect external devices to the motherboard. Common ports include universal serial bus (USB), Ethernet (used to connect computers together to form a network), video graphics array (VGA), high-definition multimedia interface (HDMI), and ports for headphones and microphones.

▽ **Motherboard**

The computer's main circuit board is called the motherboard. It allows the other components to communicate with each other. The motherboard is a thin plate that holds the CPU, memory, connectors for the hard drive and optical drive, expansion cards to control the video and audio, and connections to a computer's ports. It holds all the circuitry that ties the functions of the computer components together.

◁ **Hard drive**

A computer's software, documents, and other files are stored on its hard drive as binary code. It holds data, even if the computer is turned off or unplugged. The quicker the hard drive, the faster the computer can start up and load programs.

A computer system generally has between one and seven expansion slots.

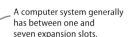

Chips provide extra processing power for specific parts of the computer.

△ **Expansion slots**

These slots allow the user to add various types of expansion card, which help to boost or update the performance of a computer. Expansion cards can upgrade the sound or video, or enable the computer to connect to networks or Bluetooth.

◁ **Power unit**

This converts the power from the wall outlet to the type of power needed by the computer. Power is sent to the motherboard and other components through cables. The power unit also regulates overheating by controlling voltage, which may change automatically or manually depending on the power supply.

Power units usually have a fan that stops the computer's components from overheating.

Peripheral devices

Any piece of hardware that enables users to interact with a computer is called a peripheral device. Without them, there would be no way to unlock a computer's potential.

SEE ALSO

❮ **14–15** Computers are everywhere

❮ **34–35** Inside a computer

Processing and memory   **42–43** ❯

Peripheral devices

A peripheral is a device that connects to the computer's motherboard. They are generally classified into three categories: input devices, output devices, and storage devices. Some devices, such as a touchscreen or a scanning printer, can be both input and output devices. Peripherals can be developed for all kinds of applications.

Camera ▽

A computer camera, commonly called a "webcam," is an input device that captures video and audio signals. Though most webcams are integrated into the computer's casing, they are still considered a peripheral device.

▷ **Headphones and microphone**

Usually connecting to the computer by a 0.14-inch (3.5mm) jack, headphones and microphones allow users to hear audio from and send audio to the computer. Some companies are eliminating physical headphone connections from their devices in favor of Bluetooth connections.

The three sections on the jack send power to the left and right audio, and ground the device.

Most modern printers connect to the computer via a USB cable.

▽ **Printer**

A printer is an output device that creates physical documents from computer files. Many printers enable users to scan documents to allow them to be manipulated on the computer.

A keyboard turns key presses into characters on the monitor.

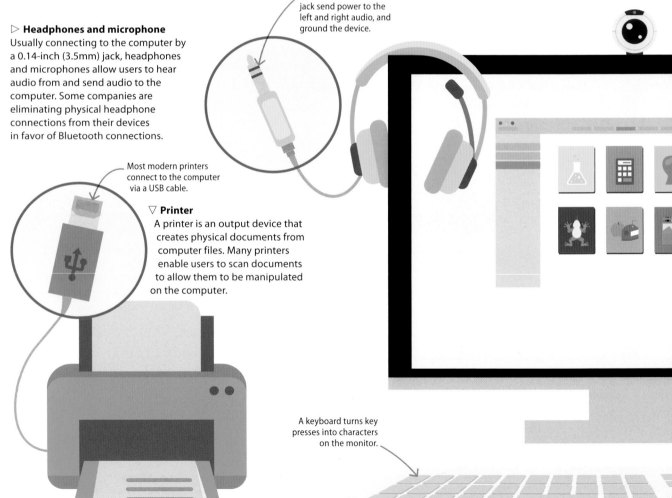

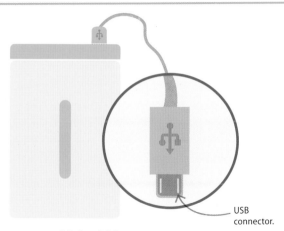

USB connector.

△ Removable hard drive

If a computer is low on storage space, or if a user needs to work on different computers at different locations, a removable hard drive is often the most efficient solution. It works just like an internal hard drive but is portable.

IN DEPTH

Controlling computers

Peripherals are crucially important to people with disabilities as they allow them to use computers. English theoretical physicist Stephen Hawking (1942–2018) suffered from motor neuron disease, which attacked his muscles and left him unable to speak or move. Engineers and software developers made it possible for him to communicate by attaching a sensor to the one muscle he could still move on his cheek. This was connected to a speech-generating machine.

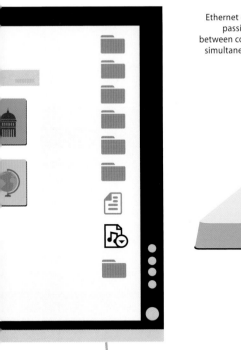

Ethernet cables control the passing of information between computers to avoid simultaneous transmission.

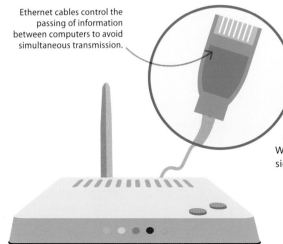

◁ Router

Routers send and receive data packets between computers, and as such, they are both input and output devices. Routers can connect devices within a home together, or they can be used to connect a home network to the Internet. It is common for most home devices to connect to a home router via Wi-Fi, but if there is a problem with the Wi-Fi signal, an Ethernet cable can often be used.

Keyboards and mouses are connected to the computer via USB cables.

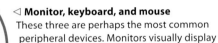

◁ Monitor, keyboard, and mouse

These three are perhaps the most common peripheral devices. Monitors visually display information processed by the computer. A keyboard and a mouse are input devices that allow users to interact with a computer. Sometimes a touch-sensitive panel called a touchpad can be used instead of a mouse.

The computer chip

Computer chips are at the heart of all modern computers.
They are found in phones, cars, and even washing machines.
But what exactly are they, and how are they made?

SEE ALSO	
❮ **14–15** Computers are everywhere	
Binary code	**82–83** ❯
Logic gates	**86–87** ❯

Integrated circuits

Computer chips are integrated circuits (ICs): silicon wafers
with millions, or sometimes billions, of tiny components
etched into them. They're much faster and smaller than circuits
constructed from individual components, and cheaper to
produce in large numbers. Chips are sealed into ceramic cases
with metal pins connecting them to the rest of the computer.
Integrated circuits can be made to carry out many tasks.

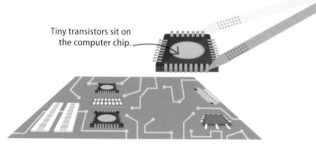

Tiny transistors sit on
the computer chip.

△ **Transistor count**
The building blocks of computer chips are transistors: tiny
devices that are used to amplify or switch electric current. The
higher the number of transistors, the more powerful a chip is.

REAL WORLD

First integrated circuit

The first integrated circuit was created in 1958 by American
electrical engineer Jack Kilby (1923–2005). Before Kilby's
invention, machines used vacuum tubes, which were bulky
and unreliable. Kilby's IC was based on tiny transistors, and
all the parts were made on the one piece of material: the
integrated chip was born.

Manufacturing chips

Chips are manufactured in semiconductor
wafer fabrication plants known as fabs. Each
fab has a "clean room" containing air with
almost all dust particles filtered out, as even
one dust mite can ruin a chip. Workers in the
clean room wear suits and masks to protect
the chips from the hair, skin cells, and any other
potential contaminants that humans shed.

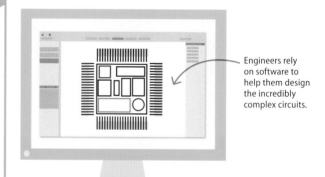

Engineers rely
on software to
help them design
the incredibly
complex circuits.

△ **1. Design**
Microprocessor circuits are designed by
teams of engineers who use software to
define how the circuit should behave. The
software then translates this definition into
a layout of components.

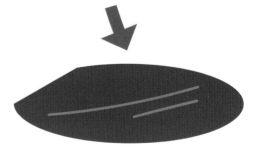

△ **2. Wafers**
The circuits are created from sheets of pure
silicon. Dozens of chips are created at the
same time from a single circular wafer.

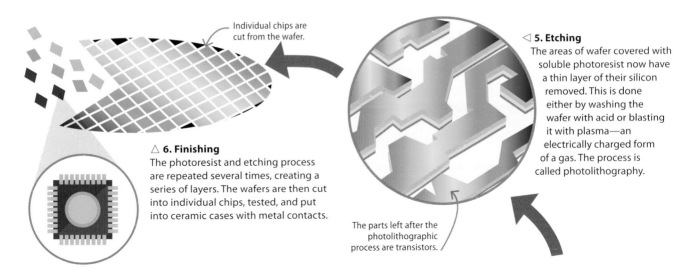

Individual chips are cut from the wafer.

6. Finishing
The photoresist and etching process are repeated several times, creating a series of layers. The wafers are then cut into individual chips, tested, and put into ceramic cases with metal contacts.

◁ 5. Etching
The areas of wafer covered with soluble photoresist now have a thin layer of their silicon removed. This is done either by washing the wafer with acid or blasting it with plasma—an electrically charged form of a gas. The process is called photolithography.

The parts left after the photolithographic process are transistors.

"There was a **space program before** there was **integrated circuits.**"
Jack Kilby (1923–2005), American electrical engineer

IN DEPTH

Moore's Law

Moore's Law is an observation made by Gordon Moore (b. 1929), co-founder of microchip company Intel, in 1965. He predicted that the number of transistors in integrated circuits would double roughly every 2 years. Many experts believe that this doubling of transistors will stop being possible in about 10 years. It's not clear yet if they are right, or what will happen if they are.

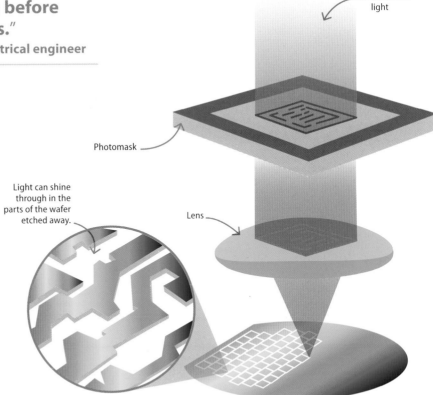

Ultraviolet light

Photomask

Light can shine through in the parts of the wafer etched away.

Lens

△ 3. Photoresist
Each wafer is coated with a substance called photoresist, which protects the wafer from chemicals such as acids. Shining ultraviolet light on an area of the photoresist, however, makes it possible for the chemicals to dissolve that area, revealing the wafer beneath.

△ 4. Mask
The design is turned into a photomask, a bit like a stencil, with some areas removed so that light can shine through them. Masks may be built up in layers, each making up part of the overall pattern.

How modern computers compute

How can an object made from millions of tiny, complex parts produce outputs like words, music, art, or motion?

SEE ALSO	
What is hardware?	**48–49 >**
Binary code	**82–83 >**
The Internet of Things	**226–227 >**

Displaying data

A computer is a machine for manipulating numbers, and to a computer, everything is numbers. Letters, symbols, sounds, and images are all represented by binary numbers. To most humans, however, binary is just a string of meaningless 1s and 0s. How have computer scientists enabled computers to display the data they work with in ways that people can understand?

IN DEPTH

Hexadecimal

Most people find binary numbers difficult to work with. The hexadecimal system is based on multiples of 16 and uses the digits 0 to 9 followed by the letters A to F. A 24-bit binary number defining a color can be written as six hexadecimal digits, making life easier for programmers.

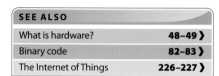

FFC0FF	8AE1FF	00F1DD	00F396	C9E151
FE9AFF	4DCAFF	00D4C3	00DA86	B2C848
F68DFF	2CC0FF	00CAB9	00CF80	A9BD44

Image
Computer screens are made up of tiny areas called pixels that are lit up to show shapes and colors. To display a pixel as white, it's lit with equal amounts of red, green, and blue light. Other colors are obtained by mixing different proportions of these three, with black being an absence of light.

00000000
00000000
11111111

Each color is made of three binary values for the amount of red, green, and blue in it.

words

Text
Letters and characters are represented by a standardized set of binary numbers. The operating system on a computer contains code that can translate these binary numbers into a pattern of pixels on a screen. Word processors and web browsers contain code for the pixel patterns of various fonts.

S

01010011

Sound
Computers produce sounds by translating binary numbers into electrical signals. These electrical signals are then fed into a loudspeaker that makes a very thin sheet of metal vibrate. The vibrations create pressure changes in the air that human ears interpret as sound.

10000110

Hardware and software

The physical parts of a computer that exist as objects in the real world are known as hardware. The combination of instructions and data telling hardware to perform tasks is called software. Software is also known as code or programs. Writing software can be challenging, as it involves writing instructions for a machine with no real understanding of the world.

▽ **Mouse input**
A computer classifies every mouse movement as an "event." Its operating system is constantly checking for events and reacts to each one by running code to deal with it specifically.

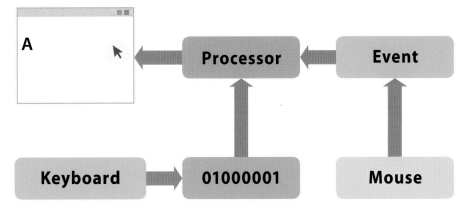

▷ **Keyboard input**
A user pressing a key on the keyboard is an event that computers recognize. Programmers often use these events to make something happen on the monitor, such as writing a letter.

Physical computing

Computers are increasingly affecting objects in the physical world, from robot helpers to apps that can control lights in people's homes. This is made possible by software containing instructions that turn numbers into signals. For instance, a smartphone app may send a signal to a nearby Wi-Fi router. This travels across the Internet to trigger a light in the user's home.

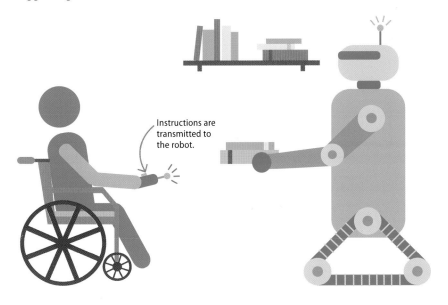

Instructions are transmitted to the robot.

How much code?

The size of programs is usually measured in lines of code. This is how many lines of code are in some well-known pieces of software:

Simple mobile app: 10,000

NASA's space shuttle: 400,000

Boeing 787 plane: 6.5 million

Firefox web browser: 9.7 million

Microsoft Office 2013: 45 million

Google: 2 billion

◁ **Robots**
A control device for a robot may send instructions as radio signals that, when received by the robot, are translated into electrical signals that operate the robot's motors and gears.

Processing and memory

Microchips process and control the flow of data and instructions inside a computer. They interact with other parts of the computer to produce outputs.

SEE ALSO

❰ **34–35** Inside a computer

❰ **36–37** Peripheral devices

What is hardware?   **48–49** ❱

Central Processing Unit (CPU)

The CPU is where all the work of the computer is done. It is made up of a control unit (CU), registers (which are temporary places in the CPU where values can be stored), and an arithmetic logic unit (ALU). The CPU has a fetch-decode-execute cycle: one instruction is fetched from memory by the control unit and translated into binary numbers, which are stored in registers. These numbers are passed into the ALU, which executes the logical or arithmetic operations necessary. Modern computers often have more than one processing unit, called a core, in the CPU.

IN DEPTH

Von Neumann architecture

The organization of computer components is known as a "von Neumann architecture." It's named after John von Neumann (1903–1957), a Hungarian-American physicist and mathematician, who described it in a report on the EDVAC (Electronic Discrete Variable Automatic Computer) computer in 1945.

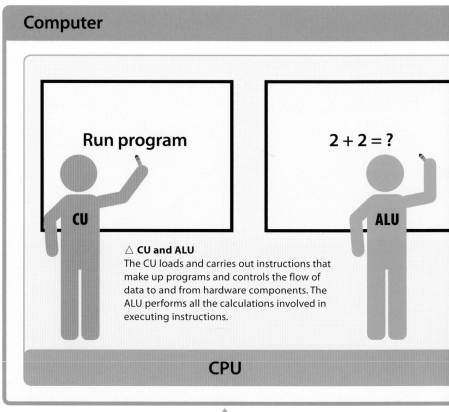

Run program

$2 + 2 = ?$

CU

ALU

CPU

△ **CU and ALU**
The CU loads and carries out instructions that make up programs and controls the flow of data to and from hardware components. The ALU performs all the calculations involved in executing instructions.

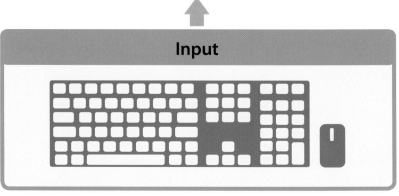

Input

Off-CPU memory

Primary memory includes read-only memory (ROM) containing instructions that start the computer. Most of the primary memory is made up of random-access memory (RAM), which contains data and instructions currently being used. Its contents are lost when the computer is turned off, so long-term data is stored on the hard drive, known as secondary memory.

On-CPU memory ▷
The CPU itself contains registers, where data currently being used is stored, and a cache containing data and instructions likely to be reused soon.

Information is contained in memory, just like books arranged in a library.

◁ **Buses**
To transfer information to the CPU, a computer has dedicated electrical connections called buses. The data bus carries data, and the address bus carries the addresses of data in memory.

Memory

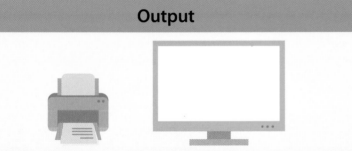

Output

What makes a computer powerful?

Computing power depends primarily on a combination of how fast the CPU can work and how much data it can store in its primary memory. It's also influenced by how fast data can be moved on the computer's buses and how long it takes to access its secondary memory. If the computer is to be used to process a lot of graphics, its speed can be improved by adding a video card containing a processor optimized for handling images.

△ **Benchmarking**
Running a set of standard tests on a computer to evaluate how quickly it completes them is called benchmarking. This makes it possible to compare the performance of different processors.

IN DEPTH

Clock-speed

The clock-speed of a processor is a measure of how many instructions it can carry out per second. This is measured in megahertz (MHz) or gigahertz (GHz). A 1.5 MHz processor can carry out 1.5 billion instructions a second. It is possible to override the setting that determines clock-speed on a computer to make it run faster. This is called overclocking, but it can cause data corruption and damage to the computer through overheating.

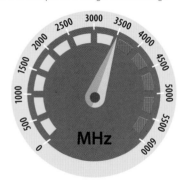

Operating systems

An operating system (OS) is a piece of software that manages a computer's hardware and software resources and makes it easier for us to use them. There are many types of OS, and they can be used for different purposes.

SEE ALSO

❰ **16–17** Computing for you

❰ **40–41** How modern computers compute

❰ **42–43** Processing and memory

Maintenance and support **174–175** ❱

How it works

A computer operating system manages a computer's resources, such as its disk space, memory, and peripherals. The OS can be thought of as an intermediary between the computer's hardware and its software. It receives instructions from applications, peripherals, and the hard drive and carries out these instructions on software, the hard drive, and other peripherals.

▽ **How it works**
The primary goal of the operating system is to provide a way of communicating with the computer that the user easily understands.

Monitor
The OS sends instructions to the monitor, which interprets these signals and displays things accordingly.

Printer
The OS uses software called a printer driver to convert the data to be printed into a format the printer can understand.

Applications
An application is a type of software that allows its user to perform a specific task. The OS provides a framework for these applications to run.

Operating system
The operating system manages the inputs and outputs to and from the computer.

Hard drive
The OS allocates storage space on the computer and sends instructions when users want to use or write to programs or files.

Keyboard
A keyboard is an input device that allows users to write and interact with programs and files.

Mouse
The OS ensures that the input from the mouse is read and results in the user being able to move and select things displayed on the monitor.

Types of operating system

As computers have progressed and developed, so have operating systems. Within the broad family of operating systems, there are generally four types. These are categorized based on the number of users or applications they can support and the type of computer they can control.

RTOS

Real-time operating systems (RTOS) are multitasking systems that are used for real-time applications. They are designed for an environment where a large number of events must be processed in a very short time, usually tenths of a second. The US space agency NASA has used RTOS on many missions, including the New Horizons probe to Pluto, launched in 2006. RTOS are cost-effective and do not require a lot of physical hardware in order to run, which is crucial when sending a probe far into space.

△ **Single-tasking and multitasking**
A single-tasking operating system runs only one program at a time, while a multitasking OS allows many programs to run simultaneously.

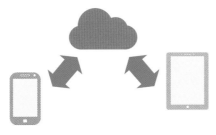

△ **Single-user and multiuser**
A single-user OS allows only one user to access the computer system at any given time. A multiuser system allows access to many users at a time.

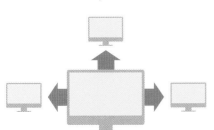

△ **Distributed**
This OS allows distributed applications to run on several machines that are connected to each other with a high-quality network.

△ **Templated**
Common in cloud computing, this refers to running multiple virtual machines off a guest OS created on a single computer.

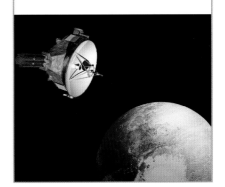

Utilities

The operating system uses applications called utilities, which allow users to manage their computer, its devices, and its programs. There are many different utility programs, and they vary across operating systems. Users can access these via a special menu or control panel.

**User accounts
and security**

**Antivirus
software**

**Deleting documents,
files, or programs**

Software updates

System clean-up

**Encryption /
decryption**

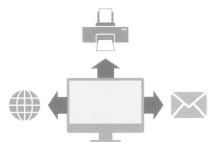

**Word
processing**

Hardware

What is hardware?

When talking about computers, people often refer to hardware, particularly in terms of upgrading or replacing it. Hardware combines with software to form a usable computing system.

SEE ALSO

❮ **14–15** Computers are everywhere

❮ **34–35** Inside a computer

❮ **36–37** Peripheral devices

❮ **38–39** The computer chip

Basic hardware

Hardware is everything in or connected to a computer that's part of the physical world and can be touched. This includes the computer itself, with a screen, keyboard, and mouse. It also includes devices connected to a computer, such as speakers and memory cards. The computer's internal components are considered hardware as well.

All electronic components in a computer are connected to a circuit board called a motherboard.

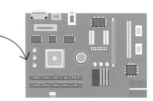

Motherboard

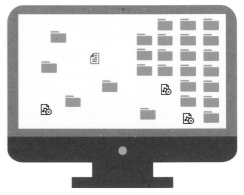

Monitor

▷ **Internal and external hardware**
Users constantly interact with external hardware devices like keyboards. Unless you have expert knowledge or assistance, it's recommended not to touch the internal hardware.

Types of hardware device

Hardware devices are grouped into several categories. They can either be integral to the computer (such as a motherboard) or attached to it via cables, Wi-Fi, or Bluetooth. Hardware devices that aren't an integral part of the main computer unit—such as keyboards, mice, screens, printers, and scanners—are called peripherals. Cell phones and tablets usually have integrated hardware devices and don't need peripherals. Here are some common hardware devices.

Scanner

Keyboard

Camera

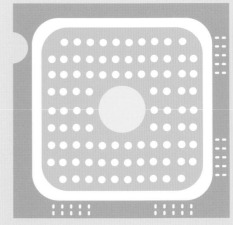

Processing chip

△ **Input devices**
These devices are used to input data or instructions. Some input devices, such as scanners and cameras, allow the input of digitized information that can be stored or processed.

△ **Processing devices**
These devices take data and instructions to produce new variations of data. Computers may also have specialized processing devices that deal with graphics or audio and video signals.

Upgrading existing hardware

Over time, computer hardware can slow down or completely stop working. When this happens, it's not always necessary to buy a whole new computer. It's often possible to upgrade a computer by buying new internal hardware for it. There are several common upgrades. These include: increasing the amount of internal memory (RAM), buying a new hard drive to increase storage space, or getting storage that can be accessed more efficiently. Gaming enthusiasts sometimes buy an improved graphics processing unit (GPU) to play games with higher-quality graphics.

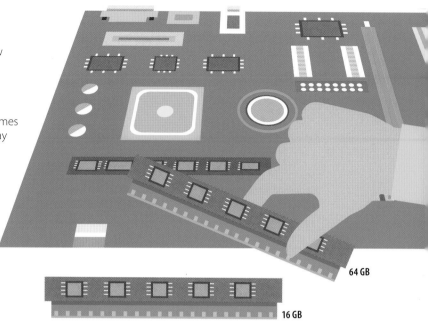

64 GB

16 GB

REAL WORLD

Recycling

When replacing components or buying a new computer, it's a good idea to find out if the old equipment can be recycled. Charities often accept old computers in good condition. Many companies recycle equipment in an environmentally friendly way.

Printer

Speaker

VR goggles

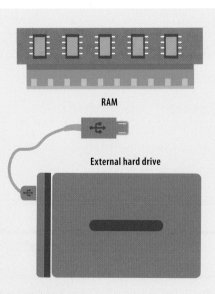

RAM

External hard drive

△ **Output devices**
These devices take data from the computer and present it to the user. Newer output devices include virtual reality (VR) goggles that immerse users in a 3D world.

△ **Storage devices**
These devices enable computers to save data when they are not powered on. Apart from hard drives and random access memory (RAM), storage devices also include USB flash drives and memory cards.

Desktop computers and laptops

SEE ALSO

❮ **16–17** Computing for you

❮ **32–33** Computing since the 1940s

❮ **36–37** Peripheral devices

The word "computer" is mainly associated with desktop and laptop computers. Each has a wide range of uses, but they also have their own pros and cons.

What is a computer?

A computer is an electronic device that manipulates data. It can receive input and perform a sequence of programmed instructions to produce a result. The original digital computers filled entire rooms, and personal computers (PCs)—small, affordable devices that individuals could own and operate—didn't appear until the 1970s. The PC revolution of the 1970s and 1980s saw an increase in computers with relatively easy-to-use software that brought computers to many homes.

▽ **Home and business**
Nowadays, the majority of homes and businesses use computers for everyday activities. These include communicating via email and social media, scheduling via calendars, shopping, and entertainment.

Desktops vs. laptops

People who need to do fairly substantial amounts of work may require a computer. Desktop computers are stationary and sit on a desk or table. They operate from a AC power supply, and usually have a separate screen, mouse, and keyboard. They are versatile and cheaper than a similarly powerful laptop. Laptop computers, on the other hand, are portable; battery- or AC-powered; and have an integrated screen or touchscreen, touchpad, and keyboard. They are usually more expensive and tend to have smaller screens and keyboards.

▷ **Which to choose?**
For most people, the choice is based on a combination of factors, such as price, portability, available space, and what the computer is to be used for.

	Pros	Cons
Desktop	Cheaper	Not portable
	More design options	Takes up more space
	Usually more processing power	Harder to set up
Laptop	Portable	More rigidly designed
	Easy to set up	Less versatile
	Takes up less space	More expensive

Windows PC vs. Mac

The two most popular types of computer are PCs and Macs. PCs usually run on the Microsoft Windows operating system (OS). They are the most widely used type of computer, particularly in businesses, and there is a wide range of software available for them. However, PCs are more prone to viruses and malware because of their popularity and the design of the OS. Macs—made by Apple Inc.—are less widely used but are particularly popular with graphic designers and photographers. They tend to be more expensive, but they are less vulnerable to viruses.

The **choice** of **desktop or laptop, PC or Mac** is a **personal** one.

	Pros	Cons
Windows PC	Usually cheaper	More susceptible to viruses
	More software available	Frequent OS updates
	More hardware available	Tend not to last as long
Mac	Better quality and design	More expensive
	Smooth user experience	Less hardware available
	Lower risk of viruses	Slightly smaller choice of software

▷ **Which to choose?**
This depends on a variety of factors: price, what system the user is most comfortable with, whether or not the software they need is available for their choice, and how the computer will be used.

Weighing the factors

Before choosing a new computer, it's worth thinking carefully about various factors. These include what it will be used for, whether portability or space is important, what the available budget is, and whether there are ergonomic issues that need to be considered. When it comes to the choice between a PC or Mac, a great deal depends on the user's familiarity with either of these types of computer. Asking family or friends for their recommendations is a good way to get help in making a decision.

▽ **Right for the job**
The choice of desktop or laptop, and PC or Mac, is a personal one. Numerous factors can influence a decision, but there is no perfect computer—just computers that are right for the tasks for which they are needed.

Smartphones and tablets

Perhaps the most popular types of computer, smartphones and tablet computers have changed the way we do just about everything online.

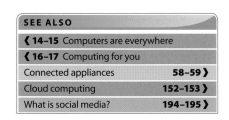

SEE ALSO	
❮ **14–15** Computers are everywhere	
❮ **16–17** Computing for you	
Connected appliances	**58–59** ❯
Cloud computing	**152–153** ❯
What is social media?	**194–195** ❯

Billions of users

There are more than 2 billion smartphones and 1 billion tablets in active use worldwide. The first smartphone appeared in 1992, with IBM's Simon Personal Computer—a mail box–sized device that featured a digital panel. The real revolution in the field was the release of the Apple iPhone in 2007. Apple also released the iPad in 2010, the first tablet computer to prove a hit, though other companies had tried the idea before. Both allow users to run software applications, or apps, to make use of the hardware and are navigated by using a touchscreen.

A speaker allows sound to be heard.

Tablets have a much bigger screen than smartphones, which is more suited to watching films and shopping online.

Users touch and drag their fingers on the tablet's touchscreen to navigate.

Some tablets and smartphones feature a fingerprint scanner that unlocks the device when a recognized finger is pressed against it.

Messaging apps may use either cellular networks or the Internet.

Smartphones often have a built-in camera that can take videos or photographs.

A microphone on the bottom can pick up or record sound.

△ **Mobile connectivity**
Smartphones are able to send and receive cellular signals but can also connect to the Internet via Wi-Fi, show the phone's GPS location, and connect to other devices over Bluetooth.

△ **Bigger and more powerful**
Tablets are bigger than smartphones, which makes them less portable. They usually have more processing power than smartphones and can handle more complex apps.

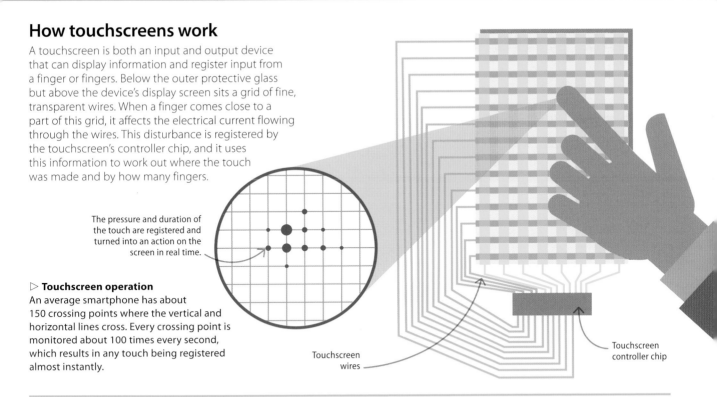

How touchscreens work

A touchscreen is both an input and output device that can display information and register input from a finger or fingers. Below the outer protective glass but above the device's display screen sits a grid of fine, transparent wires. When a finger comes close to a part of this grid, it affects the electrical current flowing through the wires. This disturbance is registered by the touchscreen's controller chip, and it uses this information to work out where the touch was made and by how many fingers.

The pressure and duration of the touch are registered and turned into an action on the screen in real time.

▷ **Touchscreen operation**
An average smartphone has about 150 crossing points where the vertical and horizontal lines cross. Every crossing point is monitored about 100 times every second, which results in any touch being registered almost instantly.

Touchscreen wires

Touchscreen controller chip

Tilt and twist

Smartphones and tablets detect changes in the orientation (position) of the phone. The accelerometer is a tiny chip that senses the tilting motion of the device. The gyroscope is a chip that adds more information to the accelerometer by measuring rotation or twists.

▽ **Accelerometer and gyroscope**
Accelerometers and gyroscopes are useful for changing the display of the device depending on how it is held, such as showing images in the right orientation, or as an additional input when playing games.

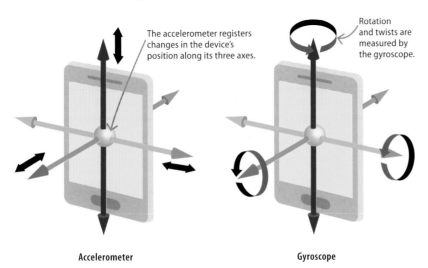

The accelerometer registers changes in the device's position along its three axes.

Rotation and twists are measured by the gyroscope.

Accelerometer

Gyroscope

Voice navigation

Smartphones and tablets have become increasingly interactive and easier to use. A lot of the applications on a modern smartphone or tablet can understand voice commands and react to them in real time. This is a huge help to disabled people who might not be able to use a touchscreen.

Which is the fastest land animal?

Build your own computers

SEE ALSO

❬ **40–41** How modern computers compute

Predicting the future   **224–225** ❭

The Internet of Things   **226–227** ❭

Most computers today are slick consumer devices that hide what's going on inside them. Several organizations are challenging this by encouraging people to build their own machines.

Equipment required

Do-it-yourself (DIY) computers are split into low-cost microcomputers, such as the Raspberry Pi, and microcontrollers, devices that hold only one program at a time. Although the devices themselves are inexpensive, they all require additional equipment. A Raspberry Pi needs a keyboard, mouse, HDMI cable, screen, power supply, and SD card. All the required software is free via the Raspberry Pi site. Microcontrollers, such as the micro:bit and Arduino boards, need another computer where the code to be uploaded to them can be written and transferred to the microcontroller via a USB cable.

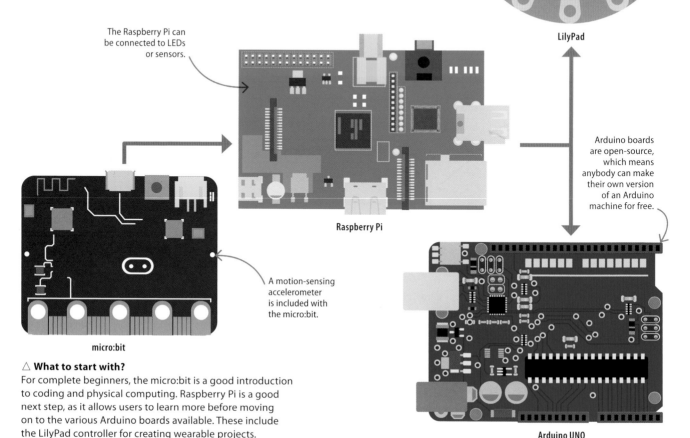

The LilyPad microcontroller can be sewn into clothes.

LilyPad

The Raspberry Pi can be connected to LEDs or sensors.

Raspberry Pi

Arduino boards are open-source, which means anybody can make their own version of an Arduino machine for free.

A motion-sensing accelerometer is included with the micro:bit.

micro:bit

Arduino UNO

△ **What to start with?**

For complete beginners, the micro:bit is a good introduction to coding and physical computing. Raspberry Pi is a good next step, as it allows users to learn more before moving on to the various Arduino boards available. These include the LilyPad controller for creating wearable projects.

Physical computing

One of the most exciting things about DIY electronics kits, such as the Raspberry Pi, Arduino, or micro:bit, is their potential for physical computing. Physical computing connects the digital world inside a computer to the physical world using cameras, LEDs, sensors, and other inputs and outputs.

Lights!

△ **Things to make**
Physical computing has been used in many projects, such as remote-controlled robots, voice-activated lights, computer-controlled cameras on weather balloons to capture photos from space, and many others.

Maker Movement

In recent years, there's been a rise in popularity of the Maker Movement, where people get together and build DIY projects using traditional crafts and modern electronics. Makerspaces, Fab Labs, Hackerspaces, and similar collaborative spaces exist in many cities, enabling people to share their ideas, time, and resources.

Online resources ▽
For people who don't have access to makerspaces, there are many project ideas and instructions available online. Free how-to guides for a variety of projects can be found on sites such as Make, Instructables, and Adafruit.

"The **Maker Movement** is about moving from **consumption to creation**, and turning **knowledge into action**."
Laura Fleming, educator and makerspace author

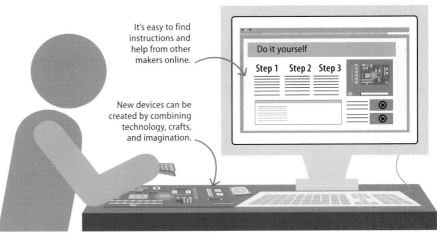

It's easy to find instructions and help from other makers online.

New devices can be created by combining technology, crafts, and imagination.

Do it yourself

Step 1   Step 2   Step 3

Wearable computers

SEE ALSO

❰ 18–19 Computing with others

Predicting the future   224–225 ❱

The Internet of Things   226–227 ❱

In recent years, computers have become small enough to wear and may be equipped with a variety of sensors. This has opened up a whole new range of uses and applications for them.

Smartwatches

The first digital watch was released in 1972. Originally a straightforward timepiece, later versions incorporated calculators, games, calendars, and memo applications. Watches that could connect to computers were available from as early as 1984, but they had limited functions. The Apple Watch, launched in 2015, has functions typical of modern smartwatches: it integrates with the owner's smartphone, allowing the user to take and make phone calls, track their fitness, and pay for things.

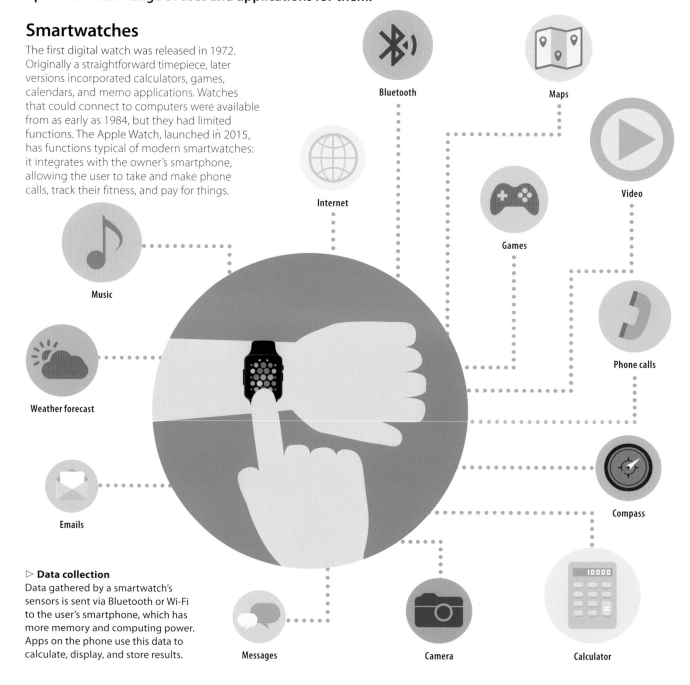

Bluetooth

Maps

Internet

Video

Games

Music

Phone calls

Weather forecast

Compass

Emails

Messages

Camera

Calculator

▷ **Data collection**
Data gathered by a smartwatch's sensors is sent via Bluetooth or Wi-Fi to the user's smartphone, which has more memory and computing power. Apps on the phone use this data to calculate, display, and store results.

Activity trackers

Since smartwatches have many integrated sensors, they often come equipped with apps that are designed to monitor health-related data. Activity trackers are also available, which function similarly to smartwatches, but without the phone or paying capabilities. Apps allow people to measure how many steps they take each day, their heart rate, and how much they sleep, among other things. Smartwatches for children allow their parents to track them via GPS.

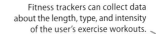

Fitness trackers can collect data about the length, type, and intensity of the user's exercise workouts.

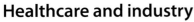

▷ **Sensors**
The integrated sensors in a smartwatch can include accelerometers, heart-rate monitors, light sensors, thermometers, and sensors that measure the level of oxygen in a user's blood.

Healthcare and industry

Wearable computers have a number of potential uses in healthcare and in the workplace. Sensors worn on the skin can be used to monitor a diabetic user's blood glucose levels. Google Glass—a pair of smart glasses that project digital information over the wearer's field of vision—is being tested as an aid to help factory workers assemble complex items.

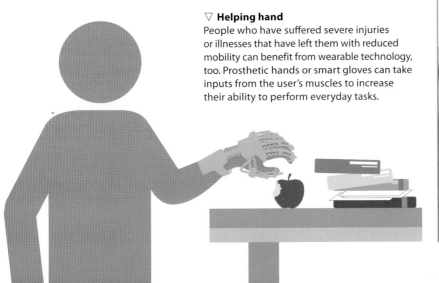

▽ **Helping hand**
People who have suffered severe injuries or illnesses that have left them with reduced mobility can benefit from wearable technology, too. Prosthetic hands or smart gloves can take inputs from the user's muscles to increase their ability to perform everyday tasks.

REAL WORLD
Criminal justice

Many countries employ an electronic tagging system that uses devices worn on the ankle to restrict people convicted of crimes to their homes or another area. The devices use GPS signals to track the convicted person and signal to police if they leave the designated area. There are even electronic tagging systems that are able to detect whether the user has consumed alcohol or drugs.

Connected appliances

Turning lights on by speaking to them may sound like science fiction, but Internet-connected household devices allow people to do this and much more.

SEE ALSO	
❮ 52–53 Smartphones and tablets	
❮ 56–57 Wearable computers	
The Internet of Things	226–227 ❯

Smart appliances and how they work

Smart appliances are home devices and gadgets that are controlled using apps on a smartphone or via interactive panels in the home. The earliest smart homes appeared in the 1970s, when a Scottish company called Pico Electronics introduced the X10 system. This system allowed people to control electrical devices in their homes using a central computer controller and their existing electrical wiring system. Nowadays, devices include tiny computers that can connect to smartphones via Bluetooth or Wi-Fi, allowing users to control their devices, even when they are not physically at home.

IN DEPTH

Benefits of a connected home

A home installed with smart devices has a number of benefits. Instead of worrying about having left a computer on, a user can check the device's status and switch it off via their smartphone. An indoor positioning system (IPS) can locate objects and people inside a house using sensory information. Smart appliance apps also give users access to data about how long they have been used for and how much energy they have used.

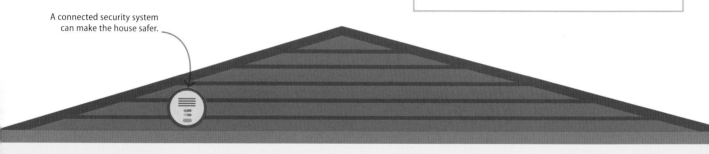

A connected security system can make the house safer.

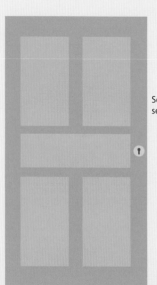

Some smart devices can send a video feed to the home owner so they can decide whether or not to open the door.

◁ **Home security systems**
Internet-connected devices can be used to keep people safe and secure at home. Smart locks can open the front door automatically for approved people but keep strangers out. Smart smoke alarms can turn electrical appliances off if they detect smoke or carbon monoxide, and even alert emergency services.

A digital assistant can send a command to close the garage door.

Voice commands can be used to operate a smart device.

Close the garage door!

▷ **Digital assistants**
A digital assistant is a small device that uses the Internet to answer questions put to them by an owner. They can also be linked up to smart devices in the home and used to control things such as lighting, doors, and temperature.

9:30 AM

Make coffee!

◁ Smart plant monitor

Smart devices and appliances contain sensors that allow their internal computers to gather data. A smart plant monitor can detect low levels of moisture in a plant's soil and either message the owner or, if they have an attached reservoir, release some water automatically.

A smartphone can tell a connected coffee machine to start making coffee.

The user can receive an alert from the smart plant monitor upstairs.

App-based appliances ▽

Connected appliances allow users to check the status of things in their home, wherever they are. A connected refrigerator can keep track of what is inside it and if the food is still safe to eat. A connected coffee machine can prepare coffee while the owner is getting dressed in the morning.

A coffee machine can receive a command from the user's smartphone.

▽ Robots in the home

Home robots include a vacuum cleaner with Wi-Fi access that can be controlled from a smartphone app, a robot lawn mower, and a robot alarm clock on wheels that drives away, forcing its owner to get out of bed to switch it off.

Digital toys

Today even the very young interact with technology, often in the form of games and apps on their parents' smartphones or tablets. Technology can help children learn through play.

SEE ALSO
❮ **18–19** Computing with others
❮ **52–53** Smartphones and tablets
Encoding audio and video **92–93** ❯

Technology for the very young

For kids aged between 2 and 5, technology is not all about computers. Anything where pressing a button makes something happen can be considered some kind of technology. Almost without exception, children find technology interesting, exciting, and motivating. Of course, too much reliance on technology can be detrimental, particularly when not supported by interaction with a parent or caregiver. However, children can gain useful skills exploring technology as part of a wide range of play activities.

▷ **Nondigital toys**
Though kids have access to digital technology, they are still interested in nondigital toys and games.

▽ **Digital toys**
Digital technology is part of today's world, and kids should use it to play and learn.

Toys containing computers

Many toys today include small, embedded computers that make the toy move or emit sounds. They may include speech recognition programs that enable them to react to a child's instructions or sensors that react when the toy is touched. These are essentially updated versions of earlier toys that played recorded phrases when a string was pulled.

▷ **A different age**
Children in earlier times also played with toys that could be made to move independently, such as wind-up train sets or clockwork cars and toy animals.

REAL WORLD

Automatons

Children's toys that try to give the appearance of being alive through technology have been popular since the 19th century. These toys, known as automatons, were usually powered by clockwork or by a user moving them directly by turning a handle.

Integrating digital and physical

Smart toys can make a useful contribution to a child's learning experience. This is particularly true when they are combined with play and learning in the real world. Toys that use technology to simulate real-world technologies such as telephones, cash registers, and office equipment can be used as part of imagination-boosting role-playing games with other children or parents. Smart toys that reinforce physical learning activities, such as counting with objects or learning to read and spell, are also beneficial.

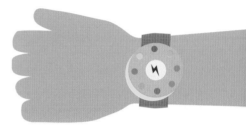

Wearable toys △
Wearable toys contain sensors that detect movement and other elements, such as lights and buzzers. Children can create games and gadgets by coding them to react to different sorts of movement.

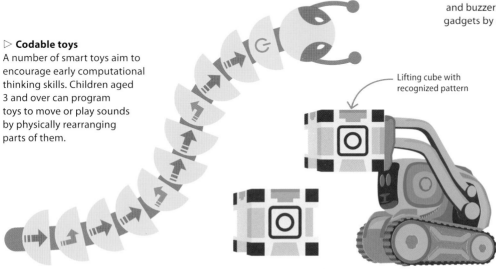

▷ **Codable toys**
A number of smart toys aim to encourage early computational thinking skills. Children aged 3 and over can program toys to move or play sounds by physically rearranging parts of them.

Lifting cube with recognized pattern

Little robots ◁
Smart toys include robots with machine-learning programs that let them recognize their owner and learn about their environment. They can also do tasks such as lifting objects or recognizing patterns.

Creative tools

Many electronic and digital tools aim to teach children literacy or numerical skills, but they can also be used to encourage creativity and exploration. One example is showing children how to make stop-motion films with modeling clay or toys using a simple digital camera and a video-editing program. They can then add a voiceover or music by recording it themselves or getting sounds from the Internet.

Children enjoy showing their creations to their parents.

▷ **Keep in touch**
Technology can be a useful tool for maintaining social links. Including children in the process of emailing or video-calling family or friends living far away is a good way to help them learn more.

Gaming consoles

Playing computer games is a popular pastime for many people. Many young people learn the basics of coding by creating their own games.

SEE ALSO

❰ **32–33** Computing since the 1940s
❰ **44–45** Operating systems
Gaming and social networks   **204–205** ❱
Computer science
and disabilities   **220–221** ❱
Careers   **240–243** ❱

Playing games

Computer gaming is often seen as a solitary pursuit, but in fact playing online multiplayer games can be a very sociable experience. Some of the earliest games, including Pong and Atari's Space Race, were for two players playing on the same computer. These days, many games offer players the ability to play each other regardless of where they are on Earth through online play. This means that friends can catch up as they play a game together, or players can find completely new people to play with. People often use headsets or onscreen text messages to communicate with each other.

▷ **Open to all**
Computer games let people of different ages and abilities connect and have fun together. They can also allow people with physical disabilities to compete in a way they aren't able to in real-world sports.

Game controllers

It's possible to play many games using a normal computer keyboard, but this isn't always easy, particularly with fast-paced action games. There are a number of dedicated game controllers available, the most familiar being the joystick (originally designed as a control for airplanes). Many controllers even incorporate haptic feedback, where the controller vibrates or resists movement, to add to the gaming experience.

Player's body movement

Dance mat

▷ **Unusual controllers**
Some controllers move away from traditional buttons and joysticks. Many are designed to look like something in the game—so a steering-wheel controller for a driving game or a guitar controller for a music-rhythm game. Others, such as Microsoft's Kinect camera or dance mats, let players control a game by body movements.

Guitar controller

Steering-wheel controller

Types of game

Books and films are often grouped by genre or type. Similarly, most computer games fall into a particular class of game. Although there can be a lot of variation within a genre, most games of a particular type will emphasize certain skills, activities, and experiences. Here are some of the most popular gaming genres.

IN DEPTH

Early computer games

Early computer games focused on collisions, explosions, and shooting. This was partly because they were relatively easy to code and play. This influenced many earlier controllers, which focused on the ability to shoot and maneuver easily.

Action
Fast-paced games where the player has to steer a character or vehicle around obstacles.

Strategy
Games like chess or simulated war games where logic and planning are required.

Adventure
Games where players explore a fantasy world or setting, solving puzzles and avoiding dangers.

Sports
Games that simulate sports. Some include controllers that mimic sports equipment.

Party games
Games where several players in the same room compete to win a series of mini-games.

Puzzles
Games where the player has to solve tricky puzzles to advance through the levels.

Role-playing games
Games where the player assumes the identity of a character undertaking a quest or mission.

Simulation
Games that allow players to experience controlling a real-life situation—for example, driving a car.

Targeting
Games where players shoot at targets.

Open world
Games where the player can explore a world and the adventures possible within it.

Computers and consoles

Computer games can be played on normal desktop computers or laptops, but regular gamers often use specialized gaming computers or consoles. The Windows operating system supports the largest number of games. A gaming PC is usually more powerful than general-purpose ones, as it has an extra processor to deal with displaying graphics. A games console is a dedicated computer that's only intended for playing games.

REAL WORLD

Data collection

Many games collect data about players and send this back to the software companies via the Internet. This data can include how long the player is playing for, game scores, and how much money they spend on items in the game. Games can also use controllers to collect data, including biometrics such as weight and facial features. Games played on smartphones can even collect location data.

◁ **Custom built**
Many serious gamers prefer to build their own gaming computer by putting together the necessary components. This allows them to hand-pick elements, such as graphics cards and RAM, that suit what they want to use the machine for.

Hidden computers

Lots of people regularly use computers for work, entertainment, or both. But there are more computers in everyday life than people may be aware of.

SEE ALSO	
❮ **14–15** Computers are everywhere	
The Internet of Things	**226–227** ❯
Biological interfaces	**234–235** ❯

Computers in unexpected places

Nowadays, computers can be found in places you might not expect. It may be in a fork that can tell if a person is eating too fast, a baby-feeding bottle that lets a user know if the baby is swallowing air, and power tools that connect to an app. On a larger scale, traffic lights in many cities can be controlled from a central location. Using data from sensors and video cameras enables controllers to react to heavy traffic or other incidents.

▽ **Internet connected**
Many smart devices are connected to the Internet by cables, Wi-Fi, or Bluetooth. This allows users to control or view data from their devices.

Controller uses data to modify traffic signals.

Smart fork

Smart bottle

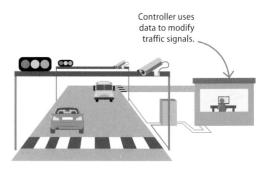

Traffic control

Shopping

Shoppers may find themselves targeted by devices that transmit ads or special offers to their phones using Bluetooth. If the user has a store's app installed, the offer will be displayed on their phone. Stores may also use facial analysis software to display ads tailored to the age or gender of an approaching customer.

An on-card computer chip encrypts a customer's bank information.

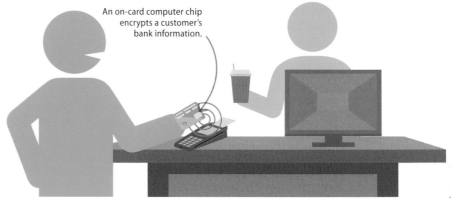

▷ **Contactless payments**
Contactless payment cards send data to a reader device using a tiny transmitter that emits radio waves. The data is encrypted by a specialized computer chip on the card.

Human health

Modern prosthetics sometimes use hidden computer technology. Some prosthetic legs have microprocessors that enable a patient to walk more naturally by adjusting the knee. Other prostheses use computer chips to take electrical impulses from nerve endings to move a leg or arm.

▽ Fitness
Many gyms have equipment that includes hidden computers and sensors. These monitor data such as heart rate, temperature, or calories burned while exercising.

▽ Programmed care
Smart IV pumps can be programmed to deliver a specific dose of medicine in intervals according to the patient's needs.

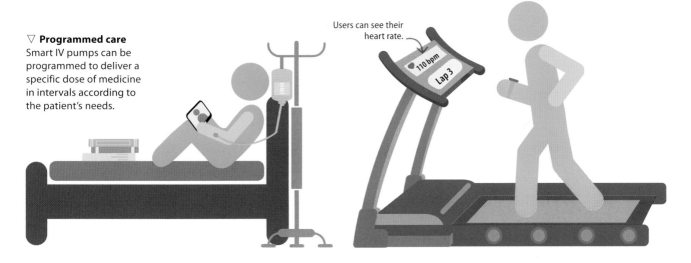

Users can see their heart rate.

110 bpm

Lap 3

Ethics and privacy

There are ethical and political issues surrounding hidden computers that could collect data on, or images of, people. As more and more devices have the ability to collect and share data, the question of consent has become a hot topic. Previously, companies assumed consent or obtained it by including it in long-winded Terms and Conditions agreements. Many countries are changing their laws so that users will have much more control over the data collected from them.

△ Facial recognition
Some smart devices use facial recognition or facial-feature analysis. These may inadvertently discriminate against racial groups or sexes because of biases in the software.

△ Spying
Spying devices are designed to look like ordinary household items but can contain hidden cameras and computers and can share their data via Wi-Fi, Bluetooth, or cell phone networks.

△ Information theft
Though experts feel the risk of this is quite low, it's possible that criminals could use devices to fool contactless cards into emitting bank details.

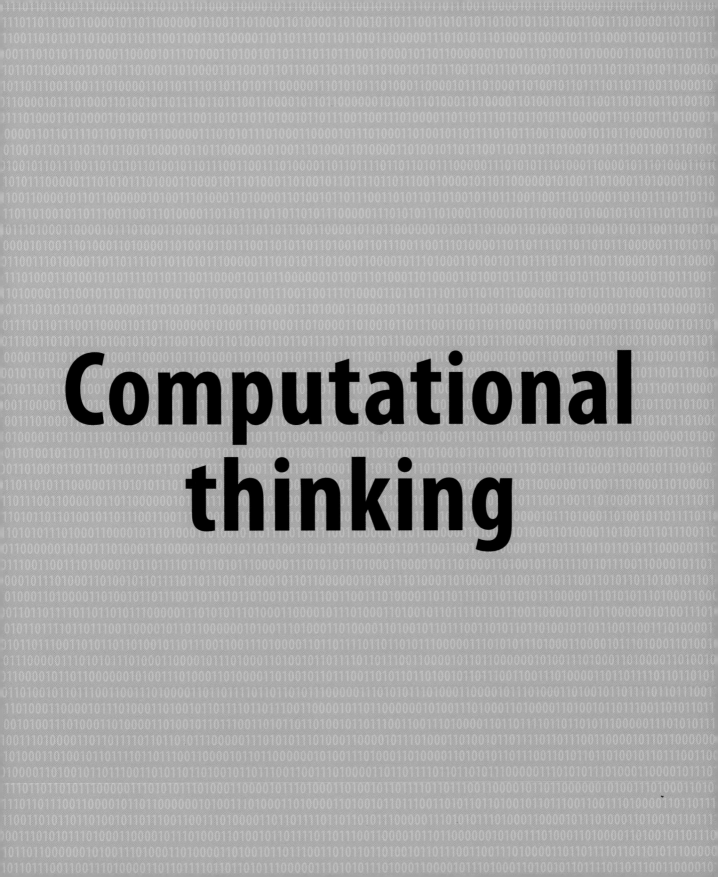

Computational thinking

What is computational thinking?

SEE ALSO

❰ 28–29 Computer science	
Decomposition	**70–71** ❱
Abstraction	**72–73** ❱
Patterns	**74–75** ❱
Algorithms	**76–77** ❱
Scratch	**136–137** ❱

Computational thinking is the collective thought process involved in figuring out problems and finding their solutions in ways that can be understood by a computer, a human, or both.

Problem solving

The goal of computational thinking is to produce instructions that enable a computer to solve a particular problem. These instructions have to be written in a language that computers understand, letting them know what they can do and how. There are four main stages to computational thinking.

3. Pattern recognition

While solving a problem, computer scientists try to find parts that are similar to problems they've solved before. Recognizing these patterns is useful, as it means that they can use or modify an existing solution to solve their current problem.

2. Abstraction

In order to write efficient sets of instructions, computer scientists need to be able to look at a situation, or problem, and work out its essential and nonessential parts. An abstraction is a model of a system, or object, that leaves out unnecessary details.

The lower pyramid is an abstraction of the one above, with details like doors and bricks removed.

The patterns in the two squares match.

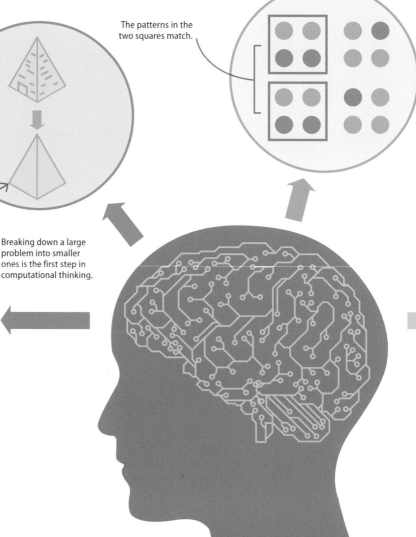

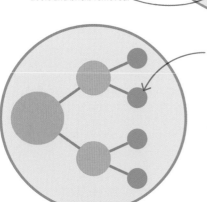

Breaking down a large problem into smaller ones is the first step in computational thinking.

1. Decomposition

Decomposition is the process of breaking down a problem into smaller subproblems. It's usually possible to break down an overwhelming task into several smaller, more manageable tasks. Tackling each of these one by one gets the original problem solved.

Thinking skills

Although computational thinking developed as a way for computer scientists to solve problems, it is useful in many areas. At work, people use decomposition—a key skill in computational thinking—by breaking down jobs into smaller tasks. Sometimes, it's possible to reuse a plan from a previous task for a new one, if there is a similar pattern to the work.

An algorithm can be written as a flowchart.

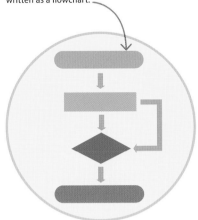

4. Algorithms
An algorithm is a series of instructions that solve a problem. Each instruction must be precise and unambiguous so that there's no doubt about what it means. Programs are algorithms translated into programming languages.

How to think computationally
A good way to practice computational thinking is to step away from the computer. Doing things in a particular order, making decisions, and repeating actions are all elements of everyday tasks. They are also the basic elements of computer programs. Writing instructions for a task that everyone does without much thought can be trickier than expected.

◁ **Precise instructions**
Writing a set of instructions accurate enough for a computer to make a sandwich can be quite a challenge. Unlike people, computers can't cope with any ambiguity. To make a jelly sandwich, it's important to write instructions that can be followed exactly—so the jelly, not the jar, ends up inside the sandwich!

▷ **Different solutions**
Often, particularly in math and science, kids learn that there's a single right answer to questions. Computational thinking is applied to open-ended problems—those that have many possible solutions.

What would you like for dessert?

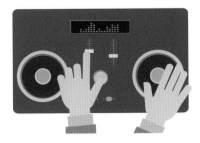

◁ **Remixing**
Another activity that promotes computational thinking is remixing—taking code that someone has shared and changing parts of it. This allows new coders to build up their understanding gradually and create something new in the process.

▷ **Getting social**
Programming is often viewed as an activity carried out in isolation. However, in the workplace, coders usually work in pairs or teams. In addition to online coding communities like Scratch, there are various coding clubs that young people interested in coding and technology can join.

Decomposition

SEE ALSO

❰ 28–29 Computer science
❰ 68–69 What is computational thinking?
What do programming
languages do?   118–119 ❱

Decomposition doesn't sound like the sort of thing anyone would want happening near a computer. Luckily, this decomposition is actually the first step in the computational thinking process.

What is decomposition?

Decomposition is the process of breaking down problems into smaller components. An effective tool in computational thinking, it allows programmers to build effective solutions. When an apple decomposes, it's breaking down into simpler chemicals that other plants can use as food. In a similar way, a problem can be solved by splitting it into smaller parts that a programmer already knows how to tackle.

▷ **Find the subproblems**
A lot of everyday problems are actually made up of smaller parts, which we can call subproblems.

Modular code

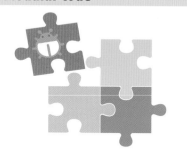

Building a program by writing small amounts of code to solve subproblems is known as a modular approach. If there is a problem with a part of the code, it can easily be taken out and fixed. Each smaller solution is tested before it's added to the main program. Breaking the original problem into subproblems also gives programmers the option of sharing the work among a team.

Computer sense

Computers, unlike people, don't have any common sense or knowledge of how things work. They do exactly what they're told to do, even if the instructions are ridiculous or totally wrong. When writing a program for a computer to solve a problem, computer scientists must include precise and detailed instructions on how to do each tiny step.

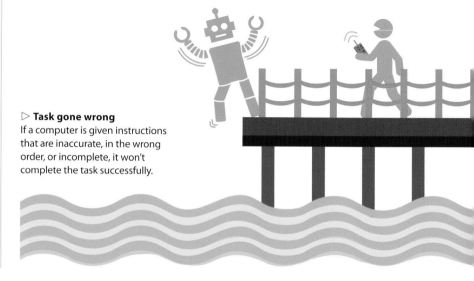

▷ **Task gone wrong**
If a computer is given instructions that are inaccurate, in the wrong order, or incomplete, it won't complete the task successfully.

Decomposition in action

Decomposition is a lot like baking a cake. Both involve a task and some tools. In baking, the task is to make a cake and the tools are the bowl, spoon, oven, and ingredients. In computing, the task might be to write a program and the tools are a computer and programming language. A good way to start is to look at the problem in more detail and break it down into smaller tasks.

△ **Getting it right**
Breaking down the steps and then successfully completing each one will result in getting the cake right. In computer science, it's important to know what the objective is before beginning to write code.

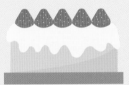

△ **Getting it wrong**
Not working in a step-by-step manner to bake a cake or build a solution will result in failure.

Important parts
Breaking down a problem into smaller parts helps find an effective solution. Each part must then be completed successfully and in the right order to get the required result.

Ingredients and preparation
To bake a cake, the first step is to buy or gather the ingredients. The right amount of each ingredient must then be prepared while the oven heats up to the correct temperature.

Timing and combining
Each ingredient must be added and combined at the right time before the mixture is put in the oven.

Baking
The next step is to ensure that the mixture is baked at the right temperature and for the required amount of time.

Finishing
Finally, the cake must be removed from the tray and allowed to cool. It can then be decorated so that it both looks and tastes nice.

Building a spaceship

No matter how complex a computer program is, it's made up of solutions to lots of tiny problems. The process of building a complicated model of a spaceship out of building blocks is similar. Each part is the solution to a subproblem, and combining the components creates the spaceship.

We often solve a **problem** by **breaking** it down into **smaller parts**.

Abstraction

Abstraction involves looking at a problem and filtering out all the unnecessary information. Identifying the essential parts of a problem helps people to figure out a solution.

SEE ALSO	
❮ 68–69 What is computational thinking?	
Storing and retrieving data	**106–107 ❯**
What do programming languages do?	**118–119 ❯**
What is a network?	**144–145 ❯**
Using social networks	**202–203 ❯**

Bare essentials

Abstraction is the process of working out which elements of an object or system are its defining features. Without them, the object wouldn't be what it is. Spanish artist Pablo Picasso often painted abstract portraits where faces look nothing like they do in the real world. Yet since they contain the essential features of a face—the eyes, nose, and mouth—they are recognizable.

The house can be recognized from the painting even without the details.

▷ **Which details are unnecessary?**
The essential details of a house are the walls, roof, door, and windows. Things like the color or number of windows are not essential details.

REAL WORLD

Railway maps

Many modern maps of train and subway systems are examples of abstraction. Earlier maps accurately showed the path a railway line took and included the distances between stations. However, they were hard to read, as they gave information that passengers didn't need, such as the exact route, and made it difficult to see information that they did need, such as the order of stations on a line. Newer maps simplify the information so passengers can see the most efficient way to get from A to B.

Finding the right level of detail

The trick with abstraction is to get the balance right between essential and nonessential information. For example, when passing on instructions for a task, too many steps can cause confusion, and too few can mean the task is not done correctly. Computer programmers need to get the balance just right in order for their programs to fix the problem.

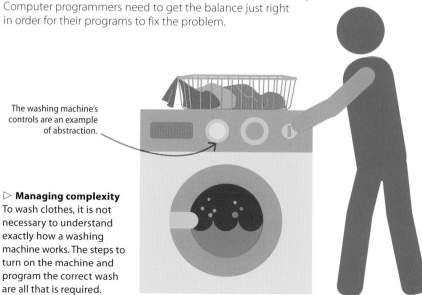

The washing machine's controls are an example of abstraction.

▷ **Managing complexity**
To wash clothes, it is not necessary to understand exactly how a washing machine works. The steps to turn on the machine and program the correct wash are all that is required.

Making a model

A model is a representation of a real-world system or object. It has the object's main features and is easy to recognize, but it's clearly not the real thing. For instance, a model of the Eiffel Tower might be really small and made of blue plastic, but it is still recognizable as the Eiffel Tower. In a similar way, a computer model of an object or system won't have a lot of the details, but it should be a recognizable representation of it—it is an abstraction of the real thing.

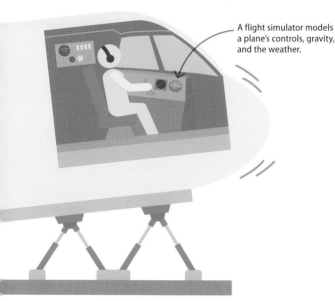

A flight simulator models a plane's controls, gravity, and the weather.

△ **Why make a model?**
A real-world model allows users to analyze the system without damaging it or endangering themselves. A flight simulator allows pilots to practice handling a variety of difficult and dangerous situations without any real danger. Likewise, a computer model allows programmers to figure out what solutions might work for the problem at hand.

TOP TECH
Programming languages

Earlier programming languages required programmers to move values around the computer's internal storage. Modern languages, on the other hand, are examples of abstraction. They allow programmers to instruct computers in a more natural way without knowing exactly what's going on inside.

Identifying variables

A model based on only the essential parts of an object or system limits the amount of analysis possible. An important step is to identify other details that change how the model behaves as the value of the details change. These nonessential details are called variables because their values vary rather than staying the same. Computer scientists have to work out which nonessential details in a system actually make a difference to the model's behavior. These can then be added to the model.

Milk, sugar, and lemon are nonessential.

Boiling water, cup, and tea bag are essential.

Essentials   Variables

△ **Tea variables**
In a model cup of tea, a cup, boiling water, and a tea bag or tea leaves are essential. The amounts of sugar, milk, or lemon are variables. The outcome depends on how much sugar, milk, or lemon is added.

"All **art is** an **abstraction** to some degree."
Henry Moore (1898–1986), English artist

REAL WORLD
Hidden networks

Stripping away nonessential details can show that two seemingly different problems can actually be the same. Social media networks seem new, but they are like any other network—simply points linked by paths. This means that existing programming solutions can be used for social network tasks.

Patterns

Recognizing patterns is an important part of everyday life, as it makes interacting with the world easier and more efficient. It's also an important part of computational thinking.

SEE ALSO

❮ **68–69** What is computational thinking?

❮ **72–73** Abstraction

Databases **88–89** ❯

Identifying patterns

A pattern involves repetition in a predictable manner and lets anyone who recognizes it draw a conclusion. It could be something as simple as a pattern of repeated shapes on a plate. This pattern helps in identifying the plate as part of a particular set of tableware. Recognizing patterns also helps people understand the world more easily. A small vehicle with an engine, four wheels, and no wings is likely to be a car. Its behavior can also be predicted—it can move at potentially dangerous speeds, but not take off and fly away.

REAL WORLD

Seeing patterns

The human brain is constantly searching for familiar patterns, so much so that people often see patterns that aren't there. This phenomenon, where a person might think a cloud looks like a particular object or see a face in a piece of toast, is known as pareidolia. Computers can only recognize faces in pictures if humans write programs that train them what to look for.

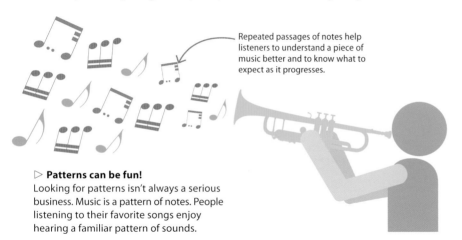

Repeated passages of notes help listeners to understand a piece of music better and to know what to expect as it progresses.

▷ **Patterns can be fun!**
Looking for patterns isn't always a serious business. Music is a pattern of notes. People listening to their favorite songs enjoy hearing a familiar pattern of sounds.

Using patterns

Computer scientists look for repeated patterns of steps in instructions. When translating the instructions into a programming language, the same code can be used each time the pattern appears. This is faster to type and easier for other programmers to understand.

This pink block appears four times in Task 1.

This bracketed pattern appears in both Task 1 and Task 2.

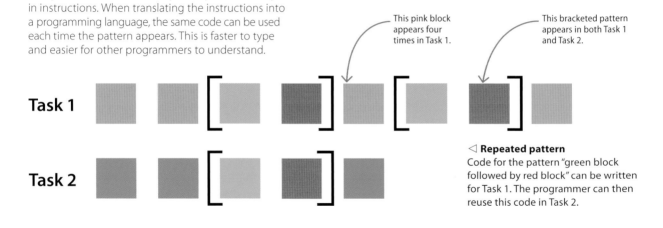

◁ **Repeated pattern**
Code for the pattern "green block followed by red block" can be written for Task 1. The programmer can then reuse this code in Task 2.

Drawing a face

A cartoonist draws a picture of a friend's face. Another friend sees it and asks for a cartoon of her own face. There are common features and shared steps that can help the artist to come up with the second illustration quickly and efficiently. The pattern from the first drawing can be used as many times as needed.

▽ **The drawing process**
The pattern of steps involved in drawing each cartoon is almost identical, but the outcome is different. In fact, the only difference is the hairstyle—spiky in one cartoon and straight in the other.

Drawing a face with spiky hair

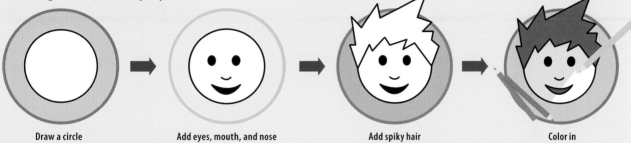

| Draw a circle | Add eyes, mouth, and nose | Add spiky hair | Color in |

Drawing a face with straight hair

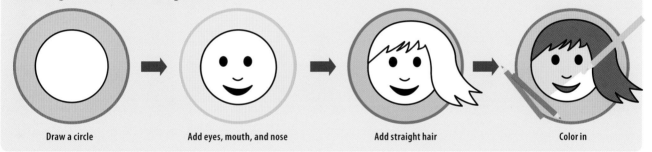

| Draw a circle | Add eyes, mouth, and nose | Add straight hair | Color in |

Reusing old solutions

If a new problem, or elements of a new problem, are similar to a problem that has been fixed before, it is possible to reuse the old solution to fix the new problem. Recognizing patterns saves time, as it cuts down on the effort needed to fix a problem.

All other elements of the cartoon remain unchanged.

▷ **Altering a pattern**
To draw the first face (above) with sunglasses, a cartoonist can take the solution used above and add one extra step. Once again, a completely different outcome is possible by slightly altering a pattern.

Success and failure

The HOLMES 2 computer system helps the UK police solve crimes by matching patterns of criminal behavior. Pattern recognition doesn't always lead to solutions, however. An unsuccessful initiative involving patterns in data was Google's Flu Trends program. It hoped to identify outbreaks of flu from clusters of flu-related searches in particular parts of the world. However, the high amount of search data didn't correspond with the outbreaks.

Algorithms

Though the word itself might sound unfamiliar, we all use algorithms every day. Baking a cake, knitting a sweater, or putting together a piece of furniture are all activities that use algorithms.

SEE ALSO

❰ **30–31** Computing before computers

❰ **68–69** What is computational thinking?

Applying algorithms **102–103** ❱

What is an algorithm?

An algorithm is a series of steps to solve a problem or carry out a task. To develop an algorithm, start by using decomposition to break down the problem into smaller tasks, then look for patterns in these tasks, and finally ignore unimportant details. This should give you the information you need to create an algorithm made of small steps that can all be described very clearly.

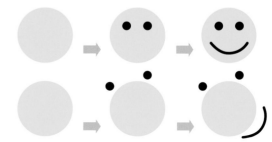

△ **Unambiguous**

Each step in an algorithm must be precise and unambiguous, with only one possible meaning. Vague instructions give incorrect results. An algorithm for drawing a smiley face might read: "draw a circle, then a curved line, and then two dots." But this doesn't tell us where the curved line and the dots should go in relation to the circle or each other.

▽ **Step by step**

Algorithms describe a series of steps that must happen in sequence in order for the problem to be solved. In athletics, the triple jump competition involves the competitor running, then performing a hop, a bounce, and a horizontal jump at specific places in order to record a successful effort.

Types of algorithm

Algorithms exist for many different computer tasks: from smartphone apps that can tell what song is being played to the algorithms used by online search engines. One area where algorithms are very influential is data processing— in particular, algorithms for searching and sorting data. There are different kinds of searching and sorting algorithms.

▷ **Linear search**

To find one item in a million, start at the first one and see if it's the right item. If it is, stop searching; otherwise, look at the next item. This isn't efficient, as it might involve looking at every item on the list.

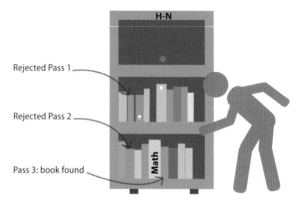

△ **Binary search**

For data that's already sorted—for instance, an alphabetical bookshelf—a binary search is efficient. At each stage, you decide which half of the data the item you want is in. The half you don't need is discarded. This is repeated until the item is found.

Describing algorithms

Algorithms can be described using flowcharts or pseudocode. A flowchart is made up of boxes linked by arrows. Each box contains a step in solving the problem or a question. Pseudocode is laid out like a computer program, but it's written in a human language.

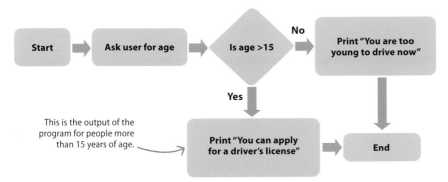

This is the output of the program for people more than 15 years of age.

Ask the user to enter their age in years

If the user's age is greater than 15

    print "You can apply for a driver's license"

else

    print "You are too young to drive just now"

◁ **Pseudocode**
Describing algorithms in pseudocode allows programmers to understand them, no matter what computer languages they are familiar with. This makes the whole range of algorithms available.

Muhammad al-Khwārizmī

The word "algorithm" comes from the name of 9th-century mathematician Abu Abdullah Muhammad ibn Mūsā al-Khwārizmī. Al-Khwārizmī lived in Baghdad, Iraq, and translated a number of scientific books from ancient Greek and Sanskrit into Arabic. He also wrote several books on mathematics, astronomy, geography, and history. These books were later translated into Latin and studied in European universities. The word "algebra" comes from the title of one of his books.

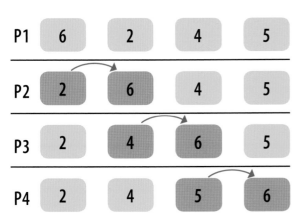

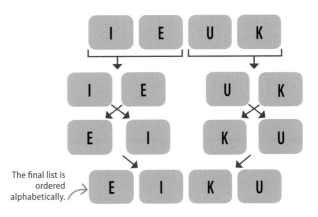

The final list is ordered alphabetically.

△ **Bubble sort**
This looks at the items a pair at a time, swapping them around if the second one of the pair is larger than the first. It's not very efficient, as it's often necessary to go through the list several times.

△ **Merge sort**
This breaks a list of items into many tiny lists. It then merges all these lists into newly sorted ones, finally producing a single sorted list. It uses more code than bubble sort, but it is more efficient.

Data

Bits and digitization

Data is often in the news, whether it's data protection or data storage. But what exactly is data, and how do computers use it and store it?

SEE ALSO

‹ **40–41** How modern computers compute

Binary code   **82–83 ›**

Streaming   **154–155 ›**

What is data?

Data is the name given to information that's processed or stored by a computer. It covers everything from instructions for the computer to carry out to text, music, photos, and more. No matter what it represents, digital data is stored as a series of binary numbers made up of the digits 1 and 0. Humans normally count in multiples of 10, in what is called the decimal system. The binary system, however, is based on multiples of two.

1 petabyte (PB)
13.3 years of HDTV video

1 bit
0 or 1

▽ **Counting bits and bytes**
A single 1 or 0 is known as a binary information digit, or bit. A byte is 8 bits, and half a byte is a nibble. One byte can store a single character of text—for example, "!," "a," or "4."

1 byte
One letter of the alphabet

1 terabyte (TB)
100 hours of video

1 kilobyte (KB)
One small text email

1 megabyte (MB)
One good-quality digital picture

1 gigabyte (GB)
240 pieces of music

Why 0 and 1?

Modern computer chips contain billions of transistors that act like tiny switches. These transistors are used to represent binary numbers. If no electrical current is flowing through a transistor, it represents a 0 in binary, while flowing current represents a 1. Nowadays, chips include transistors that are 14 nanometers long—around 500 times smaller than a human blood cell.

An open switch stops the flow of current, and the bulb does not light up. This is a 0 in the binary system.

A closed switch allows the current to flow, causing the bulb to light up. This is a 1 in the binary system.

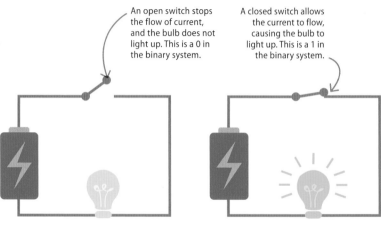

▷ **On or off**
If the switch is turned off, no current flows through the circuit; if the switch is on, a current flows through and the bulb is lit.

Data storage

The earliest form of data storage for digital computers was on punched cards or punched tape. From the 1950s, punched cards were gradually replaced by magnetic tapes and disks. The 1980s saw the introduction of compact discs (CDs), which are read using a reflected laser beam. In the past 20 years, solid-state drives have become the most popular data-storage medium.

△ **Punched cards**
Data could be entered into early computers using cards with holes punched out of them. In each position on the card, a hole represented a 0 and no hole represented a 1.

△ **Magnetic tape**
From the 1950s, data was stored on magnetic tape marked in tiny sections, where the opposing polarities represented 0 or 1.

△ **Optical disc**
Optical discs encode data in tiny indentations on the surface of the disc, called pits and lands. When a laser is shone on the disc, a pit does not reflect the light, so it represents a 0, while a land reflects the light and represents 1.

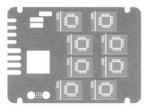

△ **Solid-state drives**
The latest hard drives are made of solid-state drives (SSDs), chips similar to those that computers use. With no moving parts, they're harder to damage.

REAL WORLD

Apollo 11

The data storage of the Apollo 11 rocket used core rope memory, where wires are wound through tiny magnetic rings called cores to represent the data. A wire going through the core is read as a 1, while a wire going around it is a 0. Retired female textile workers wove the program by hand. It landed the rocket on the moon. This led to the nickname "little old lady," or "LOL," memory.

Capacity

Hardware capacity is a measure of how much binary code a computer can store. It's usually described by two values: random-access memory (RAM) and hard drive. RAM is the storage used when the computer is executing instructions. The bulk of a computer's data, such as files and programs, are stored on the hard drive. The RAM capacity of a computer is always much smaller than its hard drive capacity.

▽ **Connection speeds**
This describes how quickly data can be transferred to or from a computer. It's measured in megabits per second (Mbps), so 20 Mbps means 20 megabits are transferred each second.

Binary code

Computers only understand electrical signals, where ON is represented by 1 and OFF is represented by 0. Binary code is used to translate these numbers into electrical signals.

SEE ALSO

❰ **38–39** The computer chip
❰ **40–41** How modern computers compute
❰ **80–81** Bits and digitization
Encoding images **90–91** ❱
Encoding audio and video **92–93** ❱

Language of computers

The binary number system uses only two digits: 0 and 1. Every operation that a computer carries out and every piece of data that it stores, or processes, is represented as binary code. Binary code uses 0s and 1s to represent a letter, digit, character, or part of another item, such as music or a picture. A binary number 8 bits long can have any value from 0 to 255. This means that an 8-bit binary number could represent any one of those 256 characters.

▷ **Binary translators**
Humans find binary numbers difficult to interpret, so most people write programs in languages closer to human languages. These are translated into binary by programs called compilers and interpreters.

Binary to decimal

People usually count using the decimal system. This makes it difficult to look at a binary number and know what it represents. In a binary number, the least significant bit (LSB) is the bit farthest to the right and the most significant bit (MSB) is the bit farthest to the left. Between these two, the range of values that can be written doubles with each digit added.

▽ **Conversion**
The first column in the binary system is the LSB on the right and is equivalent to 1. Subsequently, each column is worth double the column to its right. To get the equivalent decimal value of a binary number, multiply the value of each column with its respective binary digit and then add all the individual results.

IN DEPTH

Leibniz and the *I Ching*

The binary number system was invented by German philosopher Gottfried Leibniz (1646–1716). He highlighted its relation to the Chinese text *I Ching*, which uses arrangements of six lines to guide the user to relevant advice. The six lines are in pairs representing the concept of Yin and Yang, or, according to Leibniz, 1 and 0.

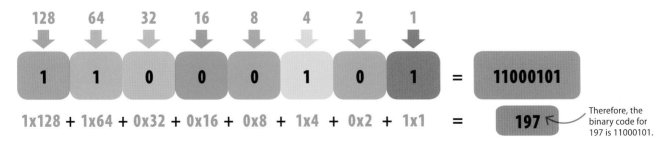

Therefore, the binary code for 197 is 11000101.

Digitization

The process of transforming information into a format that can be read by computers is called digitization. The source material can be anything from a sound, to text, to an image, and the digitization process creates a representation of it in binary code. It does this by sampling the source material thousands of times, if not more, to come up with a series of individual binary values for each part of it.

1-bit (black and white)

8-bit (black and white)

8-bit (color)

24-bit (color)

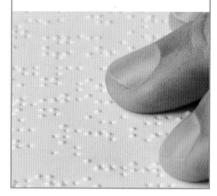

◁ **Bit depth**
If a binary number representing a digitized value has more bits, the representation will be closer to the original. Two bits allow only four colors in a digital image, while 8 bits allow 256 colors.

Binary and switches

Computers have always relied on switches to achieve the flow of electric current (representing 1) or the absence of current (representing 0). The switches in the earliest electric computers were vacuum tubes, which looked and behaved like light bulbs. They could also switch between allowing an electric current to flow through them and stopping it. Nowadays, the heart of a computer is a microchip, or integrated circuit, which is created using transistors.

▷ **Tubes and transistors**
Computers made with tubes took up a lot of space, often a whole room. Tubes were later replaced by tiny transistors made of materials such as silicon and germanium, which also allow current to be switched on and off.

Vacuum tube

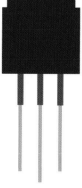

Transistor

ASCII and Unicode

SEE ALSO
❮ **40–41** How modern computers compute
❮ **82–83** Binary code
Encoding images **90–91** ❯

Turning text into binary code that can be stored on computers is useful. However, there needs to be agreement on what character each binary number represents.

What is ASCII?

First introduced in 1963, ASCII stands for American Standard Code for Information Interchange. It is a globally agreed-upon standard for representing text in binary code. The standard was developed from a code used by telegraph operators. ASCII became the official standard for computers in the US in 1968, and many other countries were also using it by the 1980s.

▷ **Extended ASCII**
Introduced in 1986, extended ASCII uses 8-bit binary numbers. This enables it to encode 256 characters, including letters with accents, making it useful for a wider variety of languages.

▽ **Standard ASCII**
Standard ASCII uses 7-bit binary numbers to represent each character. It can encode 128 characters—including letters, numbers, and punctuation.

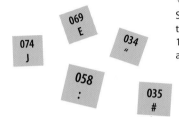

Each character in standard ASCII has an ASCII decimal code.

ASCII files

Most text files are encoded using ASCII. This means that they can be opened, read, and changed using a text editor or a word processor. The files containing code for most computer programs are also encoded using ASCII. This makes it easy for programmers to share open-source code on websites such as GitHub.

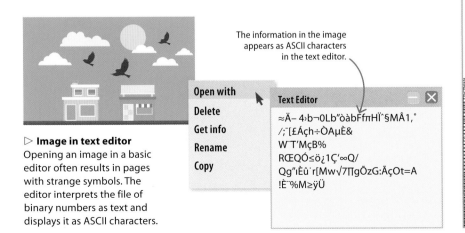

The information in the image appears as ASCII characters in the text editor.

▷ **Image in text editor**
Opening an image in a basic editor often results in pages with strange symbols. The editor interprets the file of binary numbers as text and displays it as ASCII characters.

IN DEPTH

ASCII art

It is possible to create images using long lines of ASCII characters. Often called ASCII art, these images were popular in the early days of the Internet, as computers lacked the processing power to show proper images. These days, programs can turn images into ASCII art in seconds, such as the example below.

Unicode

ASCII and extended ASCII are restricted to English and some European languages. Their creators believed every language would develop its own equivalent script, but this soon became problematic, as different scripts were using the same code. First developed in the late 1980s, Unicode is a single worldwide standard for representing text—it handles languages as diverse as Russian, Hebrew, and Japanese. Its designers were careful to ensure their system doesn't clash with ASCII. More than 130,000 characters are defined in Unicode, and more are added every year.

▷ **Why have a Unicode standard?**
Unicode provides a single agreed-on encoding for worldwide use, replacing hundreds of conflicting encodings for scripts and characters.

2022

1F27

2766

Every Unicode entry has a four- or five-character code identifier.

03C8

0908

F64D

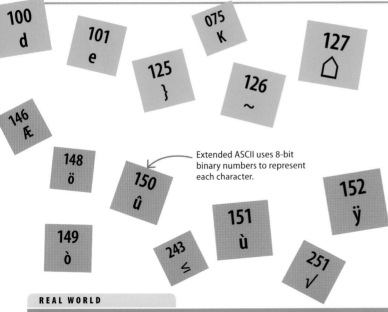

Extended ASCII uses 8-bit binary numbers to represent each character.

ASCII vs. Unicode

Unicode uses between 2 and 4 bytes to represent a character, rather than ASCII's 1 byte. While ASCII assigns a number to a whole character, Unicode assigns numbers to the parts of symbols that make up characters. The character "é" can be represented as a whole character, and it can also be expressed as two numbers—one for "e" and another for the acute accent (´) symbol.

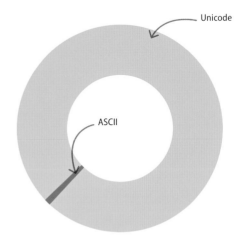

Unicode

ASCII

△ **ASCII a subset of Unicode**
ASCII is now part of the much larger set of Unicode characters. The first 127 Unicode characters and the numbers encoding them are identical to ASCII.

REAL WORLD

Emojis

One of Unicode's features is the use of emojis—a Japanese term meaning pictograph. Emojis are extremely popular, as they liven up webpages and electronic messages, and give a sense of how the writer intends the message to be interpreted. Although the content of each emoji is fixed, different browsers and devices vary in how they display them.

Logic gates

Computers carry out calculations on data represented by binary numbers. These calculations are done at the lowest level of the computer's hardware using devices called logic gates.

SEE ALSO

❰ **82–83** Binary code

Databases	**88–89** ❱
Early programming methods	**98–99** ❱
Boolean logic	**104–105** ❱

Making decisions

Logic gates are the building blocks of digital computers, as they help in making decisions. They are electronic components whose output depends on their input, following the rules of Boolean logic—a form of algebra where values are either TRUE or FALSE. All possible values of input to a logic gate and the corresponding output can be shown in a truth table. In a truth table, the binary value 1 is equal to the logical value TRUE and the binary value 0 is equal to the logical value FALSE.

▽ **Logic gates, truth tables, and circuits**
The table below shows the seven logic gates and their corresponding truth tables. Logic gates can also be combined to make circuits. Constructing a truth table for a circuit helps us to predict how it will behave.

BIOGRAPHY

Claude Shannon

American mathematician Claude Shannon (1916–2001) made real-world versions of Boolean logic by using electrical switches, with ON and OFF representing the values TRUE and FALSE. Shannon then developed combinations of electrical switches capable of making decisions or calculating numerical values—forming the basis of modern digital computing.

Logic gate	Symbol	Truth table
NOT A NOT gate's output is the opposite of its input. If the input is 0, its output is 1, and if its input is 1, the output is 0.		**INPUT / OUTPUT** 0 → 1 1 → 0
AND An AND gate's output is 1 only if both its inputs are 1.		See table below
OR An OR gate's output is 1 if either or both its inputs are 1. This is sometimes known as Inclusive-OR.		See table below

NOT truth table

INPUT	OUTPUT
0	1
1	0

AND truth table

INPUT		OUTPUT
A	B	A AND B
0	0	0
0	1	0
1	0	0
1	1	1

OR truth table

INPUT		OUTPUT
A	B	A OR B
0	0	0
0	1	1
1	0	1
1	1	1

Logic gate	Symbol	Truth table

XOR

An XOR gate's output is 1 only when both its inputs are different. This is sometimes known as Exclusive-OR.

INPUT		OUTPUT
A	**B**	**A XOR B**
0	0	0
0	1	1
1	0	1
1	1	0

XNOR

An XNOR gate is equivalent to an XOR gate followed by a NOT gate. Its output is 1 only when both its inputs are the same.

INPUT		OUTPUT
A	**B**	**A XNOR B**
0	0	1
0	1	0
1	0	0
1	1	1

NAND

A NAND gate is equivalent to an AND gate followed by a NOT gate. Its output is 1 unless both its inputs are 1.

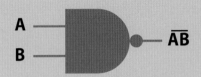

INPUT		OUTPUT
A	**B**	**A NAND B**
0	0	1
0	1	1
1	0	1
1	1	0

NOR

A NOR gate is equivalent to an OR gate followed by a NOT gate. Its output is 1 only when both its inputs are 0.

INPUT		OUTPUT
A	**B**	**A NOR B**
0	0	1
0	1	0
1	0	0
1	1	0

Combining gates

Computers carry out addition using circuits called binary adders. As computers do everything in 0s and 1s, binary adders must be combined to add numbers of several digits. They do this by having two outputs: sum and carry. The sum is the result of adding the inputs together. If both are 1, the output should be 2, which in binary is 10. The carry output becomes 1 to move the digit representing 2 into the next adder along.

▷ **Half-adders**
Each adder contains two smaller circuits called half-adders made of only two logic gates, an XOR and an AND.

The inputs (A and B) to the sum gate are the same as the inputs to the carry gate, as they are connected together.

A	B	SUM	CARRY
0	0	0	0
0	1	1	0
1	0	1	0
1	1	0	1

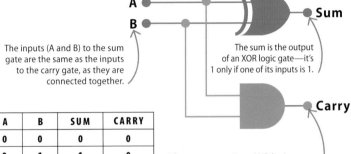

The sum is the output of an XOR logic gate—it's 1 only if one of its inputs is 1.

The carry output is an AND logic gate. Its output is 1 only if both inputs are 1. It carries a value over to the next adder when adding large numbers.

Databases

Many people keep jumbled collections of information they've gathered—for example, a folder of favorite recipes. Computers need a more organized way to store and search data collections saved on them.

SEE ALSO

❰ 86–87 Logic gates

Boolean logic   104–105 ❱

Cloud computing   152–153 ❱

The Internet of Things   226–227 ❱

What are databases?

Databases are programs that let people store and search data effectively. The most common type of database is the relational database, which stores information in tables. The tables are made up of rows, called records, and columns, called fields. Each table holds details about a particular type of item, so a library database might include a table of books and a separate table of information on the readers.

▽ **Keys**

Each record has a field containing a unique value, known as the primary key. This means that records containing the same details, such as two copies of *Matilda*, can be distinguished.

Primary key ID	Title	Author	Out of library	Loaned by
1	*Pride and Prejudice*	Jane Austen	Yes	Emma Hope
2	*Matilda*	Roald Dahl	Yes	Surinder Singh
3	*Matilda*	Roald Dahl	No	Null
4	*Frankenstein*	Mary Shelley	Yes	James Graham

Searching through databases

Searching for information in a database is called querying. The programming language used for querying relational databases is Standard Query Language, popularly known as SQL. Technically, a database only refers to the collection of organized data stored in a computer. Database management systems such as MySQL, SQL Server, Oracle, and PostgreSQL are the programs that allow users to interact with a database.

▷ **SQL query**

The most common SQL command is SELECT, which retrieves values from the database. Queries can use Boolean operators such as OR and AND to specify which values.

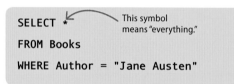

```
SELECT *
FROM Books
WHERE Author = "Jane Austen"
```

This symbol means "everything."

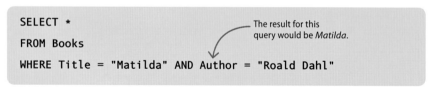

```
SELECT *
FROM Books
WHERE Title = "Matilda" AND Author = "Roald Dahl"
```

The result for this query would be *Matilda*.

REAL WORLD

NoSQL databases

NoSQL (Not only SQL) is an alternative to the traditional relational databases. It keeps track of items using a variety of methods, including keywords and graphs rather than tables. It is often more suitable for very large data collections, or those stored on the cloud.

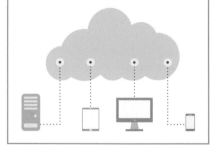

Using databases

As well as libraries, many organizations use databases to store records of staff, clients, or stock. Numerous websites, particularly those where people can keep adding content, such as social media sites, also use databases. Stores require databases to enable customers to buy items online. As databases store a great deal of sensitive information, it's very important to ensure they have adequate levels of security and are properly backed up.

Businesses
Information on staff, income, and expenditure can be stored and analyzed on databases.

Hospitals
Hospitals hold information such as patients' medical records and hospital bed allocation.

Social media
All content created, liked, or shared by users is stored on a social media site's database.

Government departments
Information on things such as income tax payment and crime statistics is stored by governments.

Schools
School databases store things such as attendance, staff information, and budgets.

Banks
Bank databases keep track of customers' accounts and their transactions.

△ **Who uses databases?**
Databases can be searched much more quickly and easily than paper records. The examples above show just some of the uses they have.

Trending tools

More than 600 million tweets are posted every day. By analyzing them as they happen, Twitter is able to identify and highlight trends in what is being discussed. People are often alerted to an event when it first starts trending on Twitter. Similarly, the Google Trends tool gives users access to data on Google searches. It's possible to see graphs of how often people across the world searched for a particular topic, or top 10 lists of popular searches in different categories. Both tools give users a picture of how people in their own vicinity and other countries are reacting to events.

Using big datasets

Massive and fast-changing collections of data, from sources as diverse as social media to scientific experiments like the Large Hadron Collider, are being created and added to every day. This data presents a challenge to traditional databases and methods of analysis. Visualization, where data is presented as graphs or images, is one aspect of big data that has become increasingly important. This can help more people to better understand patterns found in the data, which can help in everything from designing medicines to forming governmental policies.

△ **The Internet of Things**
The interconnected network of physical objects with embedded sensors and Internet connectivity that is called the Internet of Things is another source of big data.

Encoding images

Images are encoded, or changed into a sequence of numbers, so that they can be understood by a computer. These images require different methods to store and display them.

SEE ALSO

❰ **40–41** How modern computers compute
❰ **80–81** Bits and digitization
❰ **82–83** Binary code
Encoding audio and video   **92–93** ❱

Pixels and vectors

Images can be represented digitally by using two methods: bitmaps and vectors. Bitmaps are like mosaics made of lots of tiny squares called pixels, short for picture elements, arranged in a grid. Vector images are more like connect-the-dots puzzles, as the image is represented by a collection of points, along with information on what sort of lines should join to make the shapes in the image.

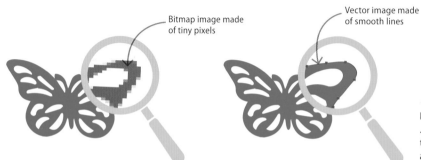

Bitmap image made of tiny pixels

Vector image made of smooth lines

IN DEPTH

Steganography

Steganography involves sending secret messages by hiding the fact that there is a message. This is like messages written in invisible ink. Information can be hidden in a digital image by using a program that changes only one bit of each binary number that represents the colors of the pixels. The same program can also extract a hidden message.

◁ **Formats**
Digital cameras produce bitmapped images as .bmp, .jpeg, and .png files. Vector images, on the other hand, are created using illustration or animation programs and are stored as .svg files.

Color and light

White light is made by mixing equal amounts of red, green, and blue light. Mixing these three primary colors in different proportions gives a wide range of other colors. An encoding called RGB (red, green, blue) is used to store color values. An RGB value is written as three numbers between 0 and 255, each representing how much of the three primary colors it contains.

LINGO

Rasterization

Because computer screens are made up of a grid of pixels, vector images have to be turned into bitmaps before they can be displayed. This process is called rasterization, after the raster scan process used in older television screens to build up pictures a line at a time. The process of keeping the screen updated when users make changes involves a lot of work for the computer's processor and is sometimes done by a specialized chip.

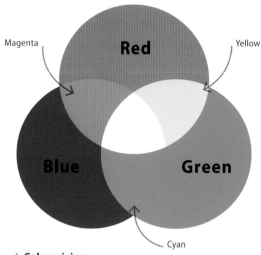

Magenta   Red   Yellow

Blue   Green

Cyan

△ **Color mixing**
Black is 0, 0, 0, as it contains no light at all, and white is 255, 255, 255—the maximum amount of all three colors. The rules of color mixing for light are not the same as those for paints.

Resolution

The resolution of a bitmapped digital image is measured in pixels or dots per inch (DPI). Expanding a bitmapped image causes the pixels to become visible. As a result, the picture looks blocky or pixelated. Vector images don't have this issue, since the math functions they contain can easily be used to generate larger versions. The bit depth of a color picture defines how many bits are used to store the binary value for the color of a pixel.

▽ **Dots per inch**
An image's DPI value defines how detailed it is. A higher value denotes a more detailed image that can be made larger, with no clarity lost.

72 DPI

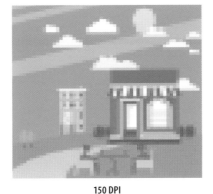

150 DPI

300 DPI

Why are image files so large?

As cameras get better at capturing detail, the resolution of pictures increases, and so does the amount of data needed to store these details. RGB images use at least 24 bits for each pixel to store color data, increasing file sizes even further. Files from professional digital cameras can be around 40 MB, and a high-resolution jpeg can be around 12 MB.

A history of data

Developed in 1956, the IBM RAMAC 350 was the first computer to have a magnetic disk drive similar to those used today. It weighed 1 ton (1 tonne) and had 50 disks that stored a total of 5 MB of data. That's around the file size of one high-resolution jpeg photo. Today, people can carry gigabytes of data in their pockets on their mobile phones.

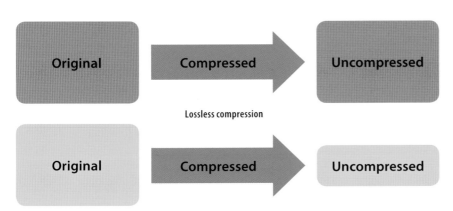

△ **Compression**
It's possible to compress files to make them easier to share or store. Compression can be either lossless or lossy. Lossless means the picture quality remains the same, with no information lost. Lossy is the opposite: some information is lost to make the file size smaller, which affects the picture quality.

Encoding audio and video

SEE ALSO
❮ **16–17** Computing for you
❮ **80–81** Bits and digitization
❮ **82–83** Binary code

Technology has transformed the way we consume and play audio and video. Digital music has completely overtaken physical storage systems, while digital video has replaced older analog systems.

Encoding audio files

To encode an audio signal, its value is recorded thousands of times a second. Each of these values is turned into a binary number, which encodes not just the pitch of the note but other information, such as how loud it is. Playing back the sample values in the same order they were recorded produces a sound that, to the human ear, is identical to the original.

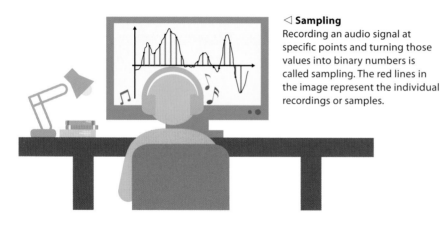

◁ **Sampling**
Recording an audio signal at specific points and turning those values into binary numbers is called sampling. The red lines in the image represent the individual recordings or samples.

REAL WORLD

How microphones work

Sounds are waves that move through the air by compressing it at regular intervals. Microphones contain a thin piece of metal or plastic called a diaphragm, which vibrates when it is hit by sound waves. Electronics in the microphone translate the change in vibration into an electrical signal. This can be amplified through a speaker or digitized and processed by a computer.

What affects audio quality?

In audio encoding, the number of samples taken per second is called the sample rate. The more samples taken per second, the more accurately the sound is represented. The number of bits used to store each sample is known as the bit depth. A higher bit depth means more information can be stored, which leads to better-quality recordings. Combining the sample rate and bit depth gives the bit rate, or bits used per second.

▷ **High values lead to better sound**
Each rectangle in these graphs represents a sample. With a higher sample rate, the rectangles are narrower and fit together to form a shape that is closer to the waveform's shape.

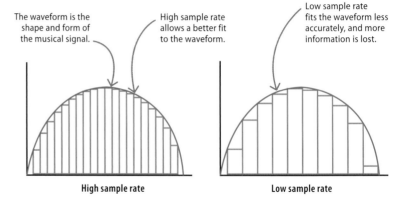

The waveform is the shape and form of the musical signal.

High sample rate allows a better fit to the waveform.

Low sample rate fits the waveform less accurately, and more information is lost.

High sample rate

Low sample rate

Encoding video files

A video is made from a series of still images called frames, which are played one after another at a high speed. Frames are displayed at a constant rate known as the frame rate—the equivalent to sample rate in an audio file. Just as with still images, a frame is made up of pixels, and data on the color and brightness of each pixel is stored as a binary number. The number of bits used to store picture and audio information per second of video is called the bit rate.

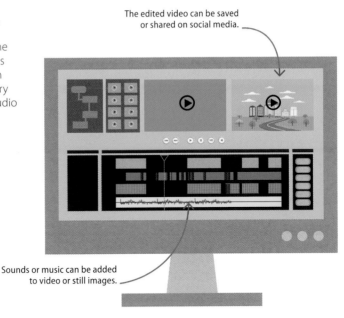

The edited video can be saved or shared on social media.

Sounds or music can be added to video or still images.

▷ **Postproduction**
Video editing software allows people to import clips of video and audio files. These can be edited and arranged in any order. Users can add transitions between sections and even include titles. Many programs also let users apply color effects.

Frames per second

The frame rate of a video affects how smooth and realistic the motion appears to the human eye. The standard frame rate for film and digital video converted from analog film is 24 frames per second (fps). Video created on digital cameras may be slightly faster, at 25 or 30 fps. People are so used to seeing 24 fps that higher rates can seem odd and unnatural.

Webcam **frame rates** are often **low**, as this creates **less data** to transfer, saving **bandwidth**.

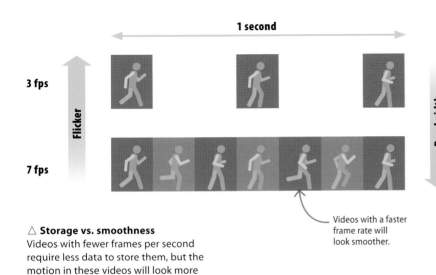

1 second

Flicker

3 fps

7 fps

Bandwidth

Videos with a faster frame rate will look smoother.

△ **Storage vs. smoothness**
Videos with fewer frames per second require less data to store them, but the motion in these videos will look more jerky and unnatural.

IN DEPTH

Codecs

Encoding allows data to be stored or transferred, and decoding allows it to be played back. A program that can be used both to encode and decode digital data is called a codec. There are audio and video codecs, and each codec decodes from and encodes to a particular file format. H.265 and Xvid are examples of video codecs, while audio codecs include MP3 and AAC.

Encryption

For thousands of years, people have sent messages that could only be understood by the intended recipients, protecting their secrets if the message was intercepted. Creating this kind of message is called encryption.

SEE ALSO

❰ 32–33 Computing since the 1940s

Connections   148–149 ❱

Artificial intelligence   236–237 ❱

What is encryption?

Encryption is the process of taking a message and making it unreadable to everyone except the person it is intended for. Historically, the most popular reason for encrypting information was to allow communication between military leaders, spies, or heads of state. More recently, with the advent of the Internet and online shopping, encryption is becoming increasingly important. For instance, it is used to keep shoppers' money safe during transactions.

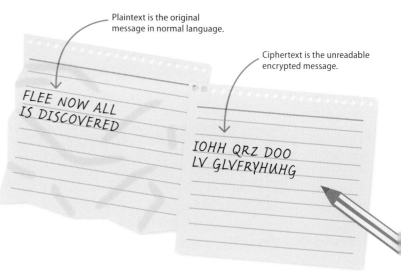

Plaintext is the original message in normal language.

Ciphertext is the unreadable encrypted message.

FLEE NOW ALL IS DISCOVERED

IOHH QRZ DOO LV GLVFRYHUHG

▷ **Plaintext to ciphertext**
Unencrypted information, or plaintext, is encrypted using an algorithm and a key. This generates ciphertext that can be decrypted using the correct key. A cipher is a key to the code.

Early encryption

A transposition cipher changes the position of the letters in a message using a specific rule, called a key. The recipient, who also knows the key, reverses the process to get the original text. Writing a message backward is a transposition cipher, although it is not a secure one, as it is relatively easy to break the code. Substitution ciphers replace each letter with another letter according to a rule or set of rules.

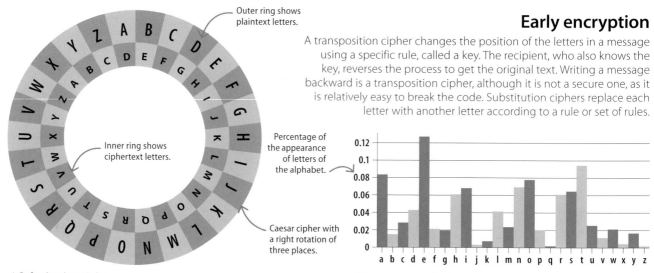

Outer ring shows plaintext letters.

Inner ring shows ciphertext letters.

Percentage of the appearance of letters of the alphabet.

Caesar cipher with a right rotation of three places.

△ **Substitution cipher**
Used by Julius Caesar, each letter in the substitution cipher is shifted by a set number of spaces along the alphabet. The key is the number of spaces a letter is shifted.

△ **Frequency analysis**
A substitution cipher can be easily broken by frequency analysis. By looking at the encrypted message and finding the most frequent letters, they can be matched to their frequency in the language. The letter "e" is the most frequent in the English language.

Public-key cryptography

The problem with early forms of encryption was that they could be easily intercepted and decrypted. Public-key cryptography was developed in the 1970s and avoids this. Essentially, both parties have two keys—a public one that is used to encrypt a message, and a private one that is known only by the sender and the recipient.

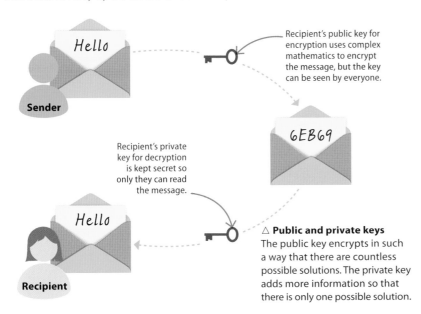

Sender

Recipient's public key for encryption uses complex mathematics to encrypt the message, but the key can be seen by everyone.

Recipient's private key for decryption is kept secret so only they can read the message.

Recipient

△ **Public and private keys**
The public key encrypts in such a way that there are countless possible solutions. The private key adds more information so that there is only one possible solution.

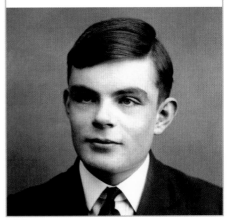
Secure Sockets Layer

Encryption is added to Internet connections by adding a Secure Sockets Layer (SSL) to the normal communication procedures. The URL of a website using SSL starts with https instead of http. Any website that wants to allow users to connect to it securely needs an SSL Certificate from a recognized provider. This includes a public and private key pair, which allows the site to encrypt the traffic between it and its users. Many email applications also use SSL to ensure users' emails are secure as they travel across the web.

Certificate Error: Navigation blocked

Problem with this website's security certificate

We recommend that you close this webpage and do not continue to this website.

Click here to close this webpage.
Continue to this website (not recommended).

▼ More information

◁ **SSL Certificate**
If a site's SSL Certificate is outdated or unrecognized, web browsers will display a warning. Some browsers will also prevent users from viewing the page.

Programming techniques

Early programming methods

SEE ALSO

❮ **30–31** Computing before computers
❮ **38–39** The computer chip
❮ **80–81** Bits and digitization

Modern programmers write code using human-readable text. The first programmers, on the other hand, wrote code in 0s and 1s, the language of the computer.

History of punch cards

Before program instructions could be stored on disks or magnetic tape, they were stored on punch cards. Programmers punched sequences of holes into stiff pieces of paper and then fed them into the computer to run a program. The design of punch cards gradually became more and more sophisticated.

"At each increase of **knowledge** … **human labor** becomes **abridged**."
Charles Babbage (1791–1871),
English mathematician and inventor

Perforated paper was used to store a specific design.

1822: The Difference Engine

English mathematician Charles Babbage was tired of typographical errors in his books of mathematical tables. These books had lists of precomputed numbers, which were used in navigation, astronomy, and statistics. Babbage drew up the design for the Difference Engine, a mechanical calculator that could produce these tables automatically. While his design was good, the engine was very expensive to make.

The Difference Engine used columns of gears to make its calculations.

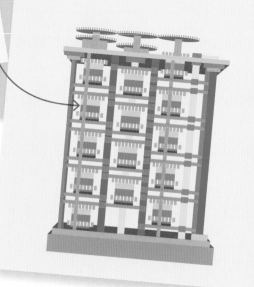

1725: Basile Bouchon

In Lyon, France, textile worker Basile Bouchon created a method to store weaving patterns in a piece of tape. Where there was a hole in the tape, the needle on the loom stayed still. If there was no hole, the needle was pushed forward and the thread was lifted. Instead of trying to memorize complicated patterns and to avoid mistakes, weavers simply shifted the tape up and down. His creation was the first semi-automated industrial machine.

1890: Tabulating Machine

American inventor Herman Hollerith invented the Tabulating Machine as an efficient way to compile population census data. An operator punched data into a card, slipped the card into the machine, and then pulled the handle. Wherever there was a hole in the card, an associated dial on the machine increased. All the data for one person was entered at the same time.

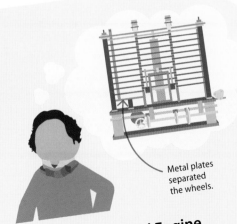

Metal plates separated the wheels.

A dial displayed the counts for a particular category.

1837: The Analytical Engine

While working on the Difference Engine, Babbage had a better idea for a machine that could calculate anything—not just numbers for mathematical tables. The Analytical Engine was composed of a store (equivalent to memory in a modern computer) and a mill (like a CPU in a modern computer). Inspired by the textile industry, Babbage proposed using punch cards to feed instructions into the engine's steam-powered mill. The engine was designed to add, subtract, multiply, and compare, but it was never built.

The IBM card

In 1928, American company IBM redesigned the punch card to have 80 columns of 12 potential holes. A light shone on each card as it was fed into the computer. If there was no hole, the light was blocked and the machine read in a 0. If there was a hole, the light shone through and was detected by an optical sensor and the machine read in a 1. Each column of potential holes therefore became a 10-digit binary number.

Cards were read column by column.

▷ **The numbers in a punch card**
The numbers in a punch card have fixed meanings. For example, 0100 could be an instruction to add or compare two numbers.

Part of an IBM punch card

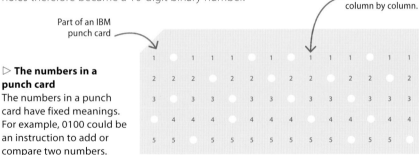

Babbage and Lovelace

English mathematician Charles Babbage (1791–1871) designed two automated calculating machines. Although his ideas couldn't be built using the technology of the time, his Analytical Engine was the first example of a computer that could be programmed to do a variety of different tasks. English mathematician Ada Lovelace (1815–1852) was the first person to see the enormous potential for the Analytical Engine in fields other than pure calculation, and became the first computer programmer as a result. A working model of Babbage's Difference Engine was built by the London Science Museum in 1991.

Analog programming

SEE ALSO
❰ 40–41 How modern computers compute
❰ 80–81 Bits and digitization
❰ 82–83 Binary code

While digital programs work with discrete data formed by 0s and 1s, analog programs can handle values between these two extremes. They both have a unique approach to programming.

Digital vs. analog data

Digital data is limited to specific values. It gives answers in yes or no. Analog data, on the other hand, gives precise and detailed answers.

▷ **Limited or precise answers**
Digital data answers questions like, "Is the door open?" with the answer being only "yes" or "no." Analog data can describe any of the points in between—and so can be used to answer the more accurate question, "How open is the door?"

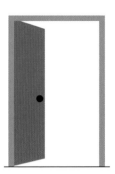

Analog computers

An analog computer stores and processes data by using physical quantities, such as weight, length, or voltage, as opposed to a digital computer, which stores data as binary code on its hard drive. While digital computers are limited to two values (0 and 1), every single unit of analog data can give precise answers.

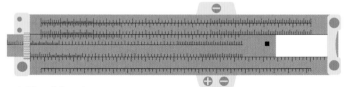

△ **The slide rule**
This mechanical analog computer was invented in the 1600s. The middle section of the ruler could be slid out to work out mathematical functions by reading the numbers on the scale.

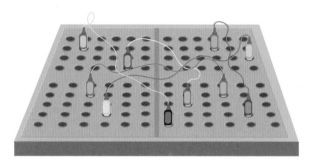

△ **Plugboard**
In analog computing, there is no concept of software. Programs are created by connecting base circuits using plugboards.

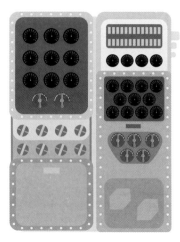

◁ **The Torpedo Data Computer (TDC)**
Used by American submarines during WWII, the TDC was an electromechanical computer that was able to work out the complex mathematics behind firing a torpedo at a moving target, such as a ship.

Noise

Electronic signals are rarely exact. Imperfections in the original medium or thermal (heat), electric, or solar interference is called noise, and can cause the signal to fluctuate. If the signal "1" is sent over a wire, it can be received as any value between 0.75 and 1.25, so the sender can never be assured that the signal originally sent is the signal received. Digital signals work in steplike increments, which means they are closer to the original signal and easier to receive. Analog circuits, however, work in tiny, smooth increments, so some precision is always lost to noise.

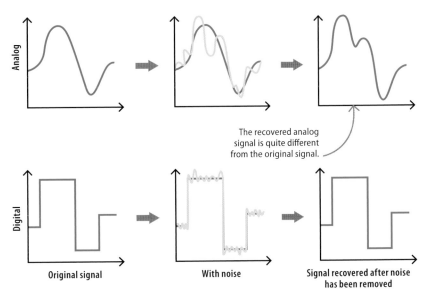

The recovered analog signal is quite different from the original signal.

Original signal   With noise   Signal recovered after noise has been removed

▷ **Signal-to-noise ratio**
Noise adds random extra information to an analog signal, making the signal less and less like the original signal. In contrast, the differences in the "on" and "off" states are so great in digital signals that it is easy to work out what the original signal was, even though there is usually some noise.

Pros and cons

Analog computers are built at the hardware level; each computer is designed for a specific task, which makes them very accurate. However, since they're so specialized, they can't be easily reprogrammed to carry out new tasks. Changing a program takes a lot of manual effort and might even require buying new components. Digital computers are more flexible and can be programmed to do unlimited tasks. Writing a new code in a digital system is easier than redesigning a motherboard.

Analog computers assure accuracy and precision.

These allow real-time operation and simultaneous computation.

Analog computers often consume less power and execute some tasks faster.

Analog signals are a natural way of storing data. There is no quantization noise.

Hybrids

Hybrid computers can combine the speed of analog programming with the accuracy of digital programming to get the best of both worlds. So far, hybrids aren't widespread beyond specialized fields, such as radar systems and scientific calculations. However, after being unused for years, analog computers are starting to make a comeback in programming.

Applying algorithms

Apart from computer science, algorithms can also be applied to real-life situations. There is often more than one algorithm for solving any particular problem.

SEE ALSO
❰ 68–69 What is computational thinking?
❰ 76–77 Algorithms
❰ 94–95 Encryption

Algorithms

Algorithms can be made to do many things, from sorting a list to finding the fastest route between two locations. They can even work out the best strategies for playing games. Every programming language implements the same algorithm differently, though the end results are the same.

A map shows only essential details like streets and buildings.

In reality, the city has streets and buildings in full 3D detail.

▷ **Algorithms vs. programs**
An algorithm can be compared to a map and a program to a city. While algorithms focus only on logic, programs contain language-specific details and syntax.

Algorithm efficiency

Two different roads might lead to the same place, but taking the highway is faster than a winding mountain path. This is true for algorithms as well. Two algorithms might produce the same result, but one may be more efficient than the other.

▽ **Adding numbers**
If you were asked to find the sum of all the numbers from 1 to 100, you could add them one by one. German mathematician Carl Gauss worked out a much quicker and more efficient way to do it that required just two simple steps.

$1 + 2 + 3 + ... + 100 = ?$

That's simple! The answer is 50 x 101 = 5,050.

REAL WORLD

Self-driving car

A self-driving car does the same tasks as a human driver: navigate lanes, detect stop signs, and respond to traffic lights. To make self-driving cars safe and reliable, programmers spend a lot of time writing the perfect algorithm for each task. Efficiency is crucial. Otherwise, the car might only detect the stop sign after it has driven past!

Selecting algorithms

While efficiency is important in an algorithm, there are other factors to consider. First is space efficiency. An algorithm may be quick, but if its speed means it takes up a lot of disk space, it may be better to choose a slower algorithm. The next consideration is how difficult an algorithm is to write. The more convoluted the algorithm, the more potential there is for human mistakes. An algorithm is useless if it's fast and space efficient but gives the wrong answers because bugs have crept into the code.

Cryptography

Every time secure data is sent over the Internet, the message is encrypted by a special algorithm that restricts who can read it. Hackers try to break the encryption to steal private data. Security companies constantly develop new encryption algorithms to stay a step ahead of hackers. Of course, safer algorithms are often slower and harder to write.

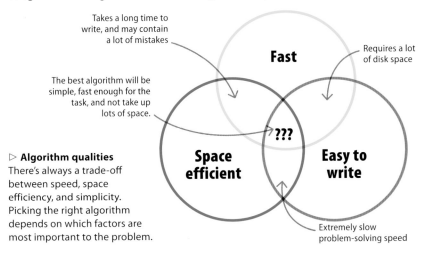

Takes a long time to write, and may contain a lot of mistakes

Requires a lot of disk space

The best algorithm will be simple, fast enough for the task, and not take up lots of space.

Fast

???

Space efficient

Easy to write

▷ **Algorithm qualities**
There's always a trade-off between speed, space efficiency, and simplicity. Picking the right algorithm depends on which factors are most important to the problem.

Extremely slow problem-solving speed

Tailoring algorithms

Because inventing new algorithms takes years of study, most developers only implement existing ones. To create a GPS system, developers will have to model the data (roads, cars, traffic lights) in a way that the algorithm understands, and then make adjustments for one-way streets, school zones, and toll routes.

▽ **Dijkstra's algorithm**
Dutch scientist Edsger Dijkstra invented an algorithm for finding the shortest path between two points. Variants of his algorithm are used by social media companies to suggest new friend connections to a user, depending on common friends, location, similar interests, and so on.

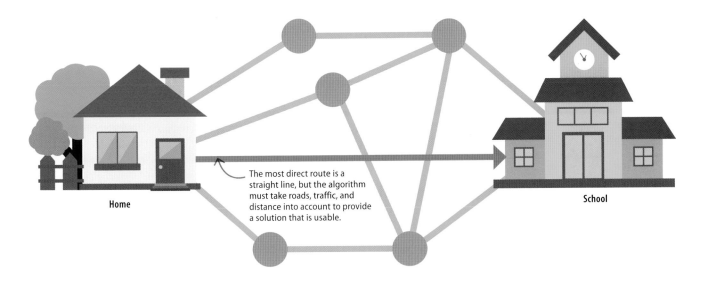

Home

The most direct route is a straight line, but the algorithm must take roads, traffic, and distance into account to provide a solution that is usable.

School

Boolean logic

Boolean logic, also called Boolean algebra, is a branch of mathematics with only two values—0 and 1. Created by English mathematician George Boole, it plays a critical role in circuit design and application design.

SEE ALSO	
❮ **86–87** Logic gates	
❮ **88–89** Databases	
Program structures	**108–109 ❯**

Boolean operators

Boolean logic is all about collections of objects, called sets. Each set can be further separated into subsets. For example, the set of all desserts can be separated into subsets like chocolate desserts and cold desserts. Some desserts, such as chocolate ice cream, belong to both groups. Others, such as carrot cake, belong to neither. While regular algebra has operators, such as add (+), subtract (−), and multiply (*), Boolean algebra has AND, OR, and NOT. These operators can be used to create more specific subgroups.

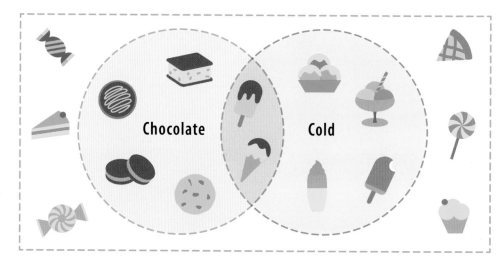

▷ **Dessert Venn diagram**
This Venn diagram shows how a set of different desserts can be divided into subsets of chocolate desserts and cold desserts. If a dessert belongs to a group, it corresponds to the Boolean value 1. Otherwise, it's 0.

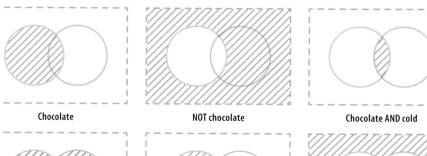

Chocolate

NOT chocolate

Chocolate AND cold

▷ **Other possibilities**
A specific type of dessert can be isolated using the right combination of Boolean operators.

Chocolate OR cold

Chocolate AND (NOT cold)

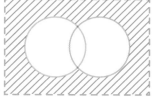

(NOT cold) AND (NOT chocolate)

Logic expressions

The AND, OR, and NOT operators used in Boolean logic correspond to the AND, OR, and NOT logic gates used in circuit design. Several logic gates can be connected together to make a logic circuit. Logic circuits can be designed to calculate anything from simple arithmetic to the physics of spaceship orbits. Understanding Boolean algebra helps programmers build and test these abstract circuits.

A	B	C	D	E	F
			NOT A	B AND C	D OR E
0	0	0	1	0	1
0	0	1	1	0	1
0	1	0	1	0	1
0	1	1	1	1	1
1	0	0	0	0	0
1	0	1	0	0	0
1	1	0	0	0	0

BIOGRAPHY

George Boole

An influential mathematician, George Boole (1815–1864) didn't have much access to formal education and was mostly self-taught. He invented Boolean logic as a systematic, mathematical approach to ancient Greek philosopher Aristotle's theory of categorical logic—rules used to determine if a statement is true or false. Boole explained his concept of Boolean logic in his work titled *The Laws of Thought* (1854).

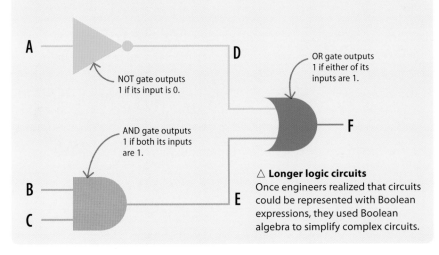

A

NOT gate outputs 1 if its input is 0.

AND gate outputs 1 if both its inputs are 1.

B

C

D

OR gate outputs 1 if either of its inputs are 1.

F

E

△ **Longer logic circuits**
Once engineers realized that circuits could be represented with Boolean expressions, they used Boolean algebra to simplify complex circuits.

Logical search

Boolean logic can also be used to search databases quickly. It eliminates the need for going through an entire database by making each search more precise. By combining keywords—such as dessert—with Boolean operators, a database search can take seconds.

Can I have a dessert with fruit AND NOT peanuts OR caramel?

▷ **Boolean query**
A Boolean query uses Boolean operators to create a more effective search by excluding irrelevant possibilities.

Storing and retrieving data

All programs, from simple calculators to flashy websites, have to store and manipulate data. The most basic programming tools used for achieving this are variables, constants, and arrays.

SEE ALSO

❰ 80–81 Bits and digitization

What do programming languages do? 118–119 ❱

Types of programming language 120–121 ❱

Variables

Variables are a storage mechanism, similar to a mug, with a name, value, and size. Just as the contents of a mug can change over time, the values inside a variable can change during the course of a program. Also like a mug, each variable has a specific size. It's important to pick the right variable size from the start, as different kinds of data stored in the variable can take up varying amounts of space in the memory.

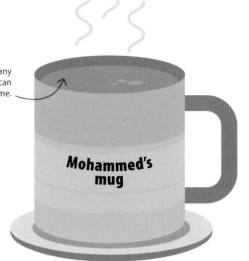

The mug can hold many different things, but it can only hold one at a time.

Mohammed's mug

▷ **Storing variables**
Variables are always labeled. To search and access data easily, programmers choose helpful, descriptive names for their variables.

Constants

Constants work like variables, but they're used for data that can't change while a program is running (if ever). They are useful when modifying programs, and are used to store tricky mathematical values (such as the value of Pi), scientific constants, or application-specific values. Anything that could be forgotten, misspelled, or changed only once every few years is best stored in a constant.

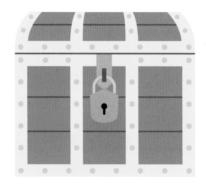

▷ **Fixed value**
Once a value is assigned to a constant, its value can't be changed unless the program is stopped and restarted. This is similar to a locked chest, whose contents can only be removed if it is unlocked.

REAL WORLD

Company banner

Let's say a library is rebranding its website. If the library has stored the image of its company banner inside a constant, they will only have to make one change to the website code for it to be changed everywhere. Otherwise, they will have to dig through hundreds of files.

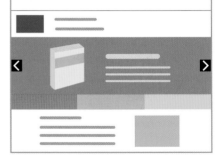

Arrays

An array is a collection of similar elements with a specific order. It is just like houses on a street or cars in a parking lot, which have a clear beginning and end. The location of an item in an array is called an array index. The first element has a name, or label, and every other piece of data is referenced based on its distance from this first element. In an array of cars, the first would be called "car," the second "car + 1," then "car + 2," and so on.

IN DEPTH

Pros and cons

Arrays are great while accessing the data as a group, such as a music app listing all the songs of an artist. However, it can be tricky to find or modify an individual element if the array is too long. A specific piece of data could be hiding anywhere—in position 1, 53, or 5,000. You don't know until you look at each element.

Arrays start their numbering system with 0 instead of 1. An array with 10 elements contains locations 0–9.

▽ **Size of an array**
Like the design of a parking lot, the size of an array is decided in advance and then filled up. A variable can also be created to keep track of the number of filled locations.

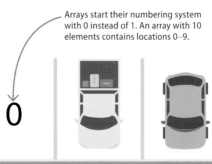

0

 4 5   8

Objects

An object is like a special, custom-sized variable. It is useful when data in a variety of sizes and shapes need to be grouped together. The key thing about objects is that the users have to write the code themselves. For this, a blueprint, called a class, needs to be defined. It includes listing all of the object's attributes, each of which is a different variable. Afterward, the same blueprint can be used every time to create a new object.

Each object contains its own unique data, based on the class blueprint.

Name:
Address:
Age:
Shopping cart

▷ **A customer object**
An object for an online shopper might contain a string of text (customer name), a couple of numbers (customer age and a unique identification number), and an array (the items in the customer's online shopping cart).

IN DEPTH

Why use objects?

The main goal of objects is to keep data in a central place. Object-oriented programming (OOP) lets you create object methods, which are special functions to manipulate object data. You can restrict which variables can be accessed by different parts of the program. This is especially useful for big software applications that have hundreds, if not thousands, of code files, each of which might process a different, unrelated type of data.

Program structures

A program can be described as a collection of possible sequences of instructions. To determine which lines of code to execute, programs use control structures such as branches and loops.

SEE ALSO

❮ **104–105** Boolean logic

❮ **106–107** Storing and retrieving data

What do programming
languages do? **118–119** ❯

Branching

A boat sailing toward a branch in the river can either go left or right. It can't sail down both streams at the same time. Similarly, the IF-THEN-ELSE control structure sends the program down a single branch of possibilities and ignores code in other branches. The choice of path typically depends on the piece of data stored in a variable.

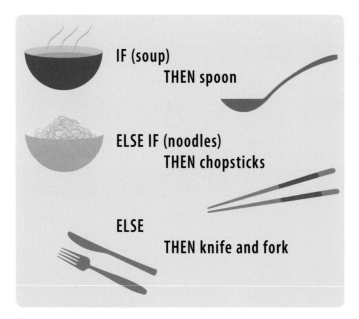

IF (soup)
    THEN spoon

ELSE IF (noodles)
    THEN chopsticks

ELSE
    THEN knife and fork

△ **Branching structure**
A spoon, chopsticks, and a knife and fork aren't all required for a single meal. Using a branching structure in a program forces the user to pick the best option, depending on the circumstances.

IN DEPTH

IF-THEN-ELSE

"If," "else if" (elif), and "else" are common programming keywords used to make decisions. "If" checks an initial condition, such as asking, "Is the sky blue?" If that condition is false, "else if" checks an alternative, such as "Is the sky purple?" The program defaults to "else" if none of those conditions can be met.

Grouping data

The IF-THEN-ELSE control structure is used as a way to sort data into groups. Programmers can also write customized code to manipulate each group differently. The ELSE statement is a "catch-all" group for data that doesn't fit into the previous categories.

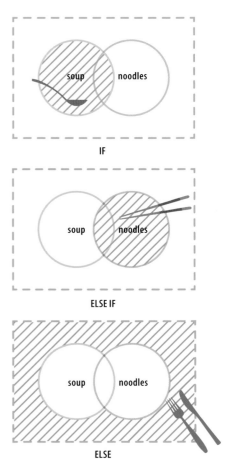

IF

ELSE IF

ELSE

△ **Boolean algebra**
Venn diagrams can be used to represent how data is separated into groups. Boolean algebra can also be used to create more complex groups, such as soup AND noodles.

Loops

Programs often need to repeat the same task multiple times. To avoid rewriting code, programmers use loops. Once a program reaches the end of a looping structure, it goes back to the beginning of the loop and starts again. There are three types of loops—FOR, WHILE, and DO-WHILE. Choosing the right one depends on the duration of the loop, the elements a user wants to change in each iteration, and how the user wants to exit the loop.

FOR loops
This loop runs a block of code a fixed number of times. If you wanted to draw a square, instead of coding for each side to be drawn, you could write the code to draw one line and then turn 90 degrees, and run this four times in a FOR loop.

WHILE loops
This is equivalent to saying "loop forever, on one condition." This condition could be "WHILE there are still cookies in the cookie jar: don't buy new cookies" or "until the user closes the program: keep recording key presses."

DO-WHILE loops
Similar to WHILE loops, DO-WHILE loops execute for an indefinite amount of time. The only difference is that this loop checks its condition at the end, so it's guaranteed to be executed at least once. For example, if a user inputs "11" into a program asking for a number between 1 and 10, the answer will be rejected and the user will be asked for a value again.

Why use functions?

Functions separate what the code does from how it acts. A function takes input data, such as numbers or coordinates, and turns it into output data, such as an answer or a full address. On the inside, functions use variables, constants, arrays, and control structures such as loops and branches. They help make code more readable.

▽ **Fahrenheit to Celsius**
A function that takes a temperature in Fahrenheit and outputs the temperature in Celsius eliminates the potential for human error, as a human does not need to do the calculation.

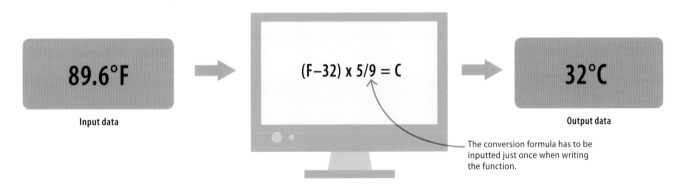

89.6°F

Input data

$(F-32) \times 5/9 = C$

32°C

Output data

The conversion formula has to be inputted just once when writing the function.

Translation

Translation is the process of converting one programming language into another. It makes coding more human-friendly by breaking down a high-level language into a low-level one.

SEE ALSO	
Assemblers, interpreters, and compilers	**112–113 〉**
What do programming languages do?	**118–119 〉**
C and C++	**126–127 〉**
Java	**128–129 〉**
Python	**130–131 〉**

High- and low-level languages

A manager of a clothing company doesn't need to know how many socks are delivered to each store. Instead, they are required to take a high-level view and only make decisions that are critical to the company's future. In a similar way, high-level programming languages don't worry about details. Memory management, converting instructions into bits, and varying voltage within physical circuits are all details hidden away from modern programmers. Instead, these are automatically handled by special programs called translators. This makes it easier for humans to focus on logic and complex algorithms and the computer to handle everything else.

"**C** is **quirky**, **flawed**, and an enormous **success**."
Dennis Ritchie (1941–2011), American creator of the C programming language

IN DEPTH

Pros and cons

High-level languages may seem like a better option, but they fall short in certain scenarios.

Pros

• Easier to learn.

• Easier to read and write. Difficult algorithms don't have to be converted into abstract strings of 0s and 1s.

• Easier to understand. Code can be shared, debugged, and augmented more quickly.

• Great for big, collaborative projects.

Cons

• Programs are bigger and slower. Since developers can't access the nuts and bolts of the code, programs are difficult to streamline.

• Security risks—developers can't check if memory is properly secured and wiped.

• The popularity of high-level languages means that many computer scientists don't fully understand operating systems and hardware. This can lead to flaws in software design.

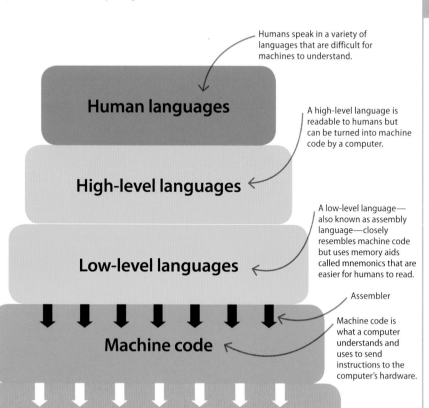

Humans speak in a variety of languages that are difficult for machines to understand.

A high-level language is readable to humans but can be turned into machine code by a computer.

A low-level language—also known as assembly language—closely resembles machine code but uses memory aids called mnemonics that are easier for humans to read.

Assembler

Machine code is what a computer understands and uses to send instructions to the computer's hardware.

Instruction set

Source code vs. machine code

Programmers write source code in languages like Java, Python, or C. These files contain the human-readable instructions that create individual programs, such as text editors, web browsers, or multimedia games. However, in order for the computer to run the code, the instructions must be translated into raw bits that a CPU can process. This is called machine code. If you open machine code in a text editor, it will look like a wall of gibberish, but this is what the computer understands.

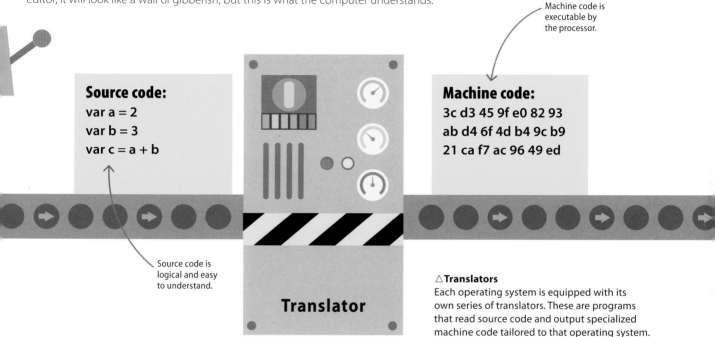

Machine code is executable by the processor.

Source code:

var a = 2
var b = 3
var c = a + b

Source code is logical and easy to understand.

Machine code:

3c d3 45 9f e0 82 93
ab d4 6f 4d b4 9c b9
21 ca f7 ac 96 49 ed

Translator

△**Translators**
Each operating system is equipped with its own series of translators. These are programs that read source code and output specialized machine code tailored to that operating system.

Opcodes and operands

In machine code, each instruction is composed of an opcode (short for operational code) and one or more operands. An opcode is a number that corresponds to a specific CPU action. For instance, the opcode 04 could mean add two pieces of data. To make opcodes more intuitive, they're given standardized nicknames, also known as mnemonics. Operands are the data being processed.

▽ **Machine-level programming**
Programming at the machine level requires programmers to memorize the opcodes of a particular operating system. Sometimes, they even work with individual bits.

Opcode	Mnemonic	Binary	Description
87	ADD *A*	10000111	Add contents of register A to that of the accumulator.
3A	LDA	00111010	Load data stored in the given memory address.
79	MOV *A C*	01111001	Move data from register A to C.
C3	JMP	11000011	Jump to instructions in specified memory address.
C1	POP *B*	11000001	Pop from stack and copy to memory registers B + C.

Assemblers, interpreters, and compilers

SEE ALSO

❮ 44–45 Operating systems

❮ 110–111 Translation

JavaScript   134–135 ❯

Translators turn high-level code into machine code, and there are three main types: assemblers, interpreters, and compilers.

Assemblers

The only difference between assembly code and opcode—the instructions to the computer to perform an operation—are the names of instructions. Assembly code is a low-level language that is written in mnemonics. Mnemonics are simple instructions that are easier for humans to remember than opcode. An assembler goes through code written in assembly code and simply swaps every mnemonic it finds for its corresponding opcode.

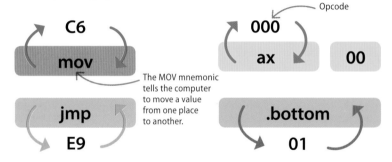

The MOV mnemonic tells the computer to move a value from one place to another.

Opcode

△ **Assembling**

An assembler is the most basic type of compiler. It simply swaps out mnemonics with the specific set of opcodes belonging to its operating system.

IN DEPTH

Assembly

Assembly is commonly used in applications such as cell phone chips, ATMs, and video-game consoles, where space and speed are important.

Pros

• Programmers don't have to remember opcodes.

• A single program can work on multiple computers.

Cons

• Programmers still work at a low level with registers, stack pointers, and heaps.

• An assembler has to be written for each OS.

• Even simple programs have many lines of code.

Interpreters

Interpretive languages can't be run without their interpreter installed on the computer. An interpreter translates and executes the source code one line at a time. While this makes code more portable, which means it can be easily adapted to run on a different operating system, it also makes it slower. In general, it's harder to guarantee that a program is error-free, but it's easier to fix errors when they crop up.

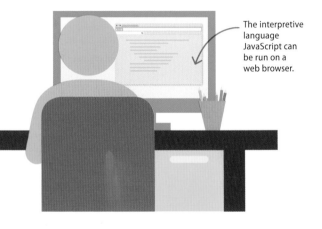

The interpretive language JavaScript can be run on a web browser.

▷ **Easy to handle**

The interpretive style makes it easy to handle interactive online pages, as it can receive new code anytime and still run it.

Compilers

A compiler translates an entire program in an OS-specific executable file in one go. Since high-level languages, such as Java and C, are very different from machine code, compiling them is a complex, multistep process.

▷ **Compilation steps**
There are four steps common to all compilers. These are lexing, parsing, optimization, and finally generation of machine code.

Source code

Machine code
The parse tree is translated into bits. This converts the program into a format that the hardware can process.

Optimization
The compiler makes the code as slick and efficient as possible. It undoes bonus steps that are added for clarity.

Lexing
This gets rid of human-readable names. Code is transformed into tokens that are easier for a computer to manipulate.

Parsing
Tokens are organized into a parse tree, which mimics the overall structure of the program, including branches and loops.

IN DEPTH

Compilation

Compiled programs are the norm except when browsing the Internet.

Pros

• Since programmers work with high-level code, they can work faster and make bigger, more complicated programs.

• There is less potential for mistakes.

• Once compiled, a program can be run at any time.

• Faster than interpreters.

Cons

• Compiled code is generally slower and bulkier than code written in assembly.

• Compiler errors can be vague and unhelpful. It's not always easy to find the errors in the program.

• A compiler must be written for each OS.

Linking

A program's code is typically spread out over many source code files, called object code, each of which is compiled separately. This makes it easier to change code, since modifying a single file doesn't require recompiling the entire program. However, this means that there's an extra step in the translation process: linking all of the object code together into a single program.

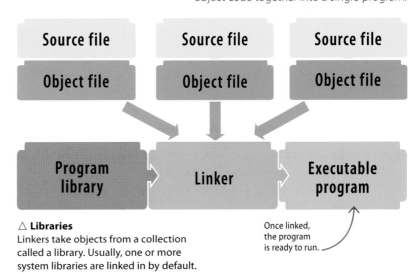

△ **Libraries**
Linkers take objects from a collection called a library. Usually, one or more system libraries are linked in by default.

Once linked, the program is ready to run.

Software errors

No program is ever entirely error-free. Luckily, there are many techniques and tools that programmers can use to detect and fix these errors.

SEE ALSO	
❮ 112–113 Assemblers, interpreters, and compilers	
Language breakthroughs	122–123 ❯
Maintenance and support	174–175 ❯

Bugs in a program

An important part of being a programmer is the ability to recognize software errors, also called "bugs," and fix them. There are three types of bugs—syntax, logic, and runtime errors. While some bugs cause obvious crashes and are easy to locate, others are subtle and can take months to find.

▽ **Syntax errors**
A syntax error is a typo or a small mistake introduced by a programmer into the wording of the program. The compiler—which translates programming languages into machine code—will not work until all syntax errors are fixed.

IN DEPTH

First bug

In 1945, computers filled entire rooms and produced a lot of heat that attracted bugs, which crawled inside the machines and caused short circuits. On September 9, 1945, American computer scientist Grace Hopper (1906–1992) found that a moth had caused a malfunction in the Harvard Mark II computer, and she taped the moth into the computer's log book. The term "bug" for a computer problem has been used ever since.

Typos and misspelled words
This includes missing brackets, semicolons, or quotation marks.

Undeclared variables
If a programmer forgets to declare a variable before assigning its value, the compiler won't be able to find the variable.

Off by one error
This includes overestimating the size of an array or forgetting that arrays start at 0 and not 1.

Forgetting to link code
If the program is not written properly, the compiler won't be able to access libraries of prewritten code.

Integer division
Integer division truncates numbers by throwing away remainders, which can cause calculation mistakes if you need precision.

▷ **Logic errors**
A logic error is a flaw in the program's design that causes unanticipated behavior. These bugs can be harder to find, as they don't always produce crashes.

What to do when an error message appears

When an error message appears, the first task for programmers is to locate the bug. The compiler usually indicates which line of code caused a crash. However, some errors have a trickle-down effect, and the actual error is several lines higher.

Error message checklist

- Review code for syntax errors. Go through the logic of the section to spot mistakes.
- If the error message doesn't make sense to you, try to find a solution online.
- Add print statements to code to display variables. A print statement is any command used to display text (including variables) to the user. Usually they appear in the programmer's console.
- Execute code and check that each value displayed in the console is correct.

Debugging

A debugger is a program used to find bugs in other programs. Most debuggers can run through the script (the program's instructions) in a step-by-step mode to isolate the source of the problem. Some debuggers can then fix the problem or offer ways in which this can be done. The program can then be run again to see if the debugger has fixed the problems it found.

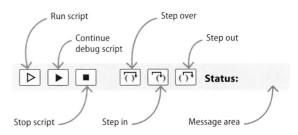

Run script · Continue debug script · Stop script · Step in · Step over · Step out · Message area · **Status:**

△ **Breakpoints**
A program freezes when it reaches a breakpoint, allowing programmers to detect the errors at their leisure. They can also check through the code one line at a time.

▽ **Runtime errors**
A runtime error is a specific type of logic error that occurs in the middle of a working program and causes it to crash. Usually, the program freezes or a pop-up box appears.

"=" instead of "=="
Mixing up "=" (assigns a value) and "==" (used for comparison) can lead to unpredictable results.

Segfault
A segmentation fault occurs when trying to access a restricted segment of memory.

Division by 0
When faced with this operation, programs usually crash.

Incorrect Boolean expressions
Using AND, OR, and NOT incorrectly can cause the program to loop forever or execute the wrong code.

Using different data types in the same operation
Mixing up text and numbers confuses a program, leading to an instant crash.

Programming languages

What do programming languages do?

SEE ALSO

❮ **76–77** Algorithms

❮ **108–109** Program structures

❮ **110–111** Translation

Types of programming language **120–121** ❯

Programming languages were developed to help humans communicate with computers. The fundamental challenge is translating instructions humans can understand into ones computers can.

Programming languages

A programming language is a formalized set of words and symbols that allows people to give instructions to computers. Just like human languages, each programming language has its own vocabulary and grammar. Translating an algorithm written in English into a programming language enables a computer to understand and carry out the instructions.

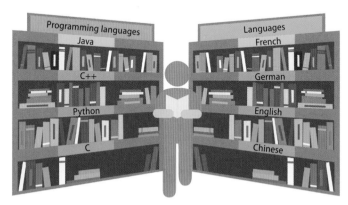

▷ **Multilingual**
It's possible to translate text into many different human languages. Similarly, computer instructions can be written in many different programming languages.

IN DEPTH

Translation

There are a variety of ways to translate programming languages into the binary code (sometimes called machine code) a computer understands. Some languages, like C and C++, use a compiler. This produces a new file containing machine code that can then be run. Scripting languages, like Python and JavaScript, use an interpreter, which translates and runs the code in a single process. Assembly languages use an assembler that, like a compiler, produces a file containing machine code.

Common features

All programming languages have certain underlying features. These are: making decisions, repeating instructions, and storing values in named containers. The words used for these features vary from language to language, but they're all doing essentially the same thing. Being familiar with these concepts in one language makes learning another language much easier.

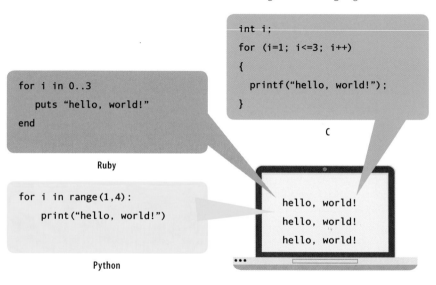

```
int i;
for (i=1; i<=3; i++)
{
    printf("hello, world!");
}
```
C

```
for i in 0..3
    puts "hello, world!"
end
```
Ruby

```
for i in range(1,4):
    print("hello, world!")
```
Python

```
hello, world!
hello, world!
hello, world!
```

▷ **Same outcome**
The three programs shown here look quite different, but they're all examples of a programming concept called "for loop" that is used to display a message three times.

High- and low-level languages

The term "programming languages" is usually used for high-level languages. These allow programmers to use a language closer to human language. Low-level languages work with internal hardware like registers and memory and are tied to a specific type of computer. Programs written in a high-level language can be run on any computer with the relevant compiler or interpreter.

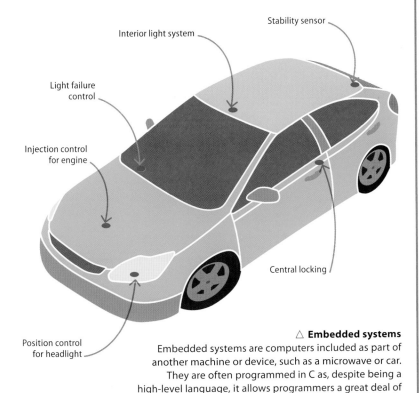

Stability sensor

Interior light system

Light failure control

Injection control for engine

Position control for headlight

Central locking

△ Embedded systems

Embedded systems are computers included as part of another machine or device, such as a microwave or car. They are often programmed in C as, despite being a high-level language, it allows programmers a great deal of control over how the code runs at the level of registers.

TOP TECH

The Mars Rover

One of the most famous devices to feature an embedded system is the Mars Rover *Curiosity*. The self-propelling robot is programmed to explore Mars and send back data. Code for the rover is written mainly in C and has been very thoroughly tested to try to ensure the rover doesn't accidentally drive into a rock and damage itself.

Special purpose

In the initial stages of computing, programs were written in binary code, or assembly language. Since then, programming languages have been developed as tools to meet a need or fulfill a purpose. Examples include languages that allow mathematicians and scientists to include formulas, languages used to teach people how to program, or languages that could be used to develop artificial intelligence.

Fortran

△ Scientific computing

Fortran was designed to allow scientists to write programs that included mathematical formulas. Its name is short for "Formula Translation."

COBOL

△ Down to business

Short for common business-oriented language, COBOL was developed to make it easier and cheaper for companies to write business-related software.

Scratch

△ Code for kids

Scratch was created as a language that would make learning to code easy and fun for children aged between 8 and 16.

Lisp

△ Thinking machines

Lisp was based on a mathematical definition of programming languages and soon became popular with researchers studying artificial intelligence.

Types of programming language

SEE ALSO

⟨ 108–109 Program structures
⟨ 114–115 Software errors
C and C++   126–127 ⟩
Python   130–131 ⟩
Scratch   136–137 ⟩

There are lots of different ways to group programming languages, and most languages fall into more than one group. A useful way of grouping is according to the features a language has.

Styles of programming language

Different styles of programming are sometimes called paradigms. They represent varied ways of thinking about computation. Some styles of programming are better at solving particular problems than others. Sometimes, there's no obvious approach, and programmers will simply choose the language they are most comfortable with.

Imperative

The imperative style of programming is best described as a recipe or a knitting pattern. It is a series of commands that are executed one after the other. The recipe changes the state, or condition, of the ingredients from uncooked to cooked. The state of a computer is the data stored in its memory. When it runs a program, the commands in the program change this state. Imperative languages include variables, which hold data, and control structures, such as loops and conditional branches.

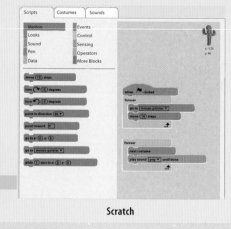

```c
#include <stdio.h>

int main()
{
    int i;
    for (i = 0; i < 5; i++){
        printf("Hello, World!");
    }
    return 0;
}
```

Hello, World!

C

Visual

The first style of programming that children encounter is often visual programming. This describes languages where the programmer fits together blocks that represent instructions. Many visual languages are designed as educational tools. They allow children, or other new programmers, to become familiar with programming concepts without needing to type in commands. This allows them to focus on solving the problem without having to worry about programming errors.

Scratch

Hello, World!

Traditionally, the first program a new programmer writes is the "Hello, World!" program. This simply prints the phrase "Hello, World!" on the screen. Even experienced programmers learning a new language often start off in the same way, and it's also a good first check to see if a newly installed system is working properly. The tradition was introduced in the book *The C Programming Language*, published in 1978.

Object-oriented

This style of programming includes the concept of objects that model real-world things. An object usually has fields (containing data) and methods (containing code) that represent behaviors. So a ball object might have the fields color and size, since these are characteristics of a ball, and the method bounce, since this is what a ball does. Objects are instances of classes—definitions of what a particular object would look like. This means the object ball is an instance of the class ball, similar to any real ball being an instance of the idea of a ball.

```python
class Ball:
    color = ""
    size = 0
        def throw(self):
            print("ball being thrown!")
        def catch(self):
            print("ball being caught!")
myball = Ball()
myball.color = "red"
myball.size = 5
```

Python

Functional

Functional languages define a program as a series of mathematical functions. A functional language is described as pure if it doesn't affect the computer's state, or impure if it does. One major feature of functional languages is that they don't use loops to repeat operations. Instead, they use a recursive function, which calls itself as part of its own definition. Another notable feature is pattern matching, where a function decides what to do by looking at the value it's been given and seeing which of the several patterns it matches.

```haskell
fac 0 = 1
fac n = n * fac (n-1)

main = print (fac 7)
```

Haskell

Natural-language programming

There are programming languages where the code looks like normal text or natural language. However, these aren't serious languages, as even tiny calculations take a large amount of code, and they're usually created just for fun. These include Shakespeare, where programs look like very confused Shakespearean plays, and Chef, where each program is written as a cooking recipe.

Language breakthroughs

SEE ALSO

❰ **110–111** Translation

❰ **114–115** Software errors

❰ **118–119** What do programming languages do?

For many tasks, high-level languages are better than machine code or assembly language. Two early programming languages, Fortran and BASIC, helped convince people of this.

Fortran

Short for "Formula Translation," Fortran was developed in 1957 by a team at IBM led by American computer scientist John Backus (1924–2007). Unlike earlier compilers, Fortran's compiler produced machine code that ran almost as fast as handwritten code. Early Fortran programs were transformed a line at a time into patterns of holes on punched cards.

```
C AREA OF A TRIANGLE - HERON'S FORMULA
C INPUT - CARD READER UNIT 5, INTEGER INPUT
C OUTPUT -
      READ(5,501) A,B,C
  501 FORMAT(3I5)
      IF(A.EQ.0 .OR. B.EQ.0 .OR. C.EQ.0) STOP 1
      S = (A + B + C) / 2.0
      AREA = SQRT( S * (S - A) * (S - B) * (S - C) )
      WRITE(6,601) A,B,C,AREA
  601 FORMAT(4H A= ,I5,5H  B= ,I5,5H  C= ,I5,8H  AREA= ,F10.2,
     $13H SQUARE UNITS)
      STOP
      END
```

▷ **Selling points**
Fortran's main selling point was that it made writing programs much easier because its syntax was much closer to English when compared with assembly languages.

What is it for?

Fortran is mainly used for writing programs involving scientific and mathematical problems. It was the first language to have built-in support for mathematical concepts such as complex numbers, used in many areas of physics. Fortran has been used for systems investigating nuclear physics, quantum mechanics, and the operation of airplanes and wind turbines.

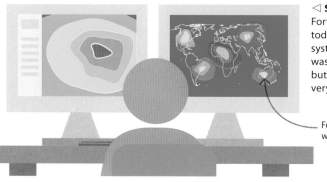

◁ **Scientific systems**
Fortran is still in use today. Many scientific systems use code that was written decades ago but has proven to be very reliable over time.

Fortran is also used for weather prediction systems.

Grace Hopper

An American mathematician and Rear Admiral in the US Navy, Grace Hopper (1906–1992) was involved in developing COBOL, a programming language for businesses. She developed one of the first compilers, and her idea of making programming languages more like English helped spread computer usage.

BASIC

BASIC (Beginner's All-purpose Symbolic Instruction Code) was developed at Dartmouth College in 1964. Math professors John G. Kemeny (1926–1992) and Thomas E. Kurtz (b. 1928) wanted a simple language that they could use to teach programming. They also developed a system where programmers could run their code immediately after entering it at a terminal. Before this, students' programs would be queued and run hours later.

"Everybody … should **learn** how to **program a computer**, because it **teaches** you **how to think.**"
Steve Jobs (1955–2011), American co-founder of Apple

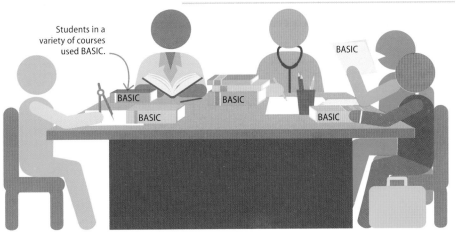

Students in a variety of courses used BASIC.

BASIC

BASIC

BASIC

BASIC

BASIC

▷ **BASIC for all**
BASIC was designed to be easy to learn for everyone, not just mathematicians. As a result, writing course-related BASIC programs became part of the syllabus for many students at Dartmouth University, regardless if they were studying to be engineers, to be doctors, or to work in the arts.

Home computers

BASIC's popularity really took off in the 1970s and 1980s, when home computers first became available. Most machines came with a version of BASIC, which became many people's introduction to programming. The syntax of the language was straightforward and easy to learn, and allowed people to write software to help them in their businesses or as a hobby. It gave people the power to "hack their own machine," enabling them to write the software they wanted rather than being restricted to what already existed.

REAL WORLD
Raspberry Pi

Since the 1990s, computers have become increasingly user friendly, to the point that this has discouraged people from experimenting with programming. English inventor Eben Upton (b. 1978) developed the Raspberry Pi in 2012, in an effort to reverse this trend. A very low-cost, simple computer, the Raspberry Pi comes with Python and Scratch as standard, and can be used for all kinds of projects.

```
READY

10 PRINT "HELLO, WORLD!"

20 GOTO 10

RUN ■
```

This program will keep printing "HELLO, WORLD!" until it is stopped.

◁ **BBC BASIC**
In 1981, BBC Micro was launched. It contained a version of BASIC that was used by schoolchildren all across the UK to learn how to code.

Application programming interface

SEE ALSO	
⟨ 72–73 Abstraction	
Python	130–131 ⟩
Cloud computing	152–153 ⟩
The Internet of Things	226–227 ⟩

Websites often feature embedded functions such as maps or social media feeds. They do not create these themselves, but use an application programming interface (API).

What is an API?

An interface describes the way a program interacts with another. The other system can be a user, through a user interface (UI), or another program, through an API. APIs make it easier for programmers to use functions and objects from other programs in their code. When an API function is requested, the computer hosting the API executes the function's code and sends the result back to the program requesting it.

▽ **Abstraction**
An API is an abstraction of the program it represents. Just as a menu only lists the names of dishes and not their recipes, an API only shows the features that can be used by other programs. All details of the program's construction are hidden.

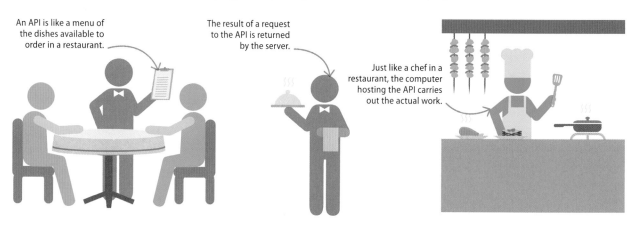

An API is like a menu of the dishes available to order in a restaurant.

The result of a request to the API is returned by the server.

Just like a chef in a restaurant, the computer hosting the API carries out the actual work.

Which languages?

APIs are written in a variety of programming languages, including PHP, Python, Ruby, and Java. Programs that are written in a different language from the one an API is written in can still use its functions. Requests to an API make use of the Hypertext Transfer Protocol (HTTP) used to transfer information across the World Wide Web. The API returns the result to the calling program in a standard format.

▷ **Helper libraries**
Many APIs provide helper libraries for different programming languages, which makes it easier to call them using another language. For example, a program written in Python can use an API's Python helper library.

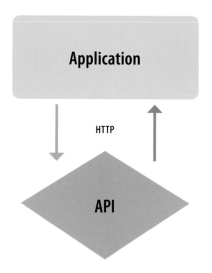

Application

HTTP

API

Cloud APIs

The cloud is the network of computers across the world connected by the Internet. The computers in the cloud provide a wide variety of services, including data storage, access to very powerful computers, and data analysis applications. Specially designed cloud APIs help programmers access these services and harness the power of the cloud. Cloud APIs are grouped according to the sort of cloud-based services they allow access to. These services include software, such as word-processing packages, and hardware, such as storage space.

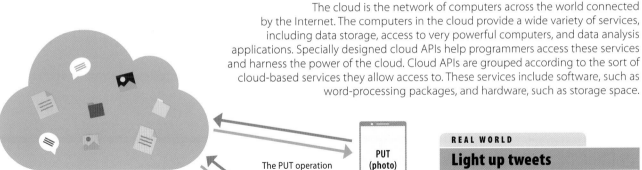

PUT (photo)

The PUT operation updates something already online, such as a blog.

The GET operation retrieves information, such as a copy of a file.

POST (tweet)

GET (file)

DELETE (status)

The POST operation adds information, such as a new social media post.

Representational state transfer

The cloud computers providing services are known as servers. Other devices, known as clients, make requests for these services using cloud APIs. Most cloud APIs are created using a format called representational state transfer (REST). This means each function performs one of the four standard web operations on data: GET, PUT, POST, or DELETE.

The DELETE operation removes information—for example, taking a photo off a social media profile.

REAL WORLD

Light up tweets

The Twitter API has been used to find out how the world is feeling. A programmer wrote code that monitored the predominant emotions mentioned in tweets from across the world. Anybody can use this code to make their own LED lights glow in a different color for each emotion.

API security and the Internet of Things

The Internet of Things is the term used for objects in the physical world that are connected to the Internet. These items all need APIs that allow programmers to interact with them—for example, by controlling an item or retrieving data created by it. These APIs could potentially all be vulnerable to attack from hackers, giving them access to items in people's homes and cars. To prevent this, APIs have to include a security system, restricting access to those who have a legitimate purpose.

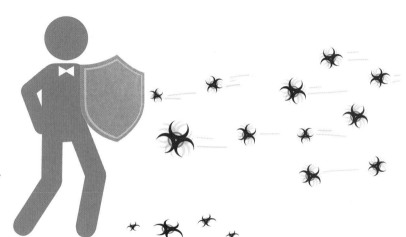

C and C++

The oddly named C and C++ are two of the most popular programming languages in existence. They have been used to create a huge amount of software we use today.

SEE ALSO

‹ 54–55 Build your own computers

‹ 110–111 Translation

‹ 118–119 What do programming languages do?

‹ 120–121 Types of programming language

The C programming language

American computer scientist Dennis Ritchie (1941–2011), a programmer at Bell Labs, released C in 1978. He developed the language while working on the Unix operating system. Unix was coded in assembly language, which tied it to a particular type of computer. This meant that the number of customers willing to buy it were limited. Ritchie created C so that a new version of UNIX could be made that could run on any machine.

▽ **IDE**
An integrated development environment (IDE) lets programmers write, compile, and run code using a single program with a graphical interface. IDEs make writing large software systems a more manageable process.

```
Claires-MacBook-Air:C claire$ clang -wall hello -o hello
Claires-MacBook-Air:C claire$ ./hello
Hello, World!
```

Command line

```
#include <stdio.h>

int main()
{
    printf("Hello, World! \n");
    return 0;
}
```

IDE

How does it work?

C is an imperative programming language and doesn't allow object-oriented or functional styles of programming. C's syntax, using curly braces { } to enclose blocks of code, has influenced many other languages. It's a high-level language that doesn't abstract away from the internal structure of the computer. This means programmers can directly access areas in a computer's memory.

Computer operating system

Robotics

NASA's core flight system

Arduino microprocessor

△ **What is it used for?**
C's combination of high- and low-level features make it popular for writing operating systems, particularly for the most essential parts. Given its flexibility, it is used in a wide variety of applications.

LINGO

Behind the names

The language Ritchie originally tried to reimplement Unix in was called B, short for BCPL (Basic Combined Programming Language). C was simply the next letter in the alphabet. Putting "++" after a variable in C tells the computer to add one to it, so 1++ = 2. The name C++ reflects the fact that the new language is C, but with additions.

This code sets a variable called "age" to 20, and then by asking for "age++" the number 21 is displayed.

```
int age = 20;
printf("Age is: %d", age);
age++;
printf("Age is now: %d", age);
```

The C++ programming language

In 1979, Danish programmer Bjarne Stroustrup (b. 1950) started working at Bell Labs. He had previously worked using Simula67, considered to be the first object-oriented programming language. Simula67 had been designed to let people model real-world systems easily, but Stroustrup found it really slow. He decided to add object-oriented features to C to create a fast language for building large systems. This resulted in C++, which was released in 1983.

Compiling program for Xcode IDE

```cpp
#include <iostream>

int main(int argc, const char * argv [])
{
    std::cout << "Hello, World!\n";
    return 0;
}
```

C++

Run Without Building	^ ⌘ R
Test Without Building	^ ⌘ U
Profile Without Building	^ ⌘ I
Test	^ ⌥ ⌘ R
Test Again	^ ⌥ ⌘ R
Profile	
Profile Again	
Compile "main.cpp"	^ ⌘ R
Analyze "main.cpp"	^ ⇧ ⌘ R

◁ **Compiled**
Similar to C, C++ is compiled to create an executable file before it is run. This can be done on the command line or through an IDE, such as Visual Studio or Xcode.

How does it work?

C++ looks very similar to C. It also allows programmers to access the computer's hardware in the same way. However, unlike C, it includes features that allow programmers to abstract away from the hardware of the computer without slowing down their code. For instance, data structures are ways of organizing data in a program. C++ includes built-in data structures, whereas C programmers have to code these themselves.

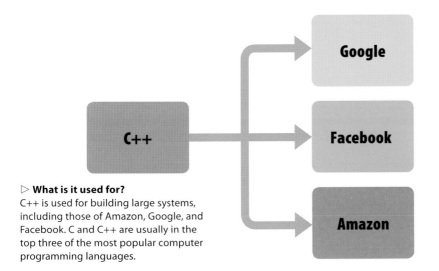

▷ **What is it used for?**
C++ is used for building large systems, including those of Amazon, Google, and Facebook. C and C++ are usually in the top three of the most popular computer programming languages.

REAL WORLD

C++ at the movies

Autodesk's Maya animation tool is written in C++. Maya has been used to create visual effects for many popular films, including *Star Wars Episode I*, *Spider-Man*, *Lord of the Rings*, and several *Harry Potter* movies. It's possible for programmers to write their own plug-ins in C++ to add functionality to Maya.

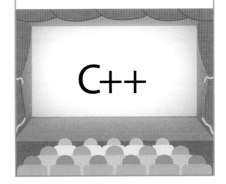

Java

Java was developed in 1995 to make it easier to write code for the range of computers available at the time. It is still a major player today.

SEE ALSO	
‹ 126–127 C and C++	
Python	130–131 ›
Scratch	136–137 ›
The Internet of Things	226–227 ›

Background

The Java programming language was developed by Canadian computer scientist James Gosling (b. 1955) for the American computer company Sun Microsystems' Java platform—a collection of software designed to allow programmers to develop a variety of systems. These ranged from tiny applications hosted on smartcards for personal banking to large systems designed for use by many people across an organization. Web browsers soon included the ability to run small self-contained applications called Java applets, which increased Java's popularity.

▷ **Language of gadgets**
The team behind Java wanted to design a language for programming the increasing number of electronic gadgets available, such as personal digital assistants (handheld personal computers) and webcams.

Personal
digital assistants

Printers

Webcams

Games

Car navigation

Smartcards

Java code

Java compiler

Java bytecode

JVM
for smartphone

JVM
for tablet

JVM
for PC

How does it work?

Java is an object-oriented language. Its syntax was designed to be similar to that of C and C++, but it doesn't include many of their low-level commands. A Java program is designed to behave in the same way on any machine. To enable this, a Java program is compiled into bytecode. Bytecode is machine code for the Java Virtual Machine (JVM), a simulated computer running on the user's real computer.

◁ **Java Virtual Machine**
The Java Virtual Machine is an abstraction that lets programmers write code without worrying about how it will work on a variety of different computers.

REAL WORLD

Bytecode verification

Users can download files containing bytecode and run them on the JVM on their computer, which could allow malicious people to send out bytecode that could cause harm to computers. To avoid this, each bytecode file is examined by the JVM's bytecode verifier, which checks it doesn't perform specific undesirable actions—for example, accessing data which it shouldn't have access to.

What is Java used for?

Java is used in many systems that people use today, including microblogging social media sites, film-streaming sites, and lots of Android phone apps. Many large banks and airlines use Java to code their systems, as it enables them to create and subsequently enlarge systems that carry out large numbers of database operations. Java is possibly the world's most popular programming language.

This code prints a countdown from 10 to 0.

```java
public class Countdown {
    public static void main(String[] args) {
        int count = 10;
        while (count > 0) {
            System.out.println(count + "\n");
            count--;
        }
        System.out.print("LIFT OFF! \n");
    }
}
```

When the count reaches 0, "LIFT OFF!" is printed.

▷ **Who can use it?**
Java is very powerful and opens up many possibilities, but it could be confusing for a new coder who may be better off learning Scratch or Python to begin with.

Internet of Things

The Internet of Things (IoT) is the name for the increasing network of objects in the physical world able to connect to the Internet. These can include smart appliances such as refrigerators, sensors on farm animals to monitor their health, or thermostats in forests to detect fires. Java has many advantages when it comes to programming these devices, as there is already a version of Java designed for programming small embedded and mobile systems.

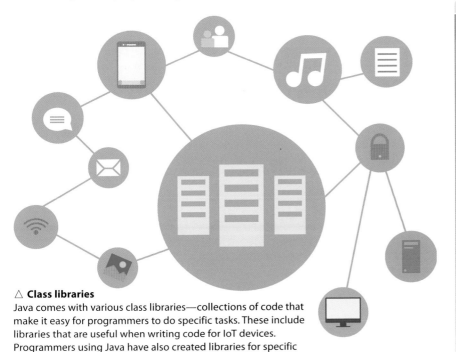

△ **Class libraries**
Java comes with various class libraries—collections of code that make it easy for programmers to do specific tasks. These include libraries that are useful when writing code for IoT devices. Programmers using Java have also created libraries for specific devices, many of which are available for other coders to use.

Minecraft

The original version of the popular game Minecraft was written in Java. Users were able to write "mods" (short for "modifications") that changed the behavior of the game world. This was done either by editing the Java source code of the game or uploading their own Java code. Microsoft recently bought the game and is moving toward a version in C++, but is currently still supporting the Java version.

Python

Released in the 1990s, Python is one of the most popular computer programming languages in the world. It takes a bit longer to learn than Scratch, but it can be used to build just about anything.

SEE ALSO

❰ **118–119** What do programming languages do?
❰ **120–121** Types of programming language
Scratch   **136–137**❱

Why Python?

Created by Dutch programmer Guido van Rossum, Python is a text-based programming language. It is extremely versatile and can be used to make many different types of program, such as apps, games, and websites. Python is a great language for getting started with computer programming and is used by many schools and universities to teach coding. Here are its most important features:

Python is **named after** the popular **British comedy** series *Monty Python's Flying Circus*.

Simple and easy to learn

A simple and minimalistic language, Python is extremely beginner-friendly. The code is written in a combination of words, numbers, and punctuation. Its easy syntax allows beginners to focus on learning programming concepts without having to worry about too many details.

Free and open source

Python is an example of a FLOSS (free/libre and open source software), which means that it can be freely distributed, its source code can be read and changed, and its code can be used in new programs. The Python community even encourages people to contribute code, documentation, and resources.

Portable

Python is extremely flexible and can run on a wide variety of hardware platforms and operating systems. Programming languages with these qualities are called "portable." From Windows to Mac, Linux, PlayStation, and more, Python works everywhere. Its interface looks the same, and the programs behave the same way on each platform.

Embeddable

Embeddable with C or C++ encoding, Python allows its users to improve their code with scripting functions. The code can be inserted into an application to provide a programmable interface. It can also be used as a scripting language for building large applications.

Extensive library

Python's greatest strength is its standard library, which supports many common programming tasks, such as connecting to web servers, reading and modifying files, and searching text with regular expressions. It also contains built-in modules that make it easier and quicker to build programs.

Great support

Python provides comprehensive and well-written documentation to its users. It has a guide to getting started, a reference section to explain what things mean, and a lot of example code. Its active support community makes sure Python projects have detailed and easy-to-understand technical documentation.

Working in IDLE

IDLE is a free application that is installed with Python. Designed for beginners, it includes a basic text editor that allows the user to write and edit Python code. It has two different windows—the editor window, which can be used to write and save programs, and the shell window, which runs Python instructions immediately. The shell window gives an immediate response, which makes it ideal for testing and exploring.

The name of the file is shown here.

Editor window

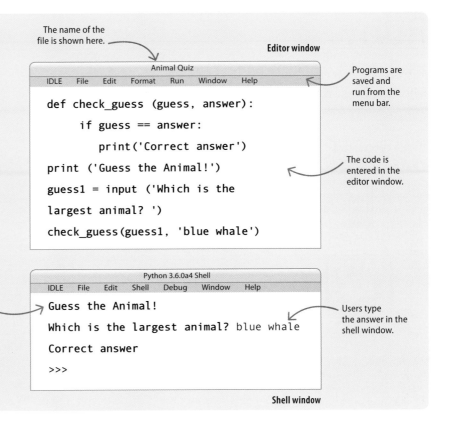

Animal Quiz

IDLE   File   Edit   Format   Run   Window   Help

```
def check_guess (guess, answer):
    if guess == answer:
        print('Correct answer')
print ('Guess the Animal!')
guess1 = input ('Which is the
largest animal? ')
check_guess (guess1, 'blue whale')
```

Programs are saved and run from the menu bar.

The code is entered in the editor window.

The output for the program appears in the shell window.

Python 3.6.0a4 Shell

IDLE   File   Edit   Shell   Debug   Window   Help

Guess the Animal!

Which is the largest animal? blue whale

Correct answer

>>>

Users type the answer in the shell window.

Shell window

▷ **Testing the code**
IDLE works in three easy steps: write the code, save it, and then run it. This program will ask the user a question and will then check to see if the answer is correct.

Python in action

A general-purpose programming language, Python has various applications in the fields of business, medicine, science, and media. It is used to test microchips, power apps, build video games, and write real-world programs.

Business
Python's special libraries and easily readable syntax make it a suitable coding language for customizing larger applications. It can be used by banks to keep track of transactions and by stores to set prices for their products.

Web development
Widely used on the Internet, Python is often used as a support language by software developers and for build control and testing.

Space
Software engineers have used Python to create tools for NASA's Mission Control Center. These tools help the crew prepare for and monitor the progress of each mission.

Game development
Python has various modules, libraries, and platforms that support computer game development. PySoy is a 3D game engine that supports Python, and PyGame provides functionality and a library for game development.

Scientific computing
Python is used for scientific computing, and it even has some libraries dedicated to specific areas of science. It can also be used to program robots to perform tricky operations.

Ruby

Ruby is a text-based language that offers a great progression when moving on from Scratch. Primarily designed to be programmer-friendly, it has a syntax that's close to English.

SEE ALSO	
❮ 120–121 Types of programming language	
Scratch	136–137 ❯
HTML	162–163 ❯
Cascading Style Sheets	164–165 ❯
Using JavaScript	166–167 ❯

Background

Ruby was released in 1995 by Japanese computer scientist Yukihiro Matsumoto, who wanted to design a simple and general-purpose scripting language. Matsumoto wanted his language to implement all the features necessary to write in an object-oriented style. Ruby was designed to make it easier for programmers to do tasks, rather than making it easier for computers to run code quickly.

```
[irb(main):007:0> puts "Hello, World!"
Hello, World!
=> nil
irb(main):008:0>
```

The prompt appears at the start of each line.

The result of the command just executed.

```
[irb(main):014:0> apples = 3
=> 3
[irb(main):015:0> oranges = 4
=> 4
[irb(main):016:0> fruit = apples + oranges
=> 7
irb(main):018:0>
```

▷ **Interactive Ruby**
Ruby has an interactive interpreter, called the Interactive Ruby Shell or IRB. It allows programmers to type individual commands that can be executed immediately.

How does it work?

Ruby has a very different approach from most languages. Almost everything in it is an object, even items like numbers and characters. These objects have methods that allow programmers to do things with them. In Ruby, it's also possible to program in a mostly imperative style. This allows new programmers to gradually come to grips with the object-oriented style.

```
"Hello, World!".swapcase.reverse.chars
```

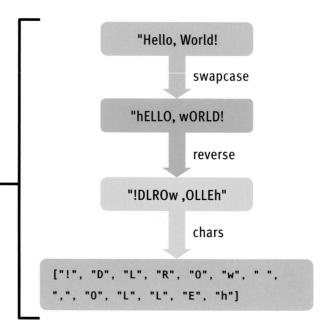

▷ **Chaining**
Ruby aims to be concise. One example of this is chaining, which applies several methods to an object. The method names are separated by periods and applied from left to right.

IN DEPTH

REPL

The Ruby interactive interpreter is an example of a REPL, a Read-Evaluate-Print Loop. This is a program that takes one command at a time, runs it, and prints the result. REPLs are a common feature of interpreted languages, which are often referred to as scripting languages. The quick feedback means it can be a useful tool for learning a language.

What is Ruby used for?

Ruby was made popular by "Ruby on Rails," a framework for making websites. It allows programmers to create websites that are connected to a database. The Rails framework simplifies retrieving and displaying data from the database and allows users to input data through the website. Rails combines Ruby with the languages of web programming: HTML, CSS, and JavaScript.

This is used for spotting and fixing spelling errors.

This sends secure messages via the web.

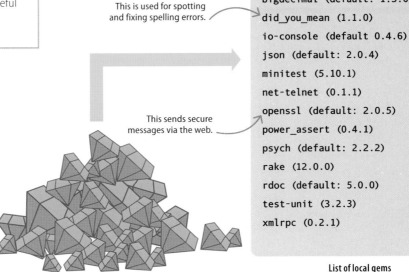

```
bigdecimal (default: 1.3.0)
did_you_mean (1.1.0)
io-console (default 0.4.6)
json (default: 2.0.4)
minitest (5.10.1)
net-telnet (0.1.1)
openssl (default: 2.0.5)
power_assert (0.4.1)
psych (default: 2.2.2)
rake (12.0.0)
rdoc (default: 5.0.0)
test-unit (3.2.3)
xmlrpc (0.2.1)
```

List of local gems

▷ **RubyGems**
Ruby's libraries, collections of ready-made code for carrying out specific tasks, are known as gems. They can be downloaded and installed using RubyGems, Ruby's built-in tool for gem management.

Why use Ruby?

Ruby was designed to reflect how people think about problems, rather than how computers think about them. All high-level languages abstract away from the way computation is done by a computer's hardware. Ruby is particularly focused on this approach, making it easy for users to program in a variety of styles.

Advantages	Disadvantages
Commands are often closer to a human language than other languages.	It is used in fewer areas in the programming world than other languages.
Thanks to Ruby on Rails, Ruby is one of the fastest-growing programming languages.	Ruby code runs slower than compiled languages like Java or C.
Ruby is still being actively developed, keeping pace with new technologies.	There are fewer libraries for coding in areas other than the web.

REAL WORLD

Sonic Pi

A free program, Sonic Pi was built using Ruby. It turns a computer into a musical instrument, which can be played by typing code. Most of its commands are specially created to allow users to do musical tasks, but it uses many of Ruby's basic features as well.

```
use_synth :piano
8.times do
  play :c4
  sleep 0.5
  sample :drum_cowbell
  sleep 0.5
end
```

JavaScript

JavaScript lets programmers create user-friendly interactive webpages. It also allows them to add animations or change a website's layout when viewed on smartphones.

SEE ALSO	
❰ 128–129 Java	
Malware	156–157 ❱
HTML	162–163 ❱
Cascading Style Sheets	164–165 ❱

Background

In the early 1990s, users couldn't interact with webpages beyond reading them. Websites were often created by amateur programmers who were interested in the new technology or by designers whose background was in art. JavaScript was designed to enable these users to add interactive elements to their pages. The name "JavaScript" was largely a marketing strategy. Java was very popular, and JavaScript's creators hoped the association would be advantageous.

```
public class HelloWorld {
    public static void main(String[] args) {
        System.out.println("Hello, World!");
    }
}
```

Java

▷ **Different from Java**
Though you might expect them to be related, Java and JavaScript are different languages, seen here in their "Hello, World!" code.

```
function helloworld() {
    alert("Hello, World !");
}
```

JavaScript

How does it work?

A JavaScript program is usually called a script. It's associated with a particular webpage and runs whenever someone loads the page in a browser. JavaScript is interpreted, not compiled, similar to Python. It's predominantly an object-oriented language but looks quite similar to C, as it uses curly brackets and semicolons.

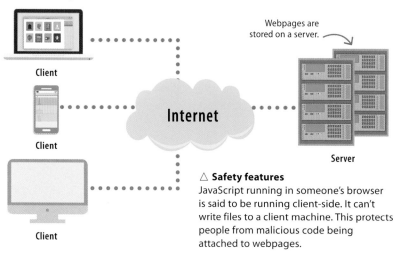

Client

Client

Client

Webpages are stored on a server.

Internet

Server

△ **Safety features**
JavaScript running in someone's browser is said to be running client-side. It can't write files to a client machine. This protects people from malicious code being attached to webpages.

Pop-ups

One of JavaScript's least popular applications may be pop-up dialog boxes. Pop-ups block the browser window and require the user to interact with them. They range from being a mild annoyance that interrupts the browsing experience to redirecting users toward malware and other online scams.

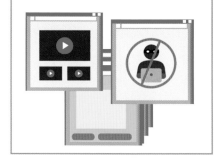

Growth of JavaScript

Professional developers looked down on JavaScript at first, largely because it was designed for and mainly used by amateur programmers. Also, unlike Java applications, JavaScript programs couldn't move data to and from a database on a server. This changed with the introduction of AJAX (Asynchronous JavaScript And XML), a collection of web technologies, including JavaScript, that allowed webpages to connect to a server. Professionals now consider JavaScript to be a useful language, and lots of code libraries have been written to make a variety of tasks easier.

▽ **Using the console**
JavaScript programs are extremely versatile. They allow programmers to create code that will help with multiple aspects of websites, such as animation, user input, auto-complete technology, and enabling the smooth flow of user interface from desktop to mobile websites.

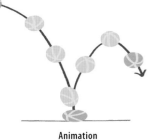

Animation

Mouse / keyboard input

How to |
How to make slime
How to prepare for hurricane
How to tie a tie

Search

Auto-complete

Mobile / desktop view

Why JavaScript?

For programmers new to web development, JavaScript is a great place to start. Using just a text editor and a web browser, programmers can add an array of interactivity and animations to their sites, from the very simple to the quite complex. It's also possible to create apps, known as web apps, using only JavaScript, HTML, and CSS. These apps run on any cell phone with a browser. There are also websites that help new programmers by allowing them to see the real-time effects of changing their JavaScript, HTML, or CSS scripts.

The "+" symbol can be used to add two numbers or two lines of code. Here, it has added cats and dogs together as a line and come up with 23 instead of 5, as expected.

```
function pets() {
  var cats = 2;
  var dogs = "3";
  console.log("Number of pets:" + (cats + dogs));
}
```

△ **Drawbacks**
A variable's type describes whether it's a number, character, or something else. JavaScript doesn't have strict rules about types, which can sometimes lead to unexpected results.

This code stores numerical values for cats and dogs and then asks to add them together.

JavaScript games

Many browser-based games, including the original version of 2048—a popular number-puzzle game—are written in JavaScript. Several free JavaScript game engines are also available, which allow programmers to easily create browser-based games. There are even games where the player has to write some JavaScript to complete each level.

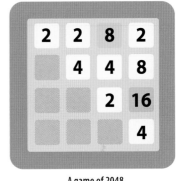

A game of 2048

Scratch

Scratch is the first programming language learned by many children. A visual language, it doesn't require users to type code. Instead, programs are made using colored blocks that represent commands.

SEE ALSO

❮ **36–37** Peripheral devices
❮ **118–119** What do programming languages do?
❮ **120–121** Types of programming language

Background

Scratch was created by the Lifelong Kindergarten group at the Massachusetts Institute of Technology (MIT). They wanted to make it easier for children aged 8–16 to learn how to code. It emphasizes the creative potential of code, allowing children to create interactive stories, games, art, and more.

Scratch cat is Scratch's mascot and the default character in projects.

▷ **Scratch worldwide**
Designed to be fun as well as educational, Scratch has a worldwide community of users who share their creations with each other.

TOP TECH

ScratchJr

This is a simplified version of Scratch for 5- to 7-year-olds. It allows users to make animations and interactive stories by clicking together colored blocks representing commands. Blocks mainly feature symbols rather than text, and there are fewer than in the standard version. It's available as an app for tablets, rather than as a desktop program.

Pop

Hi

1

How does it work?

To "write" a program in Scratch, the user drags together colored blocks that represent instructions. The instructions control images and sounds on the area of the window called the "stage." Scratch doesn't require users to have previous programming skills. The main abilities needed are basic reading, numeracy, and sufficient skill with a computer mouse to drag blocks to the desired locations.

▽ **Scratch 2.0 screen**
A program in Scratch is called a project, and its window is split into several areas, each with its own features.

Stage
The stage area is where sprites perform the actions that the code tells them to. Clicking the blue rectangle icon in the top-left corner makes this window full screen.

Sprites
Scratch programs control objects called sprites. Sprites can move around the stage area and interact with each other. Alternating between a sprite's "costumes" creates a simple cartoon animation effect.

SCRATCH 🌐 File ▼ Edit ▼ Tips

Desert life
by Vesper

Sprites   New sprite:

Stage
1 backdrop

Sprite 1   Sprite 2

New backdrop:

Using Scratch

Scratch is an excellent language for new programmers of all ages. It allows them to grasp the basic concepts of programming without the frustration of errors caused by mistyping commands. Scratch's ethos of "remixing" other users' shared code to create new projects also encourages exploration.

Advantages	Disadvantages
Gives immediate and appealing feedback in the form of animations and sounds	Only supports a limited range of computational concepts
Ability to see and modify other users' shared code is a great aid to learning	Not suitable for more advanced programming, as it doesn't include functions.
Doesn't require typing skills or memorization of commands	Restricts users' ability to write programs that integrate with other systems

REAL WORLD

Controlling code

Scratch allows users to control their programs by moving their body, either by using their computer's webcam or with devices like the Kinect games controller or the Leap motion sensor. This opens up possibilities, such as creating a game that users play without touching a keyboard or another type of controller. They can even create a new musical instrument that's played by dancing.

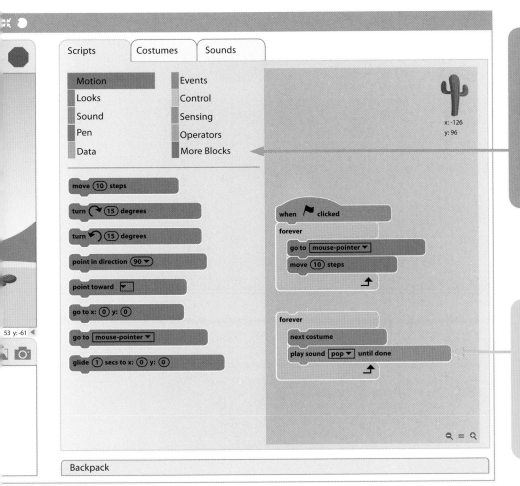

Extending Scratch
There are several extensions to Scratch that allow it to be used beyond its original scope. These include blocks to control motors, LEDs, and more from the Raspberry Pi and ScratchX, a suite of experimental blocks that lets users control robots and other devices.

Blocks
The instruction blocks fit together to make a script that controls a sprite. Blocks doing similar tasks are all one color; for example, "Sound" blocks are pink and are labeled with what it does.

Kodu

Kodu is a programming language within a game. It allows players to create their own 3D games on Microsoft's Xbox 360 game console and Windows PCs.

SEE ALSO

❰ **62–63** Gaming consoles

❰ **118–119** What do programming languages do?

❰ **120–121** Types of programming language

Background

First released in 2009, Kodu is an application for Microsoft's Xbox 360 game console. As children in the 1980s, its developers enjoyed modifying video games by altering their code. Consequently, they felt that modern games deprived children of such opportunities and decided to make a language that could be used to create a modern 3D video game world. Kodu aims to get kids to see coding as a creative tool for expressing their ideas.

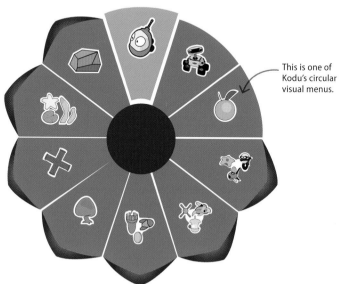

This is one of Kodu's circular visual menus.

▷ **What type of programming?**
Kodu is a visual programming language. It's also object-oriented, as each character or item in the game world is an object with features that can be recognized or changed and actions that can be done by or to them.

How does it work?

In Kodu, users write programs by creating new rules for the game world. The rules are made up of icons that represent items, actions, and properties, such as color. The rules determine how the characters in the world react to various situations, and each is in the form When: <condition> Do: <action>. Icons are selected from circular visual menus using a mouse or game controller.

The octopus says "Hello world!" when the space key is pressed.

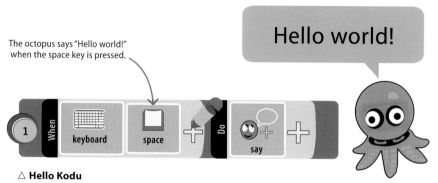

Hello world!

| 1 | When | keyboard | space | + | Do | say | + |

△ **Hello Kodu**
Kodu has a "say" command where users can type text that is displayed in speech or thought bubbles next to a character.

IN DEPTH

Built-in physics

Most game programmers have to write a lot of code to create the laws of physics that govern their game world. These laws usually mirror those in the real world. Kodu's developers decided that they would provide a game world with working physics, so that kids using Kodu can work on their own ideas without worrying about technicalities.

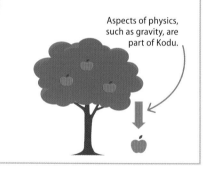

Aspects of physics, such as gravity, are part of Kodu.

Switching pages

Kodu's "switch page" feature allows programmers to make characters behave differently at different points in the game. For instance, at first, bumping a starfish might make it move away—as per a rule on Page 1 of its program. Another rule on Page 1 might make the program switch to Page 2 after 20 seconds. The rule on Page 2 might then tell the starfish to shoot purple missiles when it's bumped.

△ **Terrain**
Kodu allows users to create the terrain of their world by painting in different types of terrain blocks. It's also possible to add features such as water, hills, and walls.

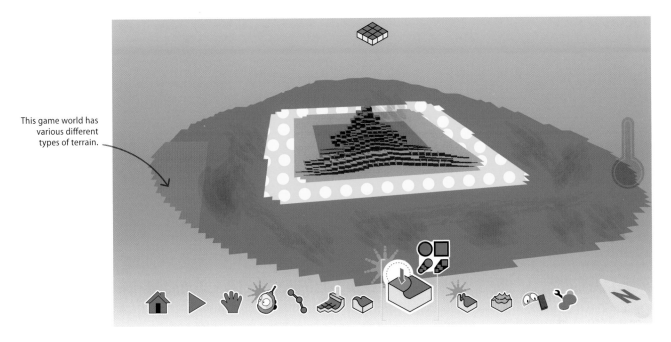

This game world has various different types of terrain.

Why Kodu?

Kodu may be easier for younger children, as it's more symbol based than Scratch. It allows children to develop computational thinking skills while creating games. Kodu puts the emphasis on inspiring creativity and making ideas come to life while enabling kids to build up complex and detailed games. As with Scratch, users can share their games with the Kodu community.

This program wouldn't work on a computer without a gamepad.

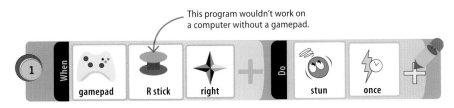

△ **Limitations**
Being a language within a game, the range of programming that can be done with Kodu is more limited than with other languages. The available options and commands are purely related to gaming.

Kodu Kinect

It's possible to control the 3D world of Kodu using body movements or speech. Microsoft's Kinect controller Software Development Kit (SDK) allows programmers to write code that connects the Kinect's input to Kodu. This means that players can control characters with their voice or make a character jump onscreen by jumping in real life. It does involve a reasonable amount of programming experience, so kids may require assistance from an adult.

Future languages

Computer programming languages have come a long way in a relatively short time. In 5 years' time, will programmers still be using the languages of today, or will they have found new ways to code?

SEE ALSO

❮ **80–81** Bits and digitization

❮ **112–113** Assemblers, interpreters, and compilers

❮ **120–121** Types of programming language

Rising stars

A number of programming languages are rapidly increasing in popularity. R is designed for statistical programming and is useful for programs that process a lot of data. Go is very readable and good for networking. It's used by many large organizations. Haskell is a functional language that encourages better programming practices. Rust is based on C, but also includes elements of Haskell. TypeScript is a version of JavaScript with stricter rules, which results in safer code.

▷ **Java Virtual Machine**
Several emerging languages can be run on any computer that has a Java Virtual Machine (JVM) implementation. This is an advantage for the Internet of Things, as the JVM can take inputs from devices that run different programming languages.

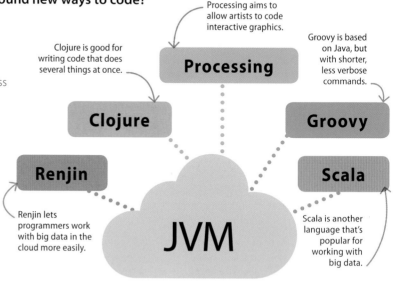

Processing aims to allow artists to code interactive graphics.

Clojure is good for writing code that does several things at once.

Groovy is based on Java, but with shorter, less verbose commands.

Processing

Clojure

Groovy

Renjin

Scala

JVM

Renjin lets programmers work with big data in the cloud more easily.

Scala is another language that's popular for working with big data.

Creating a language

A number of things have to be considered when creating a new programming language, such as the styles of programming it allows, the existing language it will be written in, and whether the language will be compiled or interpreted. The next step is to create a grammar for the language. This is a set of rules defining how programs can be constructed. Once the grammar is defined, it can be used to write a compiler or interpreter for the language.

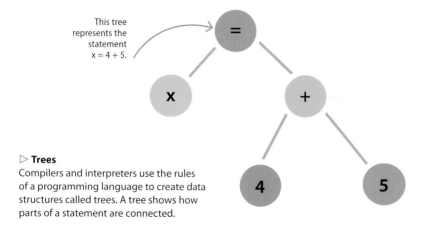

This tree represents the statement $x = 4 + 5$.

=

x

+

4

5

▷ **Trees**
Compilers and interpreters use the rules of a programming language to create data structures called trees. A tree shows how parts of a statement are connected.

IN DEPTH

Domain-specific languages

Programmers occasionally create domain-specific languages that are designed for writing programs to solve problems in one specialized area. Some examples include Verilog, used by hardware and computer chip designers; Logo, an early educational language that allowed children to move a turtle-shaped robot around the screen; and SQL, a language used for working with databases.

Future programming languages

What sort of languages would be needed to program entirely new types of computer? Quantum computers use the principles of quantum physics to do calculations, which would take an impossibly long time using normal computers. They're currently in the early stages of development, but Quantum Computing Language (QCL), based on C, has already been created for them.

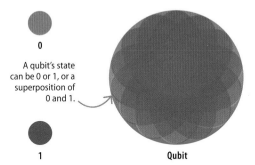

0

A qubit's state can be 0 or 1, or a superposition of 0 and 1.

1

Qubit

◁ **Qubit**
A bit in a quantum computer is known as a quantum bit, or qubit. It can be in one of three possible states: 0, 1, or a state where it is both 0 and 1 at the same time. The last state is known as a quantum superposition.

Molecular computing

Biological engineers at the Massachusetts Institute of Technology (MIT) recently developed a programming language that enabled them to construct biochemical circuits made from DNA. These circuits are placed in biological cells, enabling the cells to react to their environment in specific ways.

A universal language?

It's unlikely that programming languages will move toward a situation where there is one language used for everything. Just like with physical tools, each language is specifically designed to have particular strengths. Machine learning—the ability for computers to learn new things without being specifically programmed—is likely to have an effect on programming in the future, as programmers will make use of tools that have this ability.

```
printf("Hello, World!")
```

```
printf("Hello, World!\n");
```

```
Print "Hello, World!"
on the screen
```

```
std::count<<"Hello, World!\n;"
```

△ **Transferable skills**
Programming involves taking an algorithm and expressing it using instructions a computer can understand. It's a skill that is transferable from one programming language to another. The traditional "Hello, World!" greeting can be written in different programming languages but have the same result.

Machine learning languages

While machine learning may reduce the need for traditional programming skills, the machine learning systems themselves will have to be written by programmers. The most popular languages used to create learning systems include Python, the programming language R, and Java.

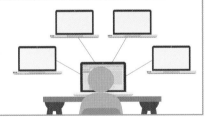

Networks

What is a network?

A network is a group of connected devices, and can include computers, smartphones, printers, routers, and hard drives. Its purpose is to share resources and data.

SEE ALSO	
❬ 36–37 Peripheral devices	
Types of network	146–147 ❭
Connections	148–149 ❭
The Internet of Things	226–227 ❭

How does it work?

A network node is any device that sends or receives data through the network. Designed and created as per the needs of its users, networks can be big or small, public or private, and can have varying levels of security. The Internet, for instance, is a massive public network that spans the entire world.

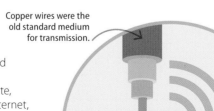

Copper wires were the old standard medium for transmission.

Wireless signals are the most practical medium over short distances.

◁ **Connectors**
A medium is needed to transmit signals between two nodes. Copper wires are a common connector, as are wireless radio waves (such as Wi-Fi, 3G, and 4G). Cell towers, satellites, and undersea cables are all part of the communication infrastructure.

An antenna helps the network adapter to reach a wireless network.

Fiber optic cables are used for fast transmissions over long distances.

◁ **Adapters**
Many media, such as telephone wires, transmit information in an analog format. Network adapters are hardware that decode analog signals into digital formats, which the computer can read. Every device with an Internet connection has its own network adapter.

Communication protocols

When two devices communicate, a protocol dictates whose turn it is to send data, what kind of data is being sent, and how this data is formatted.
Protocol: A set of rules that governs the transmission of data between devices.
HTTP (Hypertext Transfer Protocol): Used for visiting webpages.
HTTPS (Hypertext Transfer Protocol Secure): A secure HTTP.
DHCP (Dynamic Host Configuration Protocol): All computers use this to obtain their IP address from a router.

Routing ensures the computers will be connected via the shortest route.

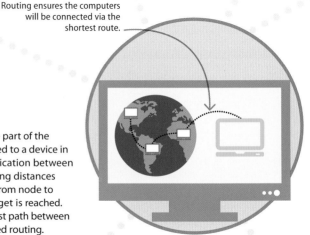

▷ **Routing**
A computer in one part of the world can't be wired to a device in another. Communication between computers over long distances involves hopping from node to node until the target is reached. Finding the shortest path between two devices is called routing.

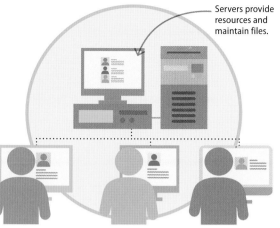

Servers provide resources and maintain files.

Client-server networks

An ordinary computer—or "client"—is designed to interact with users for tasks such as text editing, photo browsing, or video streaming. A server, on the other hand, is designed to interact with clients. Servers run specialized software and have specialized operating systems. They can be used to host websites and databases.

◁ **Client-server model in a school**
In a school network, grades are stored on a central computer called a server. Each teacher's personal computer can connect to this main server to access the grades and make changes.

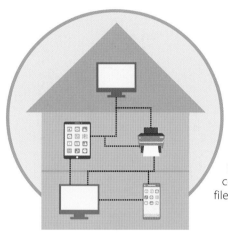

▷ **Home network**
Home networks are generally P2P. One computer might be connected to a printer, another to a scanner, while a third is connected to the TV and stores all the videos.

Peer-to-peer networks

A peer-to-peer (P2P) network has no specialized servers. Instead, each computer alternates between taking the role of client and server. P2P networks are easy to set up but hard to maintain, because each device needs to be constantly operational. If a computer crashes, all its resources and files are cut off.

Using a network

Sharing resources is a good way to save money—whether it's sharing software, data, or access to hardware. Imagine the hassle if every computer in a building needed its own printer. Unfortunately, networks come with security risks. It's easy enough to protect a network from outsiders, but once inside, it can be difficult to set up barriers.

Advantages	Disadvantages
It is easier to collaborate and communicate through a network.	Networks cost money. The more complicated it is, the more expensive a network becomes to set up.
Documents are stored in a central location where everyone can access them.	Networks require constant troubleshooting, software updates, and management.
Because there's a single copy of each file, versions can't get out of synchronization.	If the central hub breaks down, the entire network is disrupted.
Entry to the network can be restricted, and access to files can be controlled.	Viruses and malware can spread more easily through a network.
It's easy to ensure that important data is properly saved and backed up.	Streaming eats up bandwidth, so a single device can slow down the network for everybody.

Types of network

While there are many ways to classify networks, two common criteria are size and topology (layout). A small home network is organized very differently from a global network, such as the Internet.

SEE ALSO

❬ 58–59 Connected appliances

❬ 144–145 What is a network?

Connections   148–149 ❭

The Internet and
the World Wide Web   150–151 ❭

Size

The size of a network is the physical distance between its nodes. The most common network sizes are local area networks (LANs), metropolitan area networks (MANs), and wide area networks (WANs). Distance affects the number of routers needed, the kind of media used to connect the nodes, and the type of information shared over the network.

LAN (local area network)
A LAN is a small wired or wireless network. Typically, all the devices are in a single building, or even on a single floor in a large building. Too many computers in a LAN can lead to delays in sending and receiving information.

MAN (metropolitan area network)
A MAN is a network that covers a city. Essentially, it's any network bigger than a LAN but too small to be considered a WAN. Large university campuses sometimes have MANs with fiber optic connections between buildings.

WAN (wide area network)
A WAN is a network that covers more than 30 miles (48 km). It connects devices using copper wire, satellites, or fiber optic cables. Big companies, such as Google, Microsoft, and Facebook, need WANs because they have offices in different cities. The Internet is the largest WAN in existence.

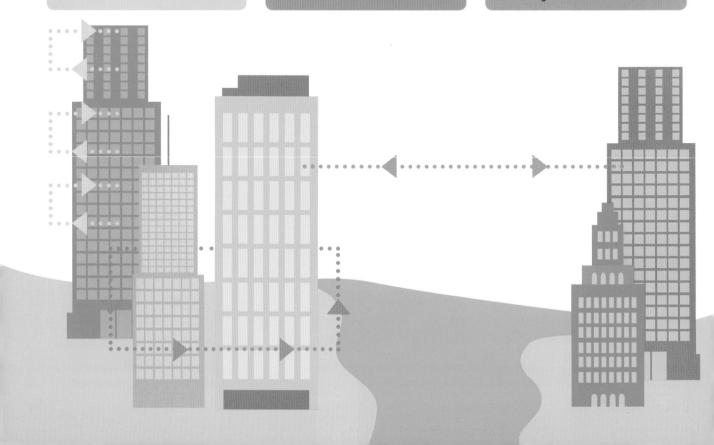

Topology

The topology of a network—also known as its layout—is the strategy used to connect devices together. The layout depends on the type of information being shared, the volume of communications, and how devices need to store data. There are pros and cons to each layout.

Many networks are **hybrids**, created by combining **multiple topologies**.

Bus topology

In this topology, devices are connected to a single main wire called the backbone, or bus. If a computer wants some data, it sends a request to all the devices in the network, but only the target device responds. Bus topology is cheap and simple to set up. However, if the backbone breaks, the network is useless. Nowadays, bus topology is considered outdated.

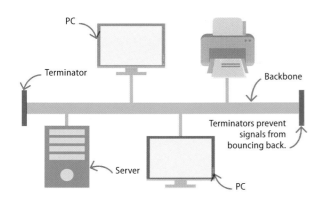

PC

Terminator

Backbone

Terminators prevent signals from bouncing back.

Server

PC

Ring topology

In this topology, devices are connected to a central ring where data flows in a single direction. When a computer sends a request, the signal travels along the ring and visits each device. Ring topology handles volume better than bus topology. It's more robust and can span greater distances. However, it's more expensive, and like bus topology, it's considered outdated.

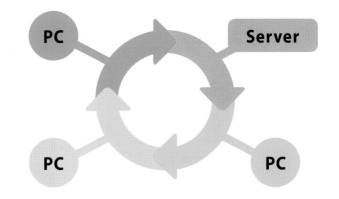

PC

Server

PC

PC

Star topology

In this topology, each device is connected to a single hub, typically a router. All communications pass through this hub. Star topology can also be called octopus topology because the hub can have many connections, or tentacles. It is cheap and easy to expand and handles breaks well—unless the hub goes down, in which case the entire network is out.

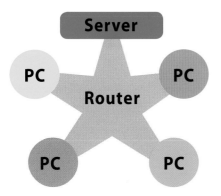

Server

PC

PC

Router

PC

PC

Mesh topology

In this topology, every node is connected to every other node. It handles breaks better than other topologies because there are many routes that data can take between any two devices. Mesh topology is very expensive and requires lots of cable. It isn't usually used for LANs, but it can be a good layout for MANs or WANs.

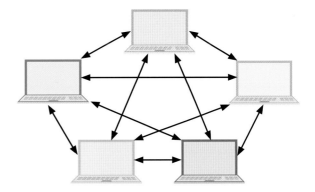

Connections

SEE ALSO
❮ **144–145** What is a network?
❮ **146–147** Types of network
The Internet and the
World Wide Web   **150–151** ❯

Many steps are involved in connecting to a website and exchanging data. The process is the same whether the two devices are next to each other or continents apart.

Connecting to a website

Each digital communication involves a request from the client and a response from the server. The format and content of each message is determined by the communications protocol, which is agreed upon by the devices used in advance. HTTP is the best-known protocol and the most commonly used over the Internet.

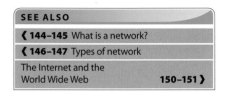

www.intrnt.com

Internet

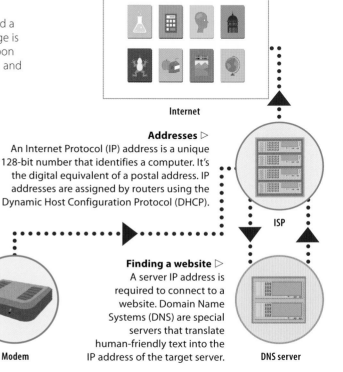

Addresses ▷
An Internet Protocol (IP) address is a unique 128-bit number that identifies a computer. It's the digital equivalent of a postal address. IP addresses are assigned by routers using the Dynamic Host Configuration Protocol (DHCP).

ISP

Start

Home-network computer

Connecting ▷
A home computer makes an initial request to connect. The message first passes through the home's router, followed by the modem, and then the Internet Service Provider (ISP), who forwards it to the appropriate website.

Router

Modem

Finding a website ▷
A server IP address is required to connect to a website. Domain Name Systems (DNS) are special servers that translate human-friendly text into the IP address of the target server.

DNS server

URLs

URL (Uniform Resource Locator), also known as a web address, is a standardized system for locating and identifying content on the World Wide Web. Each URL can be broken down into four distinct parts. Here's an example you might see in your web browser if you search for "networks" on Google:

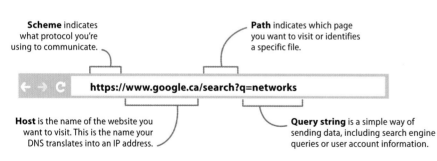

Scheme indicates what protocol you're using to communicate.

Path indicates which page you want to visit or identifies a specific file.

https://www.google.ca/search?q=networks

Host is the name of the website you want to visit. This is the name your DNS translates into an IP address.

Query string is a simple way of sending data, including search engine queries or user account information.

IN DEPTH

Other protocols

File Transfer Protocol (FTP) is used when uploading and downloading files, and Simple Mail Transfer Protocol (SMTP) plays a role in regulating emails. NoiseSocket is used by WhatsApp to create secure connections, while Real-time Transport Protocol (RTP) and Real-time Streaming Protocol (RTSP) are used for multimedia.

Packets

Transmitting large files all at once clogs up networks and prevents other computers from sending or receiving messages. To solve this issue, most protocols break data up into small packets. Pictures, text messages, and even basic HTTP requests are sliced up and transferred piece by piece. Each packet is given a header that contains its destination's IP address and a return IP address.

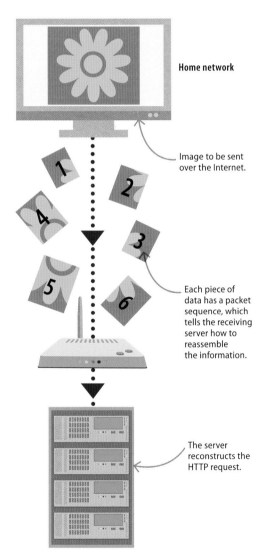

Home network

Image to be sent over the Internet.

Each piece of data has a packet sequence, which tells the receiving server how to reassemble the information.

The server reconstructs the HTTP request.

△ **Transmission Control Protocol (TCP)/ Internet Protocol (IP)**
In TCP/IP, each packet is assigned a number to help the target computer reassemble the packets into the original message.

Routing

Transmitting a message works a bit like a relay race. At each hop, the current router checks the message's target IP and determines the best router to send the message to next. This continues until the destination is reached. It's therefore possible that packets from the same message end up taking different routes to the same computer.

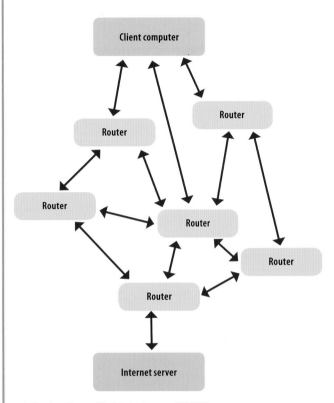

△ **Carrier-Sense Multiple Access (CSMA)**
CSMA is a low-level protocol that handles the process of transmitting packets through a wire. It includes checking that the route is clear, and helps avoid collisions.

IN DEPTH

Security and encryption

Since data packets often take convoluted routes through strange routers, there are many ways for hackers to intercept messages. Encryption is a simple way to protect data. The basic idea is to use a secret key to transform a message into gibberish. Only authorized contacts who have a matching key can recover the message. That way, even if hackers manage to steal all of the packets, the information is useless. Several protocols, such as HTTPS, have built-in encryption.

The Internet and the World Wide Web

SEE ALSO

❮ **20–21** Search engines

❮ **144–145** What is a network?

Cloud computing   **152–153** ❯

Sharing content   **198–199** ❯

People often use the terms Internet and World Wide Web interchangeably. In reality, they're two separate concepts: one is a network and the other is a file system.

The Internet

The Internet is a massive global network created from connections between billions of devices. The term refers to hardware devices and their capacity to connect and exchange data. In 2017, it was estimated that 51 percent of the world is online— more than 3.5 billion people. There are Internet users in every country on every continent, and the net's only getting bigger and faster.

History

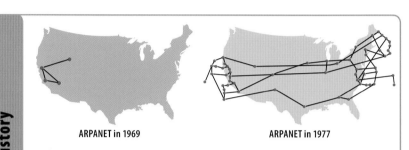

ARPANET in 1969   ARPANET in 1977

In 1969, the Advanced Research Projects Agency Network (ARPANET) connected four west-coast American universities using phone lines. By the late 1970s, more universities and private corporations had been added, so that ARPANET stretched across the country. During the 1990s, individuals began to connect, prompting the net to become more commerce-oriented.

The World Wide Web

The World Wide Web is like a global filing system that runs on the Internet. Each entry in this filing system is a website, which can consist of many webpages. Each webpage brings code, text, and multimedia files together. Hyperlinks are special interconnections between webpages that help users navigate through the World Wide Web.

History

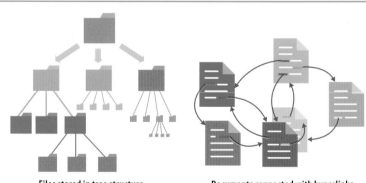

Files stored in tree structure   Documents connected with hyperlinks

As the Internet grew, it became difficult to find information. Data was stored in a tree structure, the way files are stored on a personal computer. In 1989, English engineer Tim Berners-Lee (b. 1955) came up with a solution to flatten the tree by making related files link to each other with clickable hyperlinks. This meant that to find something, users could simply jump from one relevant document to the next instead of backtracking through a maze of folders.

What does it look like?

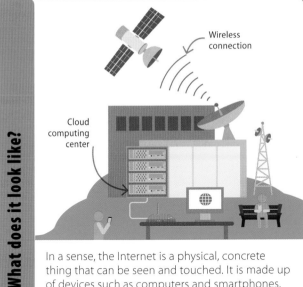

In a sense, the Internet is a physical, concrete thing that can be seen and touched. It is made up of devices such as computers and smartphones, and places where data is stored, such as cloud computing centers. An array of cell towers, home routers, communication satellites, and phone and fiber optic cables connect these devices and places together to form the Internet.

The Internet today

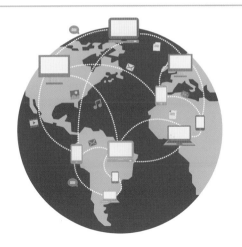

The goal of ARPANET was to improve communication. Now, with more and more devices connected to the Internet, the result is near-constant communication. It's possible to talk to anyone at any time, whether they live next door or across an ocean. Information on almost any topic can be found in an instant. Pictures and videos can be easily shared with friends. In short, the Internet has changed how people socialize, work, learn, and shop.

What does it look like?

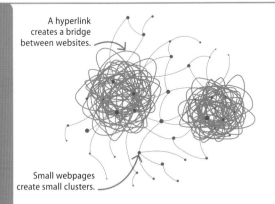

As the name suggests, the World Wide Web would look like an incredibly complex tangle if visualized. A webpage would be a dot, and a hyperlink would be a line linking two pages together. Popular websites would be incredibly knotted, as they have many webpages linking to and from them.

The World Wide Web today

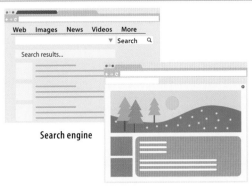

Nowadays, there are more than a billion websites on the Internet. To store all this information on CD-ROMs would require a stack of discs reaching up to the moon. Search engines such as Google, Yahoo!, and Bing are invaluable tools to help users find relevant information in a sea of advertisements, social media, and artistic content.

Cloud computing

Around since the 1950s, "the cloud" is a group of specialized computers that provide services through the Internet, such as storing files, renting software, and access to hardware.

SEE ALSO

‹ **150–151** The Internet and the World Wide Web

Staying safe online **186–187** ›

Hacking and privacy **190–191** ›

Cloud storage

Keeping files "in the cloud" helps users to save space on their computers by storing their files on a cloud provider's computer and accessing them through a network connection. Cloud storage providers buy massive hard drives and then sell, or rent, tiny pieces to clients, making it possible for the clients to upgrade and downgrade storage size according to their needs.

"I don't need a **hard disk** in my computer if I can get to the **server faster**."
Steve Jobs (1955–2011), American co-founder of Apple Inc.

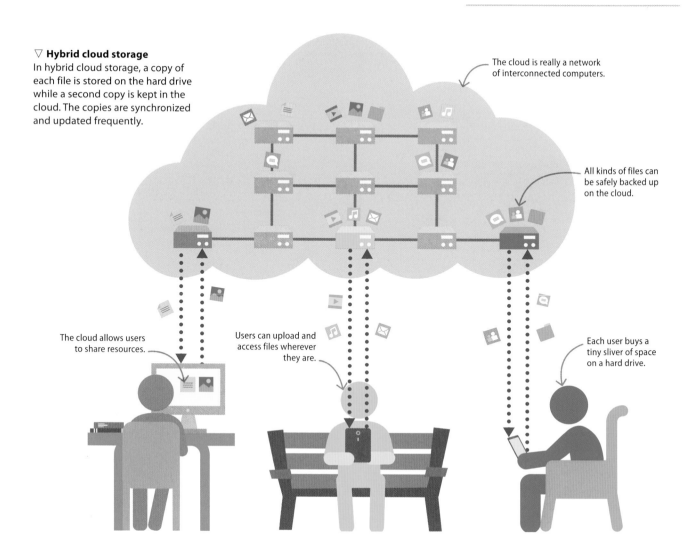

▽ **Hybrid cloud storage**
In hybrid cloud storage, a copy of each file is stored on the hard drive while a second copy is kept in the cloud. The copies are synchronized and updated frequently.

The cloud is really a network of interconnected computers.

All kinds of files can be safely backed up on the cloud.

The cloud allows users to share resources.

Users can upload and access files wherever they are.

Each user buys a tiny sliver of space on a hard drive.

How safe are your files?

Cloud storage providers are responsible for maintaining backups of the files they store. Because big companies can generally spend more money on security than their customers, data in the cloud tends to be quite secure. However, such huge volumes of protected data are more likely to be targeted by hackers, who look to gain access to the data in order to profit from it. Every time users synchronize a file over a network, there's a chance that the information could be intercepted.

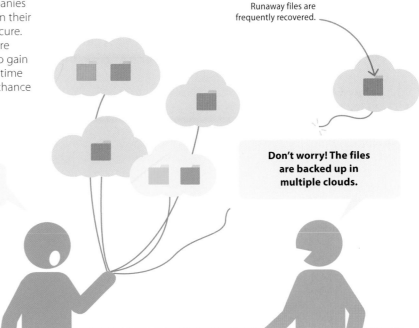

Runaway files are frequently recovered.

I lost a file!

Don't worry! The files are backed up in multiple clouds.

▷ **Multiple data centers**
Copies of files in the cloud are stored at multiple data centers located in different parts of the world. Even if a natural disaster wipes out a particular data center, files won't be lost.

Other cloud services

Apart from storage, services such as software rental and access to specialized hardware can also be provided on demand through the Internet. These services help users cut costs through resource sharing. Unlike traditional software, cloud-based programs can be used on any type of operating system. In addition, multiple people can access the same file, which makes it easy to collaborate.

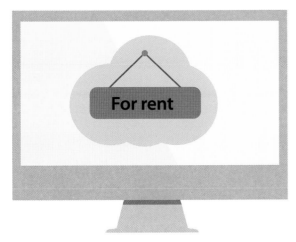

For rent

◁ **Resource sharing**
For complex, CPU-intensive calculations, users can temporarily rent someone else's system and access it through the Internet. Renting instead of buying can be great for small companies.

Streaming

Streaming allows users to enjoy music or video instantly, on demand, as long as they have a reliable network connection. It's a convenient alternative to downloading and a good option for devices with limited memory.

SEE ALSO
❮ **92–93** Encoding audio and video
❮ **144–145** What is a network?
❮ **148–149** Connections

How it works

Streaming works by breaking the streamed media into small pieces of data. These are sent over the network in a structured manner that allows the user's machine to reconstruct the media second by second. Once a segment of the media is played, its corresponding data is thrown away. This process is similar to dipping a hand in a stream—new water continuously flows past the hand, but once the water leaves, it's gone.

"The **growth** [of users] over the next **10 years** will be in **streaming**."
Reed Hastings (b. 1960),
American co-founder of Netflix

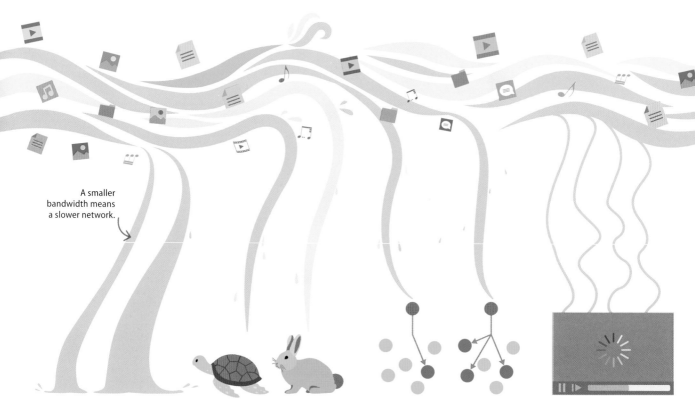

A smaller bandwidth means a slower network.

Bandwidth
Bandwidth is the amount of data that can flow into a network. In other words, it's the number of bits a computer receives per second.

TCP vs. UDP
TCP and UDP are protocols for transmitting data. Unlike UDP, TCP establishes a link between computers, making it slower but more reliable and secure.

Unicast vs. Multicast
Multicast allows a signal to be sent to multiple devices at once. Unicast, on the other hand, limits each transmission to a single receiver.

Buffering
When streaming, a computer stores a bit of data ahead of what is already playing. Buffering prevents irregular, jerky playback by controlling the rate of live streams.

Current streaming techniques

Streaming isn't just used for video or audio. Some gaming systems allow in-home streaming, where audio and video are sent to the player's system but the game is running on a machine elsewhere. The biggest challenge with streaming is to ensure that no lag is caused by a slow network connection. To address this, many streaming services offer content in different resolutions.

▽ **Adjusting the quality**
Many modern streaming services use advanced protocols that automatically detect the bandwidth. This allows them to adjust the size and quality of the data being sent.

Elevator music

The origins of streaming began with elevator music, also known as Muzak. The creator of Muzak, Major General George Owen Squier (1865–1934), invented a method to transmit music through electric cables in 1910. He later created a subscription service that let businesses play Muzak's bland, inoffensive background music for a small monthly fee.

Streaming allows users to watch live footage in real time.

Why stream?

As multimedia files get bigger and better, streaming becomes a more logical choice. People who don't want to watch the same video repeatedly need not spend a huge chunk of time and space on a download. That said, streaming can sometimes be more expensive than buying content outright. Also, with streaming, the customer never owns a copy of the content. The table on the right lists some advantages and disadvantages of streaming.

Advantages	Disadvantages
Users don't have to wait for a long download to finish.	A good Internet connection is needed throughout the streaming process.
Streaming is especially useful for handheld devices.	To watch a video again, users have to start streaming from scratch.
It helps prevent piracy, as there are no files to copy and paste.	It can end up costing more, as it eats up bandwidth.
Content quality can be adapted to the network speed.	If a provider decides to remove content, it can't be accessed again.

Malware

Malicious software, or malware, is harmful programs that gain illegal access to digital devices. They can make their way into a computer or device via email attachments or unprotected websites.

SEE ALSO

❮ 22–23 Cybersecurity

Staying safe online — 186–187 ❯

Hacking and privacy — 190–191 ❯

Types of malware

Malware can break into a computer and wreak havoc. These programs can slow down a device, send spam emails, or even steal or delete personal data. Malware is classified based on how it enters the computer and what it does once it's there. Here are the different types of malware that can attack a digital device.

◁ **Viruses**

Viruses are tiny pieces of code that sneak in by attaching themselves to preexisting files, such as email attachments. The goal of a virus is to spread to as many files on as many systems as possible. They corrupt data and slow down operating systems.

◁ **Worms**

Similar to viruses, worms tag along with legitimate downloads. They're self-replicating and can spread through networks, often via automated email spam. Unlike viruses, worms are stand-alone software. They don't need human triggers and are only installed on each computer once.

Rootkits ▷

Rootkits hide inside an operating system. They gain root (administrator) access to a computer and modify critical files, which can lower security and let in other types of malware. As they hide inside operating systems, they are difficult to detect and destroy.

◁ **Spyware**

Spyware is a general term for any program that tracks data without permission. Examples include keyloggers (programs that track what keys are pressed in order to gain access to passwords and other information) or programs that copy browser history and Google searches.

◁ **Trojans**

Named after the Greek tale of the Trojan Horse, a trojan is a malicious program that looks safe. Once downloaded, the trojan installs its payload on the computer. This could be a keylogger, a backdoor, or any number of malicious programs.

Botnets

An Internet bot is a software application that performs automated functions over the Internet. A botnet is a network of bot-infected computers. While the infected computer might run normally, there's software on it that lets a "puppet master" hijack the computer. Botnets can be used to store illegal content or mount cyberattacks without the user's knowledge.

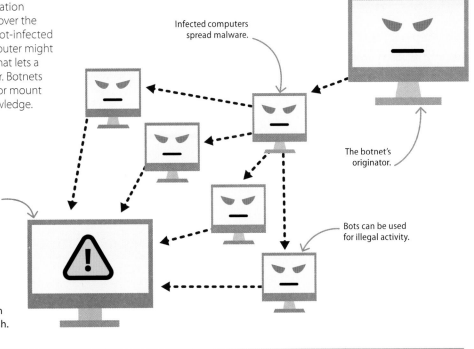

Infected computers spread malware.

The botnet's originator.

Computer under attack.

Bots can be used for illegal activity.

▷ DDoS attacks

DDoS stands for Distributed Denial of Service. A DDoS attack overwhelms a server by flooding it with data, often sent by botnets. The server receives so many requests that it can't function properly, sometimes causing it to crash.

◁ Backdoors

A backdoor allows users to bypass all regular security checks, such as passwords and permission settings. Sometimes, backdoors are created by accident when developers leave a loophole in the software. Other times, they are installed by malicious code.

◁ Ransomware

Ransomware sneaks onto a computer and encrypts files, effectively holding them for ransom. Unless attackers are paid, everything on the computer is inaccessible. Ransomware uses strong encryption protocols. It's almost impossible to break the code without paying for access to the key.

◁ Hybrid threats

Programs that have characteristics of multiple types of malware are called hybrid threats. A worm may drop a virus on a computer, or it may behave like a trojan. Classification provides a starting point for identification and defense, but each threat must be neutralized individually.

IN DEPTH

Cookies

Cookies are small files stored inside the browser cache, which is a temporary storage location for downloaded files. Websites send cookies to a computer to keep track of sessions, making it possible to log in and out of online accounts. However, some cookies track activity across multiple sites. While cookies don't contain personal information, hackers can steal a session by intercepting them. This could give them access to information, such as credit card details, stored on a user's account.

The deep web

The deep web is the segment of the Internet that is hidden. It is sometimes called the invisible Internet, as the majority of people don't ever go there or know it exists.

SEE ALSO

❰ **150–151** The Internet and the World Wide Web

Staying safe online   **186–187** ❱

Hacking and privacy   **190–191** ❱

Deep vs. dark

The deep web contains webpages that can't be found with regular search engines. These webpages include private social media accounts and corporate databases. However, the dark web is even harder to access. A special browser, such as Tor, that masks a computer's identity is required to access these heavily restricted websites.

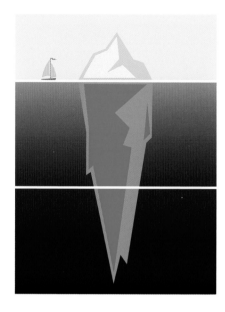

◁ **Regular web**
Between 90 and 99 percent of the Internet is hidden from view. The remaining 1–10 percent is what people browse every day.

◁ **Deep web**
Between 90 and 99 percent of the Internet is believed to be the deep web. To get to a deep web webpage, you need to know a specific URL, as the webpage will not be listed on traditional search engines.

◁ **Dark web**
The most restricted part of the deep web is called the dark web, and users need special web browser software to reach it. A lot of criminal activity happens there, as it is completely anonymous.

Onion routing

Tor, short for "the onion router," is software that allows users to browse the Internet without being identified. Normally, an eavesdropper can use a variety of ways of tracing what a user does online. Tor hides data with encryption and uses complicated routing to confuse eavesdroppers. People monitoring a network will only see packets coming in and out, but they won't know which server the user is contacting. The Tor network has its own computers, called nodes, that are run by volunteers around the world.

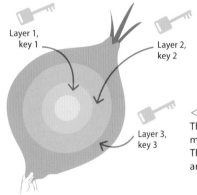

Layer 1, key 1

Layer 2, key 2

Layer 3, key 3

◁ **Layered encryption**
The browser encrypts a message multiple times using different keys. These specially encrypted packets are called "onions."

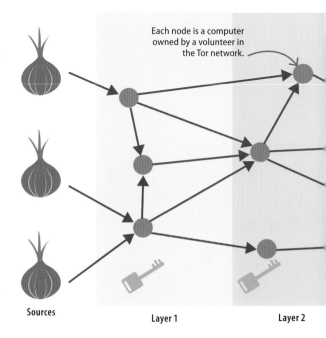

Each node is a computer owned by a volunteer in the Tor network.

Sources

Layer 1

Layer 2

The dark web

As the dark web isn't regulated, a visitor's computer has a higher risk of catching viruses and malware. Scams and botnets are also common. While visiting a criminal website isn't an offense, making a purchase on one is illegal. In short, the dark web isn't a safe place you want to visit. However, there are important uses for the dark web, especially in countries with government-restricted Internet access.

▽ **Anonymous browsing**
Using an anonymous browser is different from visiting criminal websites. Some people use these browsers to prevent governments or corporations from monitoring their browsing habits and harvesting personal data.

People hiding from authorities
Activists and persecuted minorities can use the dark web to organize support without being traced by people or organizations that could potentially do them harm.

Selling money
Criminals who produce counterfeit (fake) money often use the anonymity of the dark web to find customers.

Human trafficking
The practice of kidnapping people and selling them through the dark web is increasing. Criminals also use the dark web to sell human body organs, which is illegal in most of the world.

Whistleblowers
A whistleblower is someone who leaks confidential secrets about an organization because they believe some of its activities are illegal or immoral. Without anonymity, whistleblowers would immediately be arrested.

Drugs
The sale of illegal drugs makes up the majority of dark web transactions. For this reason, police authorities target dark web marketplaces to shut them down.

Weapons
Though the web weapons trade is relatively small, illegal weapons in the wrong hands can do a lot of damage.

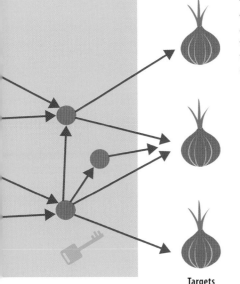

Layer 3

Targets

◁ **Complicated routing**
The browser sends the onion to its target device via multiple nodes. Each node can only decrypt one layer. Since none of the nodes know both the source and the target destination, they can't tell who is talking to whom, but the message is compiled at the other end.

Transactions on the **dark web** are usually conducted in **bitcoin—** a new **digital currency**.

IN DEPTH

Pros and cons of the deep web

Pros

• Protects against data harvesting and data theft.

• Helps protect people who really need anonymity, such as activists and whistleblowers.

Cons

• Extra security precautions make Tor a lot slower than other browsers.

• Tor requires large volumes of traffic. If only one person uses the network, it's obvious which data is theirs.

• Traditional onion routing has no encryption on its last leg.

Website and app construction

HTML

Hypertext Markup Language (HTML) is one of the three programming languages used to create every website on the World Wide Web.

SEE ALSO

‹ 148–149 Connections

Cascading Style Sheets　　　　**164–165 ›**

Using JavaScript　　　　　　　**166–167 ›**

Foundation of the web

If making a webpage can be compared to building a house, then HTML would set the foundation, Cascading Style Sheets (CSS) would take care of decorating, and JavaScript would be in charge of technical additions, such as electricity and plumbing. Each of these three languages is focused and specialized to carry out a specific set of tasks.

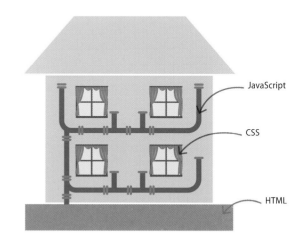

JavaScript

CSS

HTML

▷ **Special tasks**
Keeping clear boundaries between the three languages when coding a website is the key to making sure that everything runs properly. It is best practice, as it makes the code easier to understand but also ensures that the way the website displays is not a jumbled mess.

How it works

When navigating to a website, the server sends a bunch of HTML, CSS, and JavaScript code files to the user. The browser turns these into a graphic, interactive webpage by using its rendering engine. Differences in rendering engines might lead to small differences in onscreen displays.

△ **Standards**
To ensure that each website is properly displayed, the World Wide Web Consortium (W3C) created a series of international standards for writing and rendering web languages.

How to view the HTML of a webpage

It's possible to view the HTML of any page on the web. The HTML of bigger websites are optimized and can be quite difficult to understand. However, if smaller websites are checked, some of the details may be recognizable.

> **1. Open a web browser of your choice.**

> **2. Pick a website you want to view the HTML for.**

> **3. Right-click anywhere on the page.**

> **4. Click "View Page Source."**

Elements of HTML

HTML code is divided into elements, each holding a specific type of content. An HTML page can be compared to a suitcase, with separate sections for clothes, toiletries, and travel documents. These subelements make it easier to find things and arrange the suitcase in just the way a user wants.

IN DEPTH

Markup languages

HTML is considered a markup language, which means it's more limited than a regular programming language and can't be used to write a 3D game or a mobile app. Instead, markup languages are used to help process and format text. They specify things such as font, spacing, and color. They're also used to annotate the text, making it easier for other languages to manipulate sections. Examples of markup languages include XML, XHTML, and LaTEX.

Tags

〈　〉　〈 / 〉

HTML is primarily written with tags that have angular brackets. Every opening tag must have a matching closing tag, with the content between them. Common HTML tags include paragraphs (<p>), tables (<table>), and links (<a>). The "opening tag + content + closing tag" combo is collectively called an element.

```
<html>
  <head>
  </head>
  <body>
    <header>
    <title>Welcome!</title>
    </header>
    <div id="main">
      <h1>Welcome!</h1>
      <p class="centered_text">Welcome again...</p>
      <img class="fun_style" src="/Welcome.jpg"></img>
    </div>
    <footer>
      example.email@example.com
    </footer>
  </body>
</html>
```

Semantics
HTML tags are semantic, which is a fancy way of saying that the type of tag indicates the type of content it contains. A "header" tag, for instance, stores content displayed at the top of the page, while a "footer" tag is displayed at the bottom. Having different types of tag makes it easier for the rendering engine to build the final webpage. It's also easier for programmers to read the code.

△ **Nested tags**
Well-organized HTML is a series of tags within tags, each more specific than the last.

Attributes

〈━━ = "━━" 〉

An image tag might have a "size" attribute and a "source" attribute, while a font tag could have a "color" attribute. Attributes are used to pass details to the rendering engine. The value of an attribute is called a modifier. "Id" and "class" are special attributes that help the rendering engine quickly locate the elements it needs on a webpage. They're particularly important for CSS code, which uses id and class to distinguish between styles.

Cascading Style Sheets

SEE ALSO

❮ 162–163 HTML

Developing and designing   168–169 ❯

Careers   240–243 ❯

Cascading Style Sheets (CSS) describe how HTML elements are displayed in a browser. This includes placement, background color, border style, font weight, and special effects such as animation.

Readability

Until 1996, the styling of webpages was done inline, inside each individual HTML tag. This made code long and cluttered. CSS was created to separate style from content, so developers could focus on a single aspect of the code without being bogged down by other details. Style sheets were written inside an HTML style tag, or in their own separate files known as external style sheets.

```
<p id="main_text" style="color:blue;
background-color:black; font:12px arial;">…</p>
```

Before CSS

```
<style>
        #main_text {
                color: blue;
                background-color: black;
                font: 12px arial;
        }
</style>
```

After CSS

▷ **Recycling**
A single style sheet can be used for multiple different HTML files. This not only makes it easier to understand, but also saves developers a lot of time.

Flexibility

Picture a 200-page website with a unicorn theme. One day, the owner decides that a 1980s computer theme would match their products better. Without CSS, the owner would have to dig through all 200 pages and update them one at a time in order to make the switch. It would be easy to forget a section or make a small mistake. With CSS, only the style sheets need to be changed. The job becomes even easier if there's just one style sheet for multiple pages.

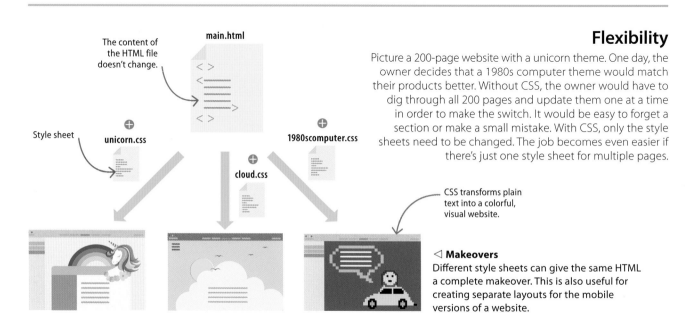

The content of the HTML file doesn't change.

main.html

Style sheet

unicorn.css

cloud.css

1980scomputer.css

CSS transforms plain text into a colorful, visual website.

◁ **Makeovers**
Different style sheets can give the same HTML a complete makeover. This is also useful for creating separate layouts for the mobile versions of a website.

CSS syntax

CSS can be split into two parts: selectors and declaration blocks. Selectors identify which elements on the webpage are going to be affected by styling. Declaration blocks, the section of code inside the curly brackets, contain the styling. Let's say you're working with a group of cats. To ensure they don't all look the same, they need to be divided into groups. CSS provides several ways to do this.

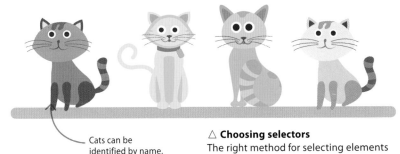

Cats can be identified by name, breed, and color.

△ **Choosing selectors**
The right method for selecting elements depends on how common a style is, how detailed it needs to be, and what other styles are being used.

Ids

Every cat has a unique name, and similarly, every HTML element can be given a unique id. This allows developers to have complete control over the styling of a single element. However, styling elements one at a time takes longer.

Elements

Just as cats can be selected by breed, the easiest way to select elements is to use the type of the tag. HTML examples include body, paragraph, table, and image tags. It's a quick and easy method, but not very flexible.

Classes

A class can be given to multiple elements. Since classes are user-defined, an unlimited variety can be created, and a single element can be given multiple classes. Examples of feline classes are "indoor cats" or "white cats."

Which selector wins?

What if an element is selected multiple times and inherits conflicting styles? Text can't be both red and blue, and a picture can't simultaneously be aligned to the right and to the left. To determine what an element's final styling is, CSS has a complicated order of precedence. A good rule of thumb is that the most specific selector wins over more general selectors. Inline styling is considered more specific than an id, which wins over a class, which in turn wins over an element. However, there's still lots of room for confusion.

Type — Id

One HTML element

```
<div id="main_text"
     class="highlighted_text
            collapsible_text">
</div>
```

Class

Inline → **Id** → **Class** → **Element**

◁ **Inline styling**
In general, inline styling makes code cluttered and inefficient. However, it's the most specific selector, so it's still used from time to time in modern web development.

Using JavaScript

With the evolution of the web, designers wanted webpages to be more interactive. Since they couldn't do this with just HTML and CSS, another programming language was created.

SEE ALSO
❮ **106–107** Storing and retrieving data
❮ **162–163** HTML
❮ **164–165** Cascading Style Sheets

How it works

JavaScript (JS) is added to an HTML webpage using the script tag, and similar to CSS, code can either be written inside the tag or in its own separate file. Each user's browser acts as a JavaScript interpreter. The biggest advantage is that JS can perform calculations and make decisions without having to send information all the way back to the server. This saves a lot of time. However, the code can't run if someone disables JavaScript in their browser.

IN DEPTH

Birth of JavaScript

In 1995, American technologist Brendan Eich was hired by Netscape (a popular web browser of the time) to create a programming language for browsers. The first draft of JavaScript was completed in only 10 days. As a result, the language has several oddities that are famous for causing frustration among developers.

JavaScript tasks

- Checking that you've filled out all the fields in an online form before sending it in
- Checking that the password field isn't empty
- Collapsing and expanding text boxes without making the page reload
- Loading images one at a time, as you need them, instead of all at once
- Allowing users to personalize their accounts
- Interactive graphics
- Video streaming

JavaScript syntax

A full programming language needs variables, functions, conditionals, and loops. Due to the popularity of Java, Netscape wanted JavaScript syntax to be similar, including brackets and semicolons. Aside from this small detail, the two languages are completely different. JavaScript was designed to be flexible and dynamic in the tradition of languages such as Scheme.

LINGO

What is a script?

A script is a code file that is executed by a program other than the computer processor. Instructions are written in a single file. Typically, scripts are used for quick, straightforward tasks, while more structured languages are used to build massive software applications. So you might write a script to automatically change the name of thousands of picture files, convert data from an Excel file into a Word file, or handle the animations on a webpage.

▷ **Limits**
JavaScript's flexibility also makes it slow and unmanageable. While a mobile photo app or a scientific program could be written in JavaScript, it's not the best language for the job.

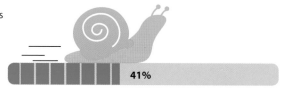

41%

Security issues

Since JavaScript is a full-featured language run in a browser, there's potential for things to go wrong. A malicious website could send a script to the browser that steals its cookies or tampers with a user's account. Not knowing any better, the browser will run the script. However, disabling JavaScript is not the solution, as that will prevent browsers from accessing most of the modern web, including websites such as Google or Facebook.

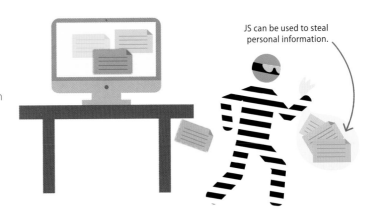

JS can be used to steal personal information.

▷ **Cross-site scripting**
Cross-site scripting (XSS) exploits vulnerabilities in JavaScript to manipulate legitimate websites and make them send out bad scripts.

Compatibility problems

The web is built on the assumption that browsers can run JavaScript. This wasn't always the case. At first, each browser implemented their JavaScript engine a little bit differently, which led to many problems and broken websites. These days, everyone is more or less up-to-date. Programming languages are constantly changing, however, and if a website uses the most cutting-edge features of JavaScript, its code may not work for all visitors.

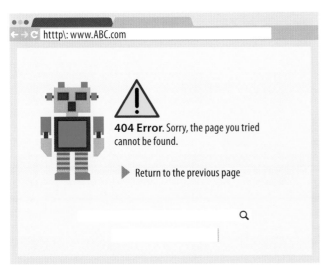

△ **Old browsers**
Since web technologies are constantly evolving, it's important to keep browsers up-to-date and to install the latest security patches. This will maximize both compatibility and security.

JavaScript plug-ins

Plug-ins are an extension of JavaScript. They are available for various things, such as making animations, drawing charts, and creating interactive maps. At a technical level, a plug-in is a file of JavaScript code that can be downloaded, added to other code files, and linked to an HTML page. JavaScript plug-ins can be written by anybody. It's important to check that you're downloading plug-ins from a legitimate source in order to prevent security breaches.

△ **The JS toolbox**
Think of plug-ins as extra tools in a toolbox. It doesn't make sense to include specialized tools in basic or default packages. That would needlessly make the toolbox bulky.

Developing and designing

SEE ALSO	
Planning ahead	170–171 ❯
Testing	172–173 ❯
Maintenance and support	174–175 ❯
Careers	240–243 ❯

Good software doesn't just appear out of thin air. A client, a concept, and a strong programming team are necessary ingredients for the final product. But how do they all fit together?

The Software Development Life Cycle (SDLC)

This is a series of steps for creating software from start to finish. Following the SDLC helps developers avoid pitfalls, such as being too ambitious or creating software that only works for a small number of users.

1. Planning
The customer describes the product they want. The project manager asks questions to get a clear picture of the requirements. If the customer asks for a new website, for instance, it's good to know how many separate webpages are needed and the type of content they need to show.

6. Maintenance
Once the final product is released, part of the development team continues to monitor the hardware and deal with any bugs that might pop up. They answer emails and calls from customers asking for help, and also create new features based on the feedback, with the client's approval.

2. Analysis
The development team turns general requirements into specifics—for instance, the website will have 10 webpages, with 50 images, 10 videos, an easy-to-update news section, and an online store. Everything is discussed and debated.

5. Testing
Developers check that all features work properly. They anticipate how the software could be misused and add mechanisms to prevent it. Sometimes a separate quality assurance team is in charge of this step. After testing is over, it is shown to the client.

3. Design
Next, it's time for the team to pick the programming language(s) and the software's architecture. These choices must take into consideration not only what the site will be used for in the near future, but also far into the future. Specific tasks are then assigned to each developer.

4. Implementation
In this step, code is written and collated. Features are added one by one until the software more or less resembles the customer's initial description. Typically, many changes to the original requirements have been made by the end of this stage.

Managing groups

There are two main management styles for software projects. Agile development involves small, 1- to 2-week sections, called sprints. Every sprint contains the whole SDLC in miniature. Agile development allows teams to be flexible and responsive. Waterfall, by contrast, is a linear, traditional method. Each step is only done once, and in order.

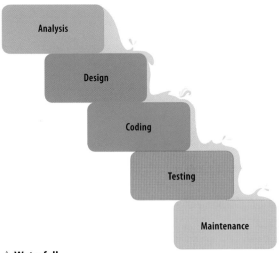

△ Agile
Under the Agile style, there is an emphasis on working in small increments to set goals as opposed to planning. At the end of each sprint, a prototype is produced. Agile projects can react to changes in the client's requirements or issues that pop up during development. The downside is that the development time is unpredictable. Plus, proper documentation is often neglected in favor of adding new features.

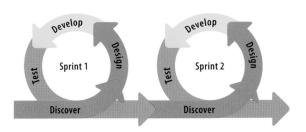

△ Waterfall
With the Waterfall style, it is easier to stay focused on the main goal. However, Waterfall style isn't flexible, as the stages must happen in a set order. Also, the requirements of the client may change over time: a company may spend a few years developing code, only to end up with software that doesn't suit the client's needs anymore.

Code collaboration

Multiple people can't edit the same file at the same time. Similarly, each file can't be restricted to a single developer, because many features overlap inside the code. But what happens if a change breaks part of the program? To resolve these issues, companies use multiple environments and special version-control software.

▽ Environments
Each programming environment has its own hardware and versions of its own code. Development contains code that programmers are currently editing. Staging contains a slightly older version whose features don't cause obvious crashes. Production contains the slick, professional, error-free code that's sold to customers.

▷ Git
Git allows programmers to save different versions of the code they're working on. It can also highlight the differences between two versions, making it easy to review each programmer's changes. In case of an error, Git can revert the code to a previous version.

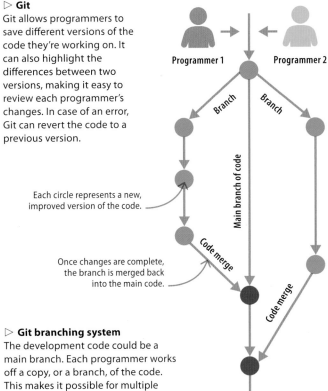

Each circle represents a new, improved version of the code.

Once changes are complete, the branch is merged back into the main code.

▷ Git branching system
The development code could be a main branch. Each programmer works off a copy, or a branch, of the code. This makes it possible for multiple people to edit the same files.

Planning ahead

Writing software is a trade-off between doing things the right way and getting things done in time. Several design techniques exist to help strike the right balance.

SEE ALSO
❮ **162–163** HTML
❮ **164–165** Cascading Style Sheets
❮ **168–169** Developing and designing
Careers **240–243** ❯

The three big pitfalls

Kids use plastic construction blocks to create an infinite variety of objects, such as castles, boats, and spaceships. A block used in an airplane can later be used in a car. Everything is flexible, versatile, and multipurpose. Keeping these qualities in mind can help to avoid common pitfalls that may pop up in the future.

IN DEPTH

Spaghetti code

This is a term for code that looks and reads like spaghetti: a tangled, twisted mess. Have you ever tried to pull a single noodle out of a jumble of spaghetti, only to have it break? Or, as you carefully removed the noodle, realized that it was way longer than expected? Neither of these are experiences you want when debugging code.

1. Scaling

Websites and apps progressively get more traffic. The software and the servers should be designed to handle a future increase in users, or at least make it easy to upgrade.

2. New features

Companies tweak their products all the time. Good code should be flexible enough for developers to make changes without wrecking the entire program.

3. New developers

People might move, retire, or get promoted. A single project has developers going in and out, so code should be written in the clearest way possible so that people unfamiliar with it can understand it with ease.

Design patterns

In computer science, a design pattern is a generally repeatable solution to a commonly occurring problem. It can be seen as a strategy that makes code more like building blocks. There's a pattern for every tricky situation, from creating objects to coordinating messages and protecting data. Each pattern isolates specific behaviors and assigns them to particular objects—or files, functions, and chunks of code—in order to make code as flexible and versatile as possible.

▽ **Changing parts**
To modify the wings of a plane made of plastic construction blocks, the entire airplane doesn't have to be destroyed. All that's required is to snap the wings off, build new wings, and snap them on. Design patterns in code creation help to make this process as seamless as possible.

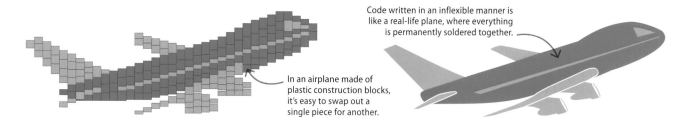

Code written in an inflexible manner is like a real-life plane, where everything is permanently soldered together.

In an airplane made of plastic construction blocks, it's easy to swap out a single piece for another.

Examples of design patterns

Design patterns have become an industry standard. Most big programs have this ability to "snap off" certain behaviors and "snap in" the replacement. However, patterns aren't a perfect solution, as each one has its drawbacks. Some programmers are critical of design patterns because they can sometimes be unnecessary and not be the right fit for the problem at hand.

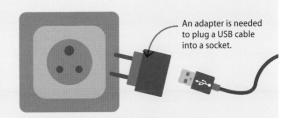

An adapter is needed to plug a USB cable into a socket.

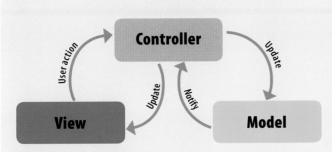

△ **Model-view-controller**

The model-view-controller design pattern is incredibly common—for example, it is used by every web browser. Essentially, it splits an application into three interconnected parts. The model is the base information. It is akin to HTML code for a webpage. The view is the visual representation of the model. For webpages, this is akin to CSS. The controller is the link between the user and the system—the way the information is shown, which is what the web browser does.

△ **Adapter (or wrapper, translator)**

Adapters bridge the gap when the format of data produced by one source does not work with the format required by another program or part of a program. The adapter takes the input data and outputs it in a way that can be used. This is similar to the way an adapter plug converts one type of plug to another.

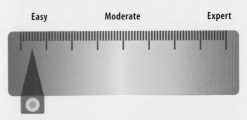

△ **Strategy**

Computer games often have different difficulty levels. The strategy design pattern makes it easier for different code to be written and organized so the player can pick the AI's difficulty level.

Planning for things to go wrong

Developers imagine how their software could be misused: people with long usernames, clients who sign up with no password, and people who click the wrong button. To handle this scenario, they might think of displaying an error message, may bring the user back to the main page, or even make the program crash.

▷ **Input validation**

This means checking the data provided by the user. If a telephone number is required, it should only contain digits, no letters or symbols. This prevents crashes down the line.

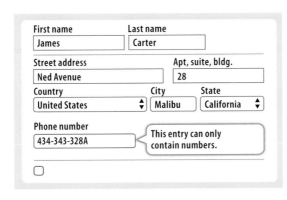

Integrated user feedback

As technology evolves, so does the development process. With the popularity of smartphones and the increase in Internet speeds, more software is becoming downloadable. It's also easier for companies to get feedback. Products tend to be released quickly and updated continuously as developers integrate user comments into new features. This means that software is becoming more responsive and more collaborative. Customers get the exact features they want.

Testing

Many things can go wrong in software, from confusing interfaces to crashes. Developers follow a multistep testing process to cover as many bases as possible.

SEE ALSO

❰ **114–115** Software errors
❰ **168–169** Developing and designing
Maintenance and support **174–175** ❱

Unit tests

These target a small block of code, usually a function, and make sure that it works under all conditions. A program to display tickets in a printable format will first test for a single ticket, then for two tickets, and then for 10,000 tickets. Each typical case, as well as edge case, is covered. Edge cases are scenarios that are unlikely but must still be checked to prevent future problems.

LINGO

Functional vs. Nonfunctional

A functional test checks if the code works. A nonfunctional test checks how well the code works. While functional tests are easier to write, they're not adequate to prove that software fulfills all of its requirements.

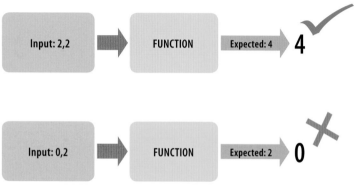

△ **What testers write**
A test is a special mini-script. Developers write unit tests for each segment of the program, specifying inputs and checking if the real output matches the expected output. Tests are often written in the same language as the main software.

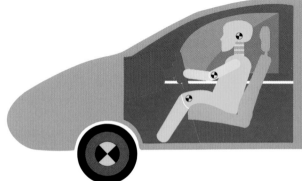

△ **Mock data**
Certain functions require specially structured data. If the data is user-provided, then it's not available in a test-case scenario, so developers create mock data to mimic what a user might enter. Crash test dummies are a real-life example.

Integration testing

Unit tests work with isolated pieces of code. New problems sometimes crop up when those pieces are fitted together. At other times, gaps are discovered in the program's functionality. Integration tests are longer, more complex test cases that combine different sections of code and make sure that everything works as expected. The goal is to model how the software will actually be used.

▷ **Simulation**
To test a virtual game of cards, you might create mock players and then simulate them to play a few fake rounds.

Regression tests

Sometimes, in the process of fixing a machine, another part may get broken. Regression tests are run after each new upgrade to make sure that the original software is in proper condition. They involve rerunning all the unit tests and integration tests one after another. Since regression tests can take a long time to run, test cases must be prioritized. Updated files are tested first, followed by critical systems that are more likely to crash.

△ **Causing new problems**
Fixing one problem sometimes creates other problems elsewhere. Regression tests are designed to make sure that all of the code works as intended.

User acceptance testing

No simulation can compare to humans testing the code. The last phase of the testing life cycle is user acceptance testing, where groups of people are handed an almost finished product and asked for feedback. These comments are handed back to the developers so they can fix any issues the human testers find.

△ **Alpha and beta testing**
User acceptance testing has multiple rounds. Alpha testing is done internally, typically by other developers. Beta testing, or field testing, is done with a select group of external customers or volunteers.

What happens when there is an error?

After a member of the testing team finds an error, they file a bug report. The report includes a description of the problem, the error message, and instructions on how to reproduce the bug. Sometimes an error is nonreproducible, which means the conditions needed to trigger the bug are too hard or too random to recreate. In this case, the bug is put on hold until more information comes up. Developers are periodically assigned to comb through the list of bugs and fix them.

IN DEPTH

Testing GUIs

Testing graphical user interfaces (GUIs) is tricky. One solution is to use automation software. These programs record a developer interacting with a webpage, and then rerun the recording on command. If an update caused a button to be moved halfway across the page, the recording won't be able to finish, and the error is detected.

◁ **Issue tracking**
Most teams use issue tracking software to keep track of bug reports. This allows them to prioritize bugs by severity and check them off as they are fixed.

Maintenance and support

SEE ALSO
❮ **16–17** Computing for you
❮ **114–115** Software errors
❮ **144–145** What is a network?

In a perfect world, software would be error-free, customers would love it, and there would be no need for maintenance and support. In reality, software is in constant evolution, guided by the interaction of developers and customers.

The support desk

The first stop toward logging a problem with software is to contact the support desk. Support staff provide assistance by phone, email, or chat. Their tasks might include walking through basic setups, troubleshooting compatibility issues, or discovering new bugs. Big companies often have specialized support staff, while developers in smaller businesses take turns at being on-call. In-person help can also be obtained at a support desk.

▷ **Support channels**
There are numerous options to connect users to support staff. Often the urgency of the problem determines which one a person needing help will use.

Phone call

Email

Chat

Video call

Documentation

Usually, new software comes with a user guide or manual. It might also come with a tutorial or how-to videos or articles. These are all called documentation. For clients, documentation covers basic tasks and common problems, such as how to reset a password or change a profile picture. Developers may also include documentation in the software for other developers to see that gives an overview of the software code. However, many companies see documentation as a bonus and neglect it in favor of bug fixes and new features.

△ **For clients**
Good documentation covers all the basics. The majority of clients should be able to solve their problems by viewing these online resources. While support staff are important, they can only help a few customers at once.

Documentation is a separate file from the code.

◁ **For developers**
Documentation talks about the logic and the design of a system. It helps new team members figure out the code and also serves as a refresher for experienced developers. Documentation is a separate resource from in-code comments.

Maintenance

In the early stages of a project, developers write lots of code and design new systems. Once the details have been hammered out and the software has matured, development becomes a matter of small tweaks. The types of improvement done on older programs can be separated into three main categories.

Issue-tracking software helps developers organize their tweaks.

▷ **More issue types**
Issue-tracking software has many options for classifying issues, including tasks, subtasks, stories, bugs, incidents, service requests, changes, and problems.

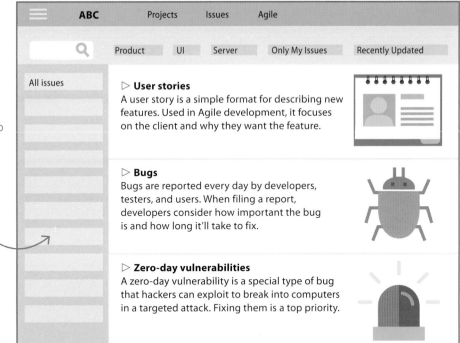

ABC   Projects   Issues   Agile

Product   UI   Server   Only My Issues   Recently Updated

All issues

▷ **User stories**
A user story is a simple format for describing new features. Used in Agile development, it focuses on the client and why they want the feature.

▷ **Bugs**
Bugs are reported every day by developers, testers, and users. When filing a report, developers consider how important the bug is and how long it'll take to fix.

▷ **Zero-day vulnerabilities**
A zero-day vulnerability is a special type of bug that hackers can exploit to break into computers in a targeted attack. Fixing them is a top priority.

Updates

A typical update includes a couple of new features and as many bug fixes as the development team could achieve. The new code is packaged into a "bundle," which clients can download. The bundle only contains code files whose instructions have changed.

Update software

◁ **Apps**
Some apps update automatically, while others request the user's permission through a pop-up window. The device's update manager is responsible for switching out old files with new ones and restarting the program.

Updated files are sent to the user's browser when they refresh.

▷ **Websites**
Often, a website can be updated without disturbing users. It's as simple as saving changes to an HTML file or replacing a script.

Upgrades

While it's important to keep software well maintained, companies want to limit the time invested in outdated programs. Even the most dependable computer can't run forever. Sooner or later it's time to upgrade to a better model with new and improved features. An upgrade, unlike an update, is completely new software with brand new code. It's designed to fully replace the older program.

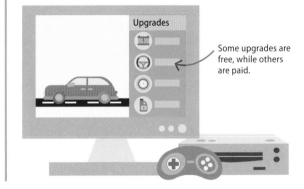

Upgrades

Some upgrades are free, while others are paid.

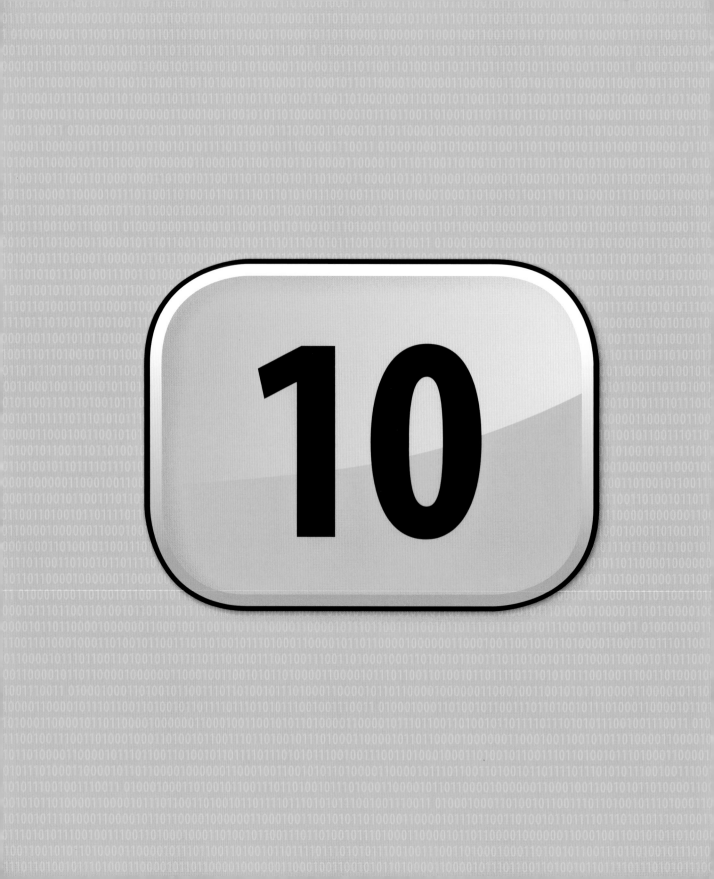

Digital
behaviors

Online and digital identities

What we think of as ourselves has become complicated by what we see in the online world. There have always been many "selves" within each person; the Internet simply makes this obvious.

Identities

There are many elements to someone's identity: the self at home; the self at school or at work; and the self as son or daughter or as parent. These "selves" are the basis for how people lead their lives, and who they interact with, and how they do it. They are also crucial for self-esteem and psychological well-being. Some may find it surprising that these factors have been imported into the virtual world.

△ **What's an online identity?**
An online identity is who we present to the online world. It is the person we curate, cultivate, and project in our digital interactions.

△ **What's a digital identity?**
A digital identity is the set of identifiers used by organizations to authenticate who we are so we can access their services.

SEE ALSO

Being a digital citizen	**182–183** ❯
What is social media?	**194–195** ❯
Social media platforms	**196–197** ❯

LINGO
Useful terms

Avatar: The virtual representation of the self, usually in visual form.

Authentication: The act of verifying a person is who they say they are, usually through a password.

End-User License Agreements (EULA): A legal agreement between a software developer or seller and the user.

IRL: In real life.

Meatspace: A term for the offline world.

Namespace collision: When the same concept is understood differently by two groups.

Profile: The public face we project to the online world.

Early online identities

The Internet allows users to control the kind and amount of information that they share with others. This was especially true in the early days of online communication, when sending images, audio, and video took a lot of time. As a result, a user could only rely on what another user said about themselves as context for online interactions, which led many people to experiment with their online identities. As the Internet has evolved, there has been a shift toward less experimentation and more self-presentation, especially with the advent of social media.

▷ **A/S/L**
In early chatrooms, when text-based communications started linking strangers, it was hard to know how to interact. A shortcut identity identifier emerged: A/S/L, or Age/Sex/Location.

Alex: ASL?
Trevor: 14 M Dublin

Multiple profiles

One of the greatest things the Internet has done for identity is to make it really obvious that each person is made up of many different selves. These days, a person can shift between their various selves in an instant, picking up a chat in one window, updating a status in a second, and replying to an email in a third.

A personal social media identity

A professional social media identity

△ **Different online selves**
People use the Internet for many aspects of their lives these days. Most people have a social media profile where they appear fun and leisurely, and a professional profile where they appear serious and hard-working on sites viewable by employers.

Digital identity

A digital identity is the information that organizations use to identify the people who use their services. As more and more services become digitized and move online for convenience, these services need ways of quickly identifying each user and having their information ready. As personal data should always be kept private, companies must be responsible with how they allow access to it. This has led to multifactor authentication to access emails or social media accounts, or requiring biometric data such as a fingerprint scan to verify if the person attempting to access information is the account holder.

△ **End-User License Agreements (EULA)**
Digital identities can be just as complicated as online ones. Most software requires you to agree to an EULA contract before using it, but most people never read them. This can be dangerous, as it can sign away rights and invade the user's privacy without them being aware.

BIOGRAPHY
Max Schrems

In 2012, Austrian law student Max Schrems sued Facebook. He wanted the US-based company to reveal the data it had collected on him. In 2015, the EU's highest court sided with Schrems and removed the safe harbor law that had allowed US companies to collect and retain data on foreign nationals.

Maintaining balance

SEE ALSO

⟨ **52–53** Smartphones and tablets

| Cyberbullying | **188–189** ⟩ |
| Social media platforms | **196–197** ⟩ |

Smartphones and tablets are changing the way we interact with each other. Though they can be helpful and convenient, it is important to develop good habits when using them.

Setting boundaries

With technology and computers embedded in so many different things these days, it is becoming increasingly difficult to set boundaries on our interaction with digital devices. Aside from sometimes being impolite, overuse of digital devices can lead to physical pain and affect sleep. It is useful to try some simple steps in order to limit the potential downside of digital devices.

△ **Short breaks**
Looking at screens for long periods can cause eye and muscle strain. Going for a short walk or simply focusing your eyes on something else for a bit can help.

△ **Nighttime use**
Studies have shown that using screens right before bedtime can affect your sleep patterns, so try to avoid them for an hour before you turn in.

△ **Longer term**
Improving your environment is important if you need to use screens a lot. Plenty of light and comfortable furniture and peripherals can help.

Problems and solutions

Having a wealth of information and potential entertainment at our fingertips can unsurprisingly be incredibly distracting. The World Wide Web never sleeps: there is an almost infinite amount of things to be notified about and to interact with. This can lead to problems when people prioritize their online life over their real-world existence, or when they experience emotional upset based on their experiences online. Here are some common problems and possible solutions.

"Technology is a **good servant** but a **bad master**."
Gretchen Rubin (b. 1965), American author

Problems

Distraction
Being unable to focus on conversations, school, lectures, or work for long periods may be a sign of someone allowing their digital devices to take precedence over real-world connections.

Narcissism
Frequently posting selfies or status updates on social media is often a sign of someone with an unhealthy obsession with themselves.

Solutions

Break the habit
Try to have device-free periods, especially when interacting with others or when your full attention is needed. Change your notification settings so that you receive less of them.

"Do I need to post?"
Take a minute to ask yourself what you are trying to achieve every time you post something. Is the information important? Is social media the right avenue for it? Is it of interest to your audience?

Fake news

While rumors and sensational reports are nothing new, the World Wide Web has accelerated the spread of what is commonly called "fake news." The term itself has become common currency, with many people using it indiscriminately to label things they don't like or agree with. In its original sense, the term means a news report or article that is not based on researched fact but is passed off as if it is. "Fake news" is often spread by people who want to exploit people's ignorance in order to build up a certain perception of something or someone.

Spotting "fake news":

- Check sources: Who is reporting the information? Are they reliable?
- Is the story being reported elsewhere?
- Does it seem too sensational to be true?
- Can the sources be checked?
- Does the person or company stand to gain something from the information presented?

Illegal content

Just about anything can be posted online, and even some highly illegal content can end up on popular sites such as YouTube and Facebook. If you have seen something that you feel is scary, upsetting, or worrying, speak to an adult about it. They may be able to explain it or configure your Internet browser or search engine so that adult content is filtered out. If it is more serious, an adult can help you report it. Reporting can be done to the site itself, or if you suspect that a law may have been broken, to the police. There are also places online and possibly in school that can help children who are traumatized by online content.

Emotional upset
The Internet can be a negative place, which can upset some people. It could be because they were criticized, or people didn't respond to them in a way they wanted, or they saw something upsetting.

Passive use
Using technology when bored or distracted is an example of passive use of digital devices. It can also distract others when engaged in a group activity, such as sharing a meal or watching a movie.

Instant gratification
The instant, at-your-fingertips accessibility of the World Wide Web has led to people expecting to be entertained all the time. With information, speed tends to be more valued than accuracy.

Protect yourself
Knowing this means you do not need to take aggressive, abusive, or provocative comments to heart. It is better to report them and avoid those sites in future if the situation doesn't improve.

Active use
The best way to use digital devices is to use them actively: before you start, have a definite task you are looking to achieve, and when it is finished, put the device away.

Take your time
Knee-jerk reactions are often inaccurate and oversimplified. It takes time to understand a complex idea or to see someone else's point of view, but in doing so, you may learn a lot more.

Being a digital citizen

SEE ALSO	
❬ **178–179** Online and digital identities	
Sharing content	**198–199 ❭**
Using social networks	**202–203 ❭**

Being a good citizen online is very similar to being a good citizen offline. The focus in both situations is on treating people and their property respectfully.

Digital citizens

More and more of our interactions with people for both work and leisure are taking place online. The behavior of a good online citizen is all about being informed on the rules, regulations, and customs of the digital world and following them. Good online citizens should welcome newcomers and report bullying or other bad behavior to relevant authorities.

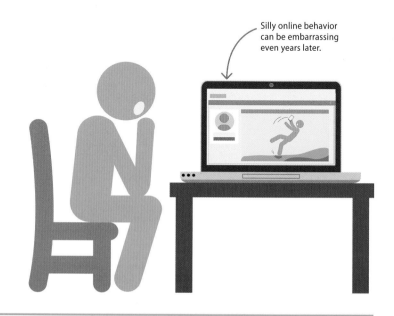

Silly online behavior can be embarrassing even years later.

▷ **Online identity**
Being a good citizen online helps build an online identity and reputation. An online identity and good reputation can be undermined by unpleasant, abusive, or dangerous online behavior, which can stick around for many years.

Digital world

The digital world allows people to do things that they wouldn't be able to in real life, such as contacting people who would be out of reach or accessing information and research. While these possibilities are largely positive, they can affect people's behavior and encourage them to act in ways they normally wouldn't. One potential danger is the temptation for people to say things they wouldn't say in person. It's also easy for remarks intended to be humorous to be taken seriously.

Abusive behavior online can result in arrest in some countries.

◁ **Digital law**
Many people are not aware that their behavior in the digital world can break the law of the country they are living in, or of another country. This is an increasingly common problem on social media and has even led to people being prosecuted.

Digital property

Online content, such as photographs or music, is usually owned by its creator. Other people aren't allowed to share it without permission or claim to have created it. Creators who are happy for others to use, remix, and share their work can release it under a "Creative Commons" agreement.

> **"Don't say** anything **online** that you wouldn't want **plastered** on a **billboard with your face** on it."
>
> **Erin Bury, marketing professional and writer**

Using content without permission is bad online behavior and can break the law.

◁ **Stealing entertainment**
People are less likely to think that consuming digital music or films without paying for them is stealing. However, doing so still deprives the creators of payment for their work.

Photographers have the right to decide who can use the photo they've taken.

A person who didn't create the original work should not use it without permission.

My Blog

▷ **Stealing ideas**
Quoting from someone's work is fine as long as they are credited. Asking permission to use someone's work is often successful, although it may involve paying a fee.

Interacting online

Interacting with people online is a great opportunity to exchange views and ideas. However, since most online interactions are carried out using text, it increases the chance of conversations running into difficulties. Not being able to see people's facial expressions or hear their tone of voice can result in misunderstandings. People can minimize the risk of encountering problems by following these basic rules for online interaction.

Be polite, truthful, and considerate. No one likes rudeness or lying.

When commenting on a forum or website, follow any rules it states.

Acknowledge when someone has been helpful and help others.

Stay positive when commenting. Say nothing rather than being unkind.

Be respectful when debating and don't resort to personal insults.

Try to keep a sense of perspective on whatever happens online.

Communicating online

Software and the Internet have opened many avenues for communication. People can now talk and send audio, text, and visual messages around the world in a matter of seconds and receive instant replies.

SEE ALSO	
Staying safe online	186–187 ❯
Social media platforms	196–197 ❯
Sharing content	198–199 ❯
Social media apps	200–201 ❯

Instant messaging

A quick and easy way of communicating, instant messaging is a process of sending real-time text-based messages from one user to another. Using a shared software client, two or more people can send messages over a network, usually the Internet or cellular. One of the most popular forms of online communication, it even allows users to create chat rooms, share links, and send photos and videos.

Video chatting

This is a popular method of live interaction, using the Internet for transmission and reception of audio-video signals. Video chats, or video calls, allow users to communicate with each other in real time. It can take place on a computer, tablet, or smartphone and requires a webcam and a specific application, such as Skype or FaceTime.

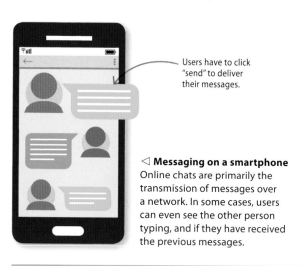

Users have to click "send" to deliver their messages.

◁ **Messaging on a smartphone**
Online chats are primarily the transmission of messages over a network. In some cases, users can even see the other person typing, and if they have received the previous messages.

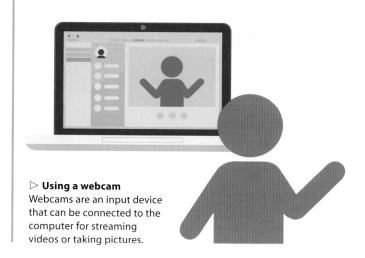

▷ **Using a webcam**
Webcams are an input device that can be connected to the computer for streaming videos or taking pictures.

Emailing

Short for "electronic mail," emails are the digital equivalent of exchanging letters. They are text-based messages that can be sent or received by anyone with an email account. Users can create a unique email address from which messages can be sent back and forth. Emails can even include attachments, such as documents, images, and videos. A sender can choose to "cc" (short for carbon or courtesy copy) an extra person or people into an email, or "bcc" them (blind carbon copy), which conceals the person's identity from other recipients.

◁ **@ sign**
Email addresses are recognizable by the "@" sign. The first part of an email is called the local part of the address. The part after the @ sign is usually a domain name that hosts the email program.

More than
205 billion emails
are sent every day worldwide.

Making connections

There are a number of websites and applications available these days where one can communicate informally, find people, and share similar interests. These platforms allow users to connect directly with others based on their groups, interests, and location. For most of these websites, users have to follow a simple online registration process and create a user profile indicating their details.

Pros and cons of online communication

While having a variety of methods for communication can contribute to an increase in the speed and quantity of interpersonal communication, it can also lead to misinterpretation and other negative effects.

Advantages

• **Flexibility:** Accessible 24/7 from any location, as long as there is an Internet connection.

• **Documented:** Unlike verbal communication, online communication is archived and can be revisited anytime.

• **Easier to give opinion:** People who usually don't speak out in real-life situations can say what they want without interruption.

• **Community:** Facilitates the creation of a community regardless of geographical distance.

Disadvantages

• **Security threats:** Information can be destroyed or stolen, either through a virus or hacking.

• **Information overload:** The volume of information online can sometimes make it hard to focus and be heard.

• **Misinterpretation:** As it is nonverbal, online communication lacks the interpersonal context that can help make meaning clear.

• **Connectivity issues:** Communicating online requires constant Internet access—which is not always possible.

Blogging
An online personal journal, a blog is used for recording and sharing opinions, stories, articles, and links on the web.

Microblogging
This involves posting very short entries or updates on a social networking site. Microblogging sites allow users to subscribe to other users' content, send messages directly, and reply publicly or privately.

Video sharing
This involves publishing videos in order to share them. It also allows users to embed media in a blog or social networking post.

Photo sharing
These websites and applications allow users to publish their digital photos. These can be shared with others either publicly or privately.

Crowdsourcing
This process entails obtaining services, funding, ideas, or content by seeking small contributions from a large group of people online.

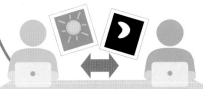

Staying safe online

The Internet is a useful tool both socially and educationally, but it also has its pitfalls. It's essential that users are aware of the dangers and ways to avoid them.

SEE ALSO

❰ **22–23** Cybersecurity

❰ **36–37** Peripheral devices

Hacking and privacy **190–191** ❱

Keeping devices safe

The first stage in staying safe online is to keep computers and cell phones secure. All devices should have up-to-date virus protection. If using a public computer in a library or at school, remember to log out of accounts before leaving.

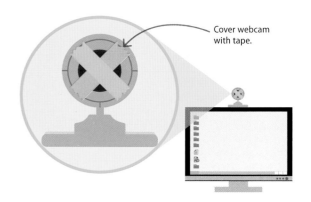

Cover webcam with tape.

▷ **Webcam**
It's possible for hackers to take control of your webcam and film without permission. Cover the webcam on a computer or phone with stickers, tape, or a cover when not in use.

Dangerous content

The Internet gives access to many sites that parents would prefer young people not to see. These can include hate sites, websites that encourage anorexia or self-harm, and pornography. Discussing these issues with young people can help counteract this kind of negative influence, as can encouraging them to evaluate what they read critically, comparing it with other sources of information.

REAL WORLD

Sharing personal information

It's important for young people to develop a healthy level of distrust when interacting online, particularly if websites or people ask them for personal information. Contact details—such as email address, phone number, home address, and school—shouldn't be given out to strangers. These can all be used to identify someone's location, which could potentially put them in danger.

◁ **Bigoted material**
Young people are often anxious to find a group where they belong, but this can make them prey to unpleasant ideologies. Sites that promote racism or sexism, or encourage prejudiced views against minority groups such as gay people, can encourage bad behavior and, in some cases, criminal acts.

◁ **Drugs**
The dark web is an underground part of the Internet where illegal drugs are readily available. It's also easy to obtain potentially dangerous substances known as "legal highs" online.

◁ **Self-harm**
Young people who are under stress or struggling with their mental health are particularly at risk from websites that encourage self-harm or suicide. Sites that promote anorexia also exist and can endanger vulnerable teenagers.

◁ **Pornography**
It's very easy for young people to access sexually explicit content on the Internet, as many sites don't require any payment. Activating parental controls on devices and Internet connections can help restrict access to these sites at home.

Social media

Although it is a positive way to connect with friends, social media can often be stressful for young people. This could be due to unrealistic pressures to look a certain way, or unkind comments from others. There's also the danger of private messages or pictures being circulated widely. Parents can help by making kids aware of these issues and discussing practical ways to avoid feelings of inadequacy. Boosting their confidence and making them aware of their right to say no can also help.

▷ **Privacy settings**
Social media privacy settings allow users to hide their posts so that strangers can't access them. Disabling location settings can stop people from identifying where a person is.

False identities

While chatting with new people on the Internet can be a great way to make friends and connect with people with shared interests, it can also present some dangers. People don't have to use real photos of themselves or their real name, or be telling the truth about anything they say. While this can be a way for users to explore their identities, it is unfortunately also possible for criminals to use it as a way to contact young people.

▽ **Fake profiles**
People who want to insult or antagonize others online—also known as "trolling"—often set up a new profile under a fake name so their activities are hard to trace back to them. As a result, it's usually relatively easy to spot these social media profiles.

A fake profile often doesn't include a photo or uses a very artificial-looking generic photo.

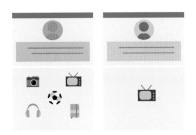

Fake profiles may not include much personal information, while real profiles list information like interests or job.

Having an extremely small number of friends or followers is another feature to be wary of.

Fake profiles sometimes use screen names made of a series of random letters and numbers.

An account that posts abusive content only is most likely a fake account.

Cyberbullying

Coupled with the rise of instant online communication is an increase in online bullying, but support from parents and teachers can really help with upsetting interactions.

SEE ALSO

❮ 180–181 Maintaining balance

❮ 182–183 Being a digital citizen

What is social media? 194–195 ❯

What is cyberbullying?

Threatening or embarrassing someone using Internet-connected devices is called cyberbullying. This can happen in many forms, including sending threatening or unpleasant text messages, impersonating someone online in order to obtain information, posting personal information without someone's consent, setting up a poll about someone, passing on secrets, and threatening to make information public.

▷ **How it feels to be a victim**
Cyberbullying can make the victim feel scared and isolated. They may feel embarrassed and ashamed about what is being said about them, which can make it harder for them to ask for help.

What makes it different?

Unfortunately, bullying is fairly common in schools and among groups of young people, but cyberbullying has features that mark it out as different. Some of these make it easier to identify the bully and deal with the problem, but others make it much more difficult.

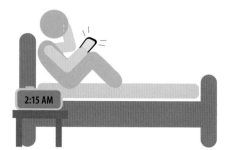

△ **Anytime**
Cyberbullying can happen around the clock, even in the victim's home where, before Internet and handheld devices, they would have been safe from this kind of abuse.

△ **Anonymous**
Cyberbullies have the ability to remain anonymous, and tracing the source can be extremely difficult, meaning that the victim doesn't know who to trust or blame.

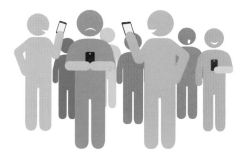

△ **Large audience**
Cyberbullies can reach large audiences very quickly, increasing the victim's distress. Many people can become complicit by passing on a bullying image or remark.

Dealing with cyberbullying

There are a number of ways to deal with cyberbullying. The best way for young people to respond to the problem is by blocking bullies on social media and reporting offensive behavior to the site. Contacting a bullying helpline can also be useful, along with telling family or friends so that they can provide support.

Cyberbullying and the law

Cyberbullying isn't a specific criminal offense in most countries, but there are often laws that relate to behavior or communications that can apply to cyberbullying. As the problem becomes more widespread, police and prosecutors are starting to issue guidelines on these laws. Remarks made on social media may also lead to people being sued for defamation in civil court.

Save online conversations and screenshots of websites that contain bullying messages or images as evidence.

Contact a helpline for young people struggling with issues like bullying to access advice and support.

Block and report the bully if they are using social media or a public website.

Tell family members, friends, or teachers, as they can provide support and practical help.

Don't retaliate or reply to the bully, as this may simply encourage them to continue.

The ability to **make comments anonymously** often **brings out the worst** in people.

△ **Evidence**
In cases where the bullying isn't anonymous, online messages or incidents are evidence of the bully's behavior and can be shown to teachers or the police.

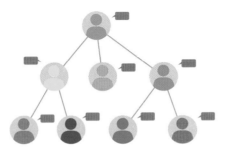

△ **Thoughtless remarks**
Some instances of cyberbullying aren't intentional. A thoughtless remark might unintentionally hurt someone after it is shared by many people.

Why do people do it?

There are a variety of reasons why young people may become involved in cyberbullying behavior. If they have been the victims of bullying or have problems at home, they may take it out on others. Some see it as a way to increase their popularity at the expense of others. Young people may feel uncomfortable about being involved in a group that's picking on someone, but don't have the confidence to point out and stop the bad behavior.

Hacking and privacy

SEE ALSO
❮ 22–23 Cybersecurity
❮ 156–157 Malware
❮ 186–187 Staying safe online

Every Internet user creates data that could be harvested for malicious purposes. It's important to understand the potential pitfalls in order to minimize the risks.

Nothing is private

As a rule of thumb, assume that nothing posted on the Internet will be kept private. Account settings might restrict who can view posts on social media, but it's easy enough to download pictures or take screenshots. The pictures can then be shared and reuploaded at any time. Many websites also have automatic backups, so deleting content only removes it from the main website directory and doesn't necessarily get rid of copies.

▷ **Privacy on the Internet**
To stay safe, avoid posting anything online that you wouldn't be comfortable having strangers know about you.

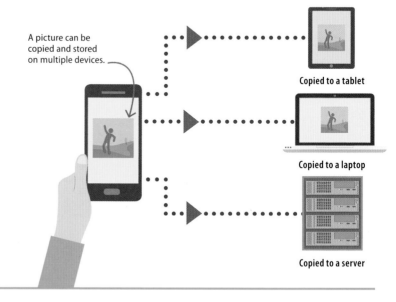

A picture can be copied and stored on multiple devices.

Copied to a tablet

Copied to a laptop

Copied to a server

Hacking

Making a piece of technology do something it wasn't designed to do is called hacking. A common example is bypassing software security to illegally access someone else's account. There are many types of hacking, but they can all be avoided with the right precautions.

▷ **Social engineering**
Studying a person's social media account to gain information that could be used to help guess or steal a password.

▷ **Password grabbing**
If a user tends to reuse the same password for many sites, stealing it once from a low-security website means that they have access to all the sites the password has been used for.

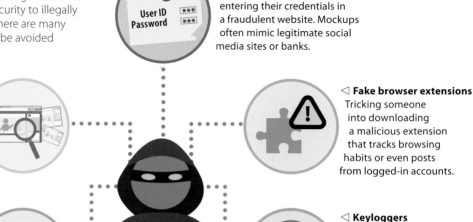

◁ **Phishing**
Tricking a person into entering their credentials in a fraudulent website. Mockups often mimic legitimate social media sites or banks.

◁ **Fake browser extensions**
Tricking someone into downloading a malicious extension that tracks browsing habits or even posts from logged-in accounts.

◁ **Keyloggers**
Once downloaded, keyloggers record user key presses and send data, such as passwords, back to the original hacker.

Browsing habits

Online browsing can be compared to dropping crumbs. A single crumb isn't a big deal, but many crumbs create a mess. Most users aren't even aware of what information they're giving away when browsing the Internet. Continuously harvesting these small, harmless pieces of data can lead to serious privacy breaches. To prevent this, it's important to understand how user data is created and monitored.

Cookies
Cookies are small pieces of data that websites use to store information about a user's browsing session. Along with the IP address and search history, they can be used to create a detailed portrait of a user's habits and interests.

Privacy settings
When installing a new app, many people hit the "I agree" button without reading the software license agreement. This potentially makes it possible for apps to collect personal information without the user's knowledge, but with their permission.

IP addresses
An IP address is a 32-bit or 128-bit unique number used to identify a computer. An eavesdropper on a network can use this IP address to monitor the websites a user is visiting.

Targeted Advertising

Targeted advertising is designed to show people content they're interested in. If someone's browsing history contains a lot of travel websites, they might be shown ads for flight discounts and vacation packages. While targeted advertising isn't a violation of privacy, it reveals how much information can be obtained by studying search histories.

Prevention

The best advice for preventing data theft is obvious: only visit trusted websites; be selective about social media posts; if a problem is identified or even suspected, address it right away. For advanced protection, consider two-factor authentication (2FA) and encryption services. While it might be annoying to go through extra security steps online, in the long term, it's a small price to pay for maintaining privacy and preventing problems.

◁ **Anonymous browsing**
When browsing in a private or incognito window, no cookies are stored. Your search history, download history, and search queries aren't recorded and therefore can't be stolen.

◁ **Proxy servers**
These servers are used to hide the IP address, making it difficult to tell what websites the user is visiting. It's just like using someone else's phone to call a taxi—the taxi will still turn up, but they have no information about you.

◁ **Clearing data**
When using a regular browser, make sure you clear the history, cache, and cookies periodically. You can also configure the browser to automatically clear these after each browsing session.

Parental advice

Keeping kids safe online means teaching them responsible browsing habits. Update the browser settings to block adult content and periodically check their browser history. Have conversations about online safety. Parents of younger kids may also want to have access to their passwords, but for teenagers, there's a fine line between safety and privacy. If you decide to use GPS tracking apps or monitoring software, it's better to be open about it.

Social media

What is social media?

Though it might seem like a recent concept, social media is really the World Wide Web's version of a town square. Social media creates virtual places where people can interact with each other.

SEE ALSO

❮ 18–19 Computing with others
❮ 150–151 The Internet and the World Wide Web
Social media platforms 196–197 ❯
Sharing content 198–199 ❯

Using social media

Social media platforms or social networks are websites and apps that allow users to connect to each other. They also allow users to upload their own content in the form of text, images, audio, and video. There is a variety of social media platforms, and each has its own flavor in terms of how it works and what it is centered around. Since their inception in the early 2000s, social media platforms have become more and more a part of everyday life.

"The **Internet** is becoming the **town square** for the **global village** of tomorrow."
Bill Gates (b. 1955), American co-founder of Microsoft

◁ Business
Many businesses pay social media companies to spread the word of their products and services on social media platforms. Social media allows for people to share and like the things they see, which helps businesses to reach new customers.

Entertainment ▷
All kinds of entertainment are available on social media, from watching videos and participating in debates, to playing computer games with others.

◁ Building community
It has become fairly easy for people to find others with similar interests in their local area through social media.

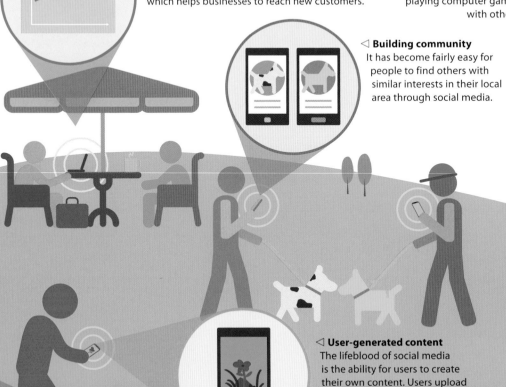

◁ User-generated content
The lifeblood of social media is the ability for users to create their own content. Users upload images, video, or text usually by using their smartphones.

Profiles and newsfeeds

Whether using an app or a website, social media platforms have similar layouts. Users can upload a picture of themselves, called a profile picture, that makes them identifiable to others. When users log in, they have a newsfeed of what their connections have been uploading to the site since they last checked in, sometimes along with news on what has been trending (popular recently) on the site. There might be ads or sponsored posts there, too. Many platforms also offer users the opportunity to talk to each other in private, play games together, take part in competitions, and other things.

LINGO

Selfie

A self-portrait, usually taken with a digital camera or smartphone, is called a "selfie." Though self-portraits are nothing new, the rise of social media has led to an explosion in the number of people taking them. Selfies can be taken by hand or by attaching a "selfie stick" to the smartphone, which allows the picture to be taken from farther away.

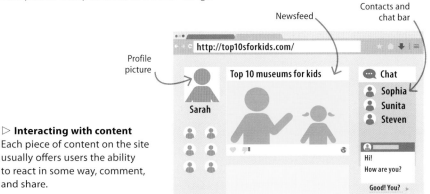

Profile picture

Newsfeed

Contacts and chat bar

▷ **Interacting with content**
Each piece of content on the site usually offers users the ability to react in some way, comment, and share.

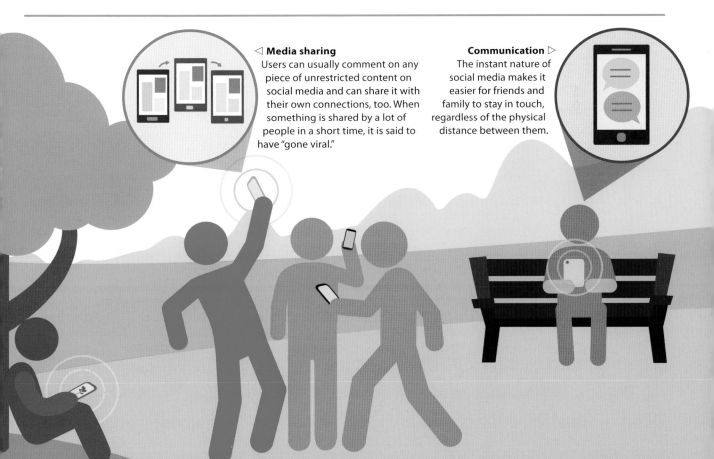

◁ **Media sharing**
Users can usually comment on any piece of unrestricted content on social media and can share it with their own connections, too. When something is shared by a lot of people in a short time, it is said to have "gone viral."

Communication ▷
The instant nature of social media makes it easier for friends and family to stay in touch, regardless of the physical distance between them.

Social media platforms

SEE ALSO

❰ 150–151 The Internet and the World Wide Web

❰ 194–195 What is social media?

Using social networks 202–203 ❱

A social media platform is an online place where communities can gather to make connections and share user-generated content. There are different types of social media platform.

From bulletin boards to Facebook

The Internet was the original social media platform. It connected people to one another via their computers. Soon, topic-based newsgroups and listservs (mailing list software applications) emerged, so people with specific interests could gather together to chat and share information. When the World Wide Web launched, some of the most popular sites were aimed at helping people to connect with long-lost friends, create new connections, and showcase their interests. By the mid-2000s, the platforms that served the function of connecting people became some of the most important platforms in the world. Here is a timeline of the types of social media platform that have developed since 1978.

1978 Bulletin boards

1985 The WELL

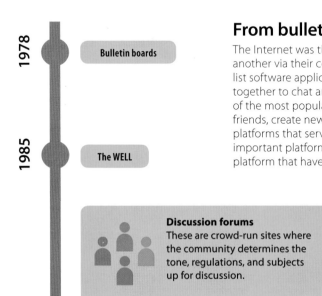

Discussion forums
These are crowd-run sites where the community determines the tone, regulations, and subjects up for discussion.

Online reviews
These platforms allow people to post their thoughts about everything from dentists to restaurants to help others choose where to go and what to do.

Social publishing platforms
The function of social publishing platforms is to create content that is meant to be shared and responded to widely.

Relationship networks
Personal relationship networks connect people. Professional networks connect current or future colleagues. Dating networks connect people romantically.

1996 ICQ

Digg

Vimeo

Friendster

Yelp

Reddit

TripAdvisor

last.fm

LinkedIn

Facebook

YouTube

2000   **2002**   **2003**   **2004**   **2005**

BIOGRAPHY

Mark Zuckerberg

Mark Zuckerberg (b. 1984) is the founder of Facebook, currently the most popular social network. He developed it as a dating app but quickly realized that it had a social function greater than that. Facebook was only intended to be used by students at a few universities while they were at college, but in 2006, the network was opened to everyone. This allowed anyone over the age of 13 to create a profile and connect and share with people around the world.

Media-sharing networks
Social media-sharing networks let users publish videos, images, and audio and connect users with audiences and collaborators.

Interest-based networks
These networks connect people who share hobbies or need specific information. This might be a particular kind of literature or where to find social services.

Snapchat

2011

Goodreads

Twitter   Tumblr   Quora

2010

2006   **2007**

Different platform, different self

Each social media platform is different. For this reason, different aspects of a person's interests or personality might be more prevalent on one and less on another. The work self might be served by one medium, and cake-baking skills might be showcased on another. The two contexts share the same user, but social media allows everyone to isolate each aspect of the self and to explore and express them in their own fully formed ways.

△ **Multiple selves**
People appear different on different platforms, and the online world lets each of these personas thrive.

Useful terms

Social network: A social media platform that shows users who they and their friends are connected to.

Web 2.0: A term sometimes used to refer to developments in the Internet and programming languages that made it easier for users to interact with websites.

Direct message (DM): A private message sent from one user on a social network to another.

Lurker: A person who reads other people's posts on social networks but rarely posts themselves.

Newsfeed: A list of content created by people a user is connected to.

Sharing content

Content is the most important asset in the world of social media. It is used to make and keep connections, and companies use it to get a better idea of who their customers are.

SEE ALSO

❮ **18–19** Computing with others

❮ **144–145** What is a network?

❮ **150–151** The Internet and the World Wide Web

Access to the world

The World Wide Web was devised to solve a problem— English computer scientist Tim Berners-Lee wanted a place where he could get information about computer systems without having to stand up and walk across the room or phone someone to get it. He created a hypertext protocol that allows anyone to create webpages and store content that anyone can access from anywhere.

▽ **The web's network**
The web is made up of content creators, storage spaces for content, and the people who access it. Everyone and everything is directly or indirectly connected to one another, resulting in a very resilient network.

BIOGRAPHY

Tim Berners-Lee

English computer scientist Tim Berners-Lee (b. 1955) invented the World Wide Web. In the 1990s, he created an information distribution system at CERN (European Organization for Nuclear Research) whereby Internet users could access information via a computer. His invention, Hypertext Transfer Protocol (HTTP), made the Internet a much more accessible place for people who weren't able to access huge databases or mainframe computers. Today, he campaigns to keep access to information on the web free.

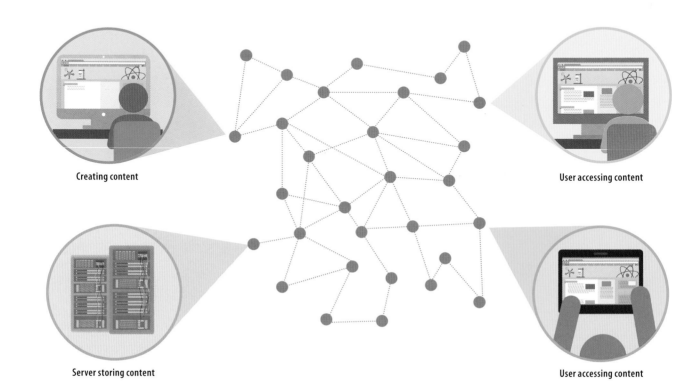

Creating content

User accessing content

Server storing content

User accessing content

Sharing is caring

The online world is mostly text, images, and video, which makes it difficult to express emotions. Users can bond with their close friends by sharing information with them. Though this can be a very positive thing, it's worth bearing in mind that there are things that probably should not be published online.

△ **Making friends**
Making friends online is very similar to making friends offline. People need to be able to meet (whether it's in the online or offline world) and spend time doing shared activities.

△ **Oversharing**
Sometimes, people publish information about themselves or others that is probably best left unsaid. This is called oversharing. It might be personal opinions, images, or videos that other people simply do not need to know or see.

△ **Sharing is forever**
When something is shared with another person, it's theirs. When it's shared online, it's stored by the company who made it possible to share the information in the first place, so be careful with what you put online.

Content control

The web is like a giant photocopying machine that can make a copy of most things, including content owned by other people. It is also easy to share content widely. This has disrupted industries that have traditionally relied on intellectual property: they have lost the ability to control their content and to make money from it.

▽ **Creative Commons**
Creative Commons is a content license that lets the creator determine who can access and publish their work. It can be totally free and open—even allowing others to financially profit from the content—or it can be completely closed, as well as everything in between.

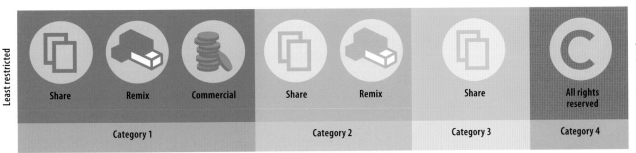

Least restricted — Most restricted

Category 1			Category 2		Category 3	Category 4
Share	Remix	Commercial	Share	Remix	Share	All rights reserved

Social media apps

The rising popularity of social media has changed the way people communicate with each other. Thanks to various social media apps, it's now possible to stay connected with family and friends all the time.

SEE ALSO

❮ 18–19 Computing with others
❮ 194–195 What is social media?
❮ 196–197 Social media platforms

Mobile first

In the early days of the Internet, people used desktop computers or laptops to access the Internet. These days, handheld devices such as smartphones and tablets are now primarily used to access the web. The upside of this is that people are always connected, always on, always capturing, and always uploading and downloading content—wherever they are. The downside, however, is that this may lead to information overload.

▷ **On the go**
Social media can be accessed from anywhere. Portable devices are as powerful as desktop computers and allow users to stay connected on the go.

Downloading social media apps

There are various ways to connect to a social media app. The first step is to download the app from an app store. Apps may be released by recognized developers, such as Facebook or Google, or by smaller companies. Most apps are free, but some may have paid services or features. Bear in mind that some apps have age restrictions. Google Play, the Apple App Store, and the Microsoft Store are some of the popular distribution platforms.

Apple App Store
The Apple App Store is where social media for iOS devices can be downloaded from. The Apple App Store has a very stringent policy for the apps that are uploaded there, and each one undergoes rigorous testing.

Google Play
Android users can download a social media app from the Google Play store. This store allows anyone to upload apps, and therefore doesn't offer quality control. The apps uploaded are open source, which means that they can be tinkered with and adapted by anyone.

Microsoft Store
People using Windows on their tablets and smartphones can visit the Microsoft Store for social media apps. Though big social media companies usually offer their apps on the Microsoft Store, some smaller companies may take a while to have a version for Microsoft devices.

Using social media apps

Most social media apps are not as flexible or sophisticated as their web versions. Some may offer reduced interactivity or require a separate app to be downloaded to access things like direct messaging. Mobile social media apps make it easier to be more immediate with social media in comparison to their web counterparts. This might be a good thing when giving important information to others in real time, such as reacting to a natural disaster. However, this immediacy can be a bad thing if a user posts something without thinking about it first.

"As users **replace** usage of the web with a mobile, **app-centric ecosystem**, the phone becomes the center of gravity."
**Keith Teare (b. 1954),
British technology entrepreneur**

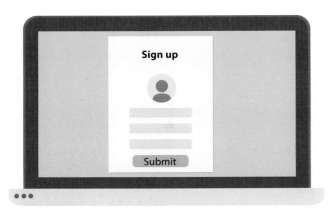

△ **Signing up**
Once an app has been downloaded on a device, the first step to access it is to link it with a new or an existing account. The same account can be used to view the app on different devices.

△ **Two-factor authentication**
Many social media apps require two-factor authentication. This means that, in addition to a username and password, users must also enter a unique code to prove their identity. This is designed to minimize the chances the account can be broken into by an unauthorized person.

▷ **Leaving a social media app**
Deleting the app does not delete your social media account. Different apps have different terms and conditions required for completely terminating an account. Usually this is done by looking in the app settings.

REAL WORLD

Location tracking

One of the benefits of accessing a social media app through a handheld device is that users can get information based on their current location. The app creators can track the users' locations and create more customer-specific features. However, there is a downside to this: app creators can sell this location information to third parties for their own benefit.

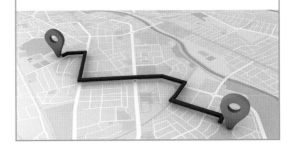

Using social networks

Social networks are some of the most popular ways people connect with friends and families. But just because everybody's using them doesn't mean caution isn't needed.

SEE ALSO
❮ **18–19** Computing with others
❮ **178–179** Online and digital identities
❮ **194–195** What is social media?

What do you get from a social network?

Social networks are places where you can meet new people and keep up to date with friends and family. They are also where we get a lot of our news, discover what's going on in our local area, and find new trends in things we find interesting. Some social networks are aimed at helping users find a job. Others are to help users find new friends. There are social networks online for pretty much anything and everything.

IN DEPTH

Digital footprint

Everything you do on a social network is collected by the company who runs it. This information is called your digital footprint, and it is used by the company to show you information—such as ads—that might appeal to you. This footprint might be shared between companies to create an even more detailed profile of you and your connections. This is a controversial thing, and governments around the world are grappling with the question of who should own a user's digital footprint data—the user, or the companies whose services they are using?

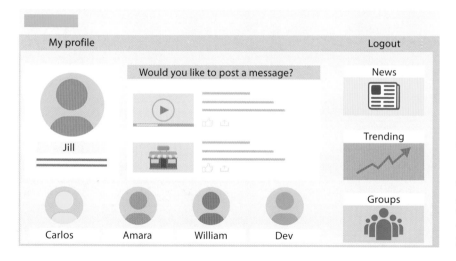

◁ **Your profile**
Your profile is the most important thing on your social network: it tells people who you are (or what you want to tell them about who you are), and it shows your connections and content.

Managing relationships on social networks

As a user connects with more people, their social network expands. To make a connection, one person submits a request to connect with another. If it's accepted, the connection is made. But just like offline, it's important to maintain that connection—this might be by sharing information and responding to theirs, or creating content that's useful to other people. Social network connections can also be broken. If someone chooses to sever contact, their information won't be viewable by the other anymore.

△ **Muting**
If someone uses social media a bit too much for your liking, you can often mute them. It doesn't stop them from saying things, but their posts will no longer be visible to you anymore.

△ **Unfriending**
When a connection is disconnected, a user's content won't be published to a former friend's newsfeed. Sometimes the unfriended person may still see the other's content.

Publishing on a social network

People can judge the content that their connections publish to social media by liking or sharing it. If the content a user publishes is perceived by others to have value, their reputation increases and they become a valuable resource for others. Viewed through this lens, social media is like a popularity contest.

Being "super-me" △
People tend to create a "super-me," or someone that's a little bit better than they are, when publishing on social media. They might share their best vacation pictures or the fancy food they have eaten. Their posts may not fully reflect reality though.

◁ **Public vs. private chat**
Studies show that two people who communicate via private message are more likely to be closer than people who only communicate via public "walls." That said, some people prefer public chatting, as everyone connected can see it.

IN DEPTH

Comparing ourselves

Some people use the content they see on social media—whether it has been created by family or friends, sports stars, movie stars, or other celebrities—to reflect negatively on their own lives. It is worth remembering that social media users present an edited version of their lives to the network, and that it isn't real life, but just what someone wants you to see.

Social networks and news

One of the primary uses of social networks is sharing news stories among friends and connections. Social network connections are likely to be interested in the same things as one another, and so sharing news stories is an easy way of sharing information that might be useful to a network. News and other media organizations learned this quickly and became active members of these networks, creating content that would be easily shareable on these platforms.

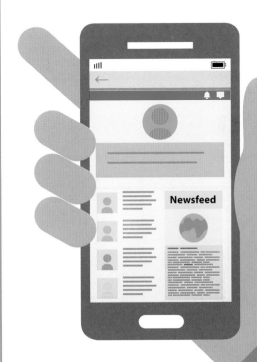

△ **Social networks in your area**
You can configure your social networks to only send you news and information based on your local area. Your local area might be your country, town or city, or even your street. This way, information you do not need is filtered out.

"Social media [is] not only **sharing** the news, but **driving it**."
Dan Rather (b. 1931), American journalist

Gaming and social networks

SEE ALSO

❰ 180–181 Maintaining balance
❰ 188–189 Cyberbullying
❰ 202–203 Using social networks

Social networks and computer games have converged to a point where most games give players a chance to play with others online, and many social networks offer embedded games.

Social network gaming

Many social networks allow their users to play games within their network and to share their progress with those they are socially connected to. These simple games usually run via Flash animation within the website or app. They tend to feature uncomplicated tasks, such as farming or building, that take time to develop and motivate users returning to the site to check on their progress.

IN DEPTH

Microtransactions

Whether in a social media game or app, many games offer players the ability to unlock special abilities or levels. These in-game purchases are called "microtransactions" and are charged to the account holder, who should be aware of this if others are using their devices. Microtransactions can be disabled in all major gaming platforms, usually by looking in the settings or account menus, or you can require a password to be given in order to make an in-app purchase.

Microtransactions
The player can make in-game purchases to increase their ability to play the game: usually to speed time up or give them special abilities for a set period of time.

Continuous goals
These games feature objectives that get progressively more difficult. The goals are relatively straightforward, but it may take time or in-game money to be able to achieve them.

Achievements
Each completed goal is rewarded with some form of prize or feedback, so the player is encouraged to keep playing. There are usually no victory conditions in these games, so this is how the player "wins."

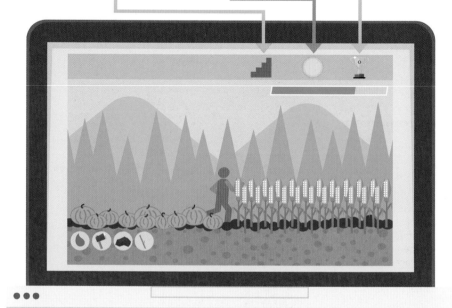

Gaming networks

The Internet has made it possible for people to play games with each other regardless of where they are in the world. Dedicated gaming networks also allow users to buy games, upload videos of them playing, and share achievements.

Steam

Steam is a digital storefront that sells games and also allows players to play those games online on Windows, Mac, and Linux operating systems. It started in 2003, with seven games, but currently has tens of thousands of titles.

PlayStation Network

With 110 million members worldwide, PlayStation Network is the largest gaming platform. It is designed to allow players of Sony's PlayStation consoles to interact with each other over games, films, and music.

Xbox Live

Designed to run on Microsoft's Xbox console range, Xbox Live allows users to play games with each other online and use an array of apps, including video-streaming, sports, music, and video chat.

Advantages of playing games online

Gaming online can be thought of as being a social network centered around the activity of playing games. On the big online gaming networks, gamers can create an avatar and make friends. Some networks and games limit the ability for players to interact with each other, especially if the players are likely to be young.

Making friends
Playing games and socializing with new people online is a way of making friends and developing social skills, and even learning about different countries and cultures.

Maintaining friendships
A great way of staying in touch with friends—particularly friends who do not live in the same area—is by having shared experiences. Online gaming can be one of these.

Having fun and relaxing
It can be a very enjoyable experience to step inside the new worlds that gaming offers. In moderation, gaming can help reduce stress and improve cognitive function.

Online hate

Gaming networks are no different from other kinds of social networks when it comes to negativity and abuse. Users can even face aggressive or threatening behavior at times. Thankfully, gaming network providers advise gamers to report abusive players and take action on receiving these reports.

▷ **Trolls**
A troll is someone who communicates in a deliberately offensive or provocative way online. A troll may try to anger other players by being loud, aggressive, or destructive.

Gaming terms

FPS: First-person shooter.

Griefing: When an online player intentionally causes irritation or anger to other players when playing a game together.

MMORPG: Massively multiplayer online role-playing game—a game where a player creates a character and can interact with large numbers of other players in an online world.

Rage quitting: When someone gets so angry that they quit their game.

RPG: Role-playing game—a game where the player either makes or becomes a character and usually interacts with a fantastical environment.

Social media bubbles

Social media platforms allow us to see what we want to see and filter out the stuff we don't. But it's not just the technology that does it: it's part of our psychology, too.

SEE ALSO

❮ 180–181 Maintaining balance
❮ 194–195 What is social media?
❮ 196–197 Social media platforms

What is a social media bubble?

A social media bubble, also known as a filter bubble, is the phenomenon of only seeing the things we like on social media. This is caused by two things. Users can block, ignore, and sometimes delete things that they don't agree with or dislike, which tailors their social media feed in a certain way. Second, many social media platforms use algorithms that are geared toward showing users things that they're likely to want to see. A person who shows support for a political party is unlikely to see anything that is critical of that party or point of view.

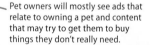

Pet owners will mostly see ads that relate to owning a pet and content that may try to get them to buy things they don't really need.

Those in a home-cooking bubble are more likely to see content critical of fast food and the people who eat it.

▷ **Bubbles**
If all people see on social media are things that they like and agree with, they run the risk of being isolated from other groups and perhaps gradually losing the ability to understand others.

Fans of soccer are likely to see content that reaffirms their view that it is the best sport.

Why we like who we like

We are drawn to people who are similar to us: perhaps they look like us or they dress like us. They may have similar backgrounds to us or have had similar experiences. These become the foundations for friendships because we can relate to these people and what they think. While this is a positive thing, it can limit how much we understand those that are not like us.

▷ **Trust**
We are more likely to trust information that comes from people we trust—even if they don't have any relevant expertise in the topic!

LINGO
Useful terms

Strong ties: People we connect to who are part of our social circle, and with whom we have lots of direct or indirect connections.

Weak ties: People we connect to by chance or accidentally, with whom we have few or no other connections.

Confirmation bias: Being more likely to like or believe something that confirms your existing beliefs.

IN DEPTH
Closed and open networks

There are two kinds of social network—open and closed. An example of an open network is Twitter: you can connect with anyone you want to, and they don't have to connect back to you to make the friendship official. But in closed networks, like Facebook, you have to reciprocate an invitation to be a friend before you are connected and can access all their information.

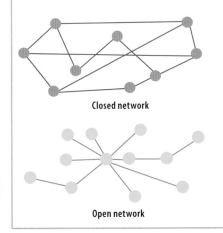

Closed network

Open network

How bubbles are created

A social media platform's main aim is to keep as many users interacting with their service as possible. Social media's main revenue comes from showing users advertisements, and the longer users are on the site, the more ads they will see. The best way to keep you focused on something is to confirm your biases, because it feels good. Social media feeds users things they want to see through complex algorithms. These algorithms guess what a user will like based on what they have expressed a like for before, and also what their friends like.

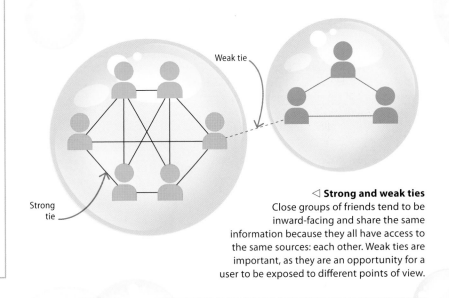

◁ **Strong and weak ties**
Close groups of friends tend to be inward-facing and share the same information because they all have access to the same sources: each other. Weak ties are important, as they are an opportunity for a user to be exposed to different points of view.

Fake news

Since people confirm their biases online through their social networks, it's easy to create a story or opinion that will resonate with a particular set of people, even if it's untrue. All it needs to do is use the generally assumed beliefs of one group and extend them in a believable way. This can then quickly spread, as people with similar beliefs will share it to prove themselves right. The more people share it, the more it's believed to be true. Also, people can claim that something is fake news when it isn't, purely because they don't agree with it.

▷ **Eiffel abduction**
A fake news report might say that a UFO has abducted the Eiffel Tower in Paris, France. Cross-checking the story with other news sites is advised before believing it!

REAL WORLD
Filtered reality

During the 2004 US presidential election, American scientist Lada Adamic wanted to find out how much people on opposite sides of the political spectrum interacted with each other online. What she found was that each side tended to listen to only their own side's points of view, and there were very few people who took the time and effort to listen to and understand the views of others. This results in a polarization of opinions, where each side becomes increasingly more opposed to the other's political views, making it harder for people to trust each other, and harder for politicians to reach agreement.

Digital issues

Digital literacy

Getting the most out of digital technology is becoming increasingly important in the modern world. Digitally literate people are those who are able to participate fully in the world of digital technology.

SEE ALSO
❮ 48–49 What is hardware?
❮ 50–51 Desktop computers and laptops
❮ 52–53 Smartphones and tablets

Using computers

A huge part of digital literacy is what used to be called computer literacy in the pre-Internet age. This is basically the ability to understand and use a computer as a tool to get things done. As more and more computers have connected to the Internet, the term "digital literacy" has become more common.

IN DEPTH

Why it's important

Being computer-literate is about being able to use computers. Digital literacy is about having the tools to make the most out of the Internet. Digitally literate people are able to find reliable and accurate information online and are responsible in their use of that information.

△ **Finding**
The first part of computer literacy is using computers to search for and navigate toward information. The information may be stored on the computer or online.

△ **Using**
There is a lot of information out there, and not all of it is relevant, accurate, or up-to-date. Being able to think critically and to analyze information is a huge part of modern computer skills.

△ **Sharing**
Having found and evaluated information, the next step is being able to create and communicate your own thoughts to the body of information—sharing an opinion on social media or writing a school report.

Different platforms

In the digital world, the hardware you use both requires different skills and also changes the type of thing you can do and experience. People who are digitally literate may not think twice about switching from a laptop to a touchscreen, or Windows to macOS machine, but these things might be a problem for some. Developers and designers should create software and hardware with simplicity in mind and offer friendly support to people who want to learn to use their products.

◁ **Mouse trap**
People who have always used a mouse may find it difficult to navigate tablet computers by using the touchscreen hardware. Similarly, people who find touchscreens to be second nature may find it difficult to use a physical keyboard and a mouse.

Examining information

Every day, hundreds of thousands of articles are shared online. With so many claims made about everything from the NASA Moon landings to current events, it is increasingly difficult to evaluate and understand what to take as fact and what to discard as fiction. Information online may be wrong on purpose, by mistake, or be opinion passed off as fact. Here are some tips that may help when scrutinizing online information.

REAL WORLD

Snopes

Snopes.com is one of the most respected websites for sorting fact from fiction. It was set up in 1994 to investigate and fact-check online information. If you want to find out the truth behind a particular story you've seen online, it is worth searching Snopes to see if there is an article on there covering it.

Purpose
Most sites have an "About this site" section that explains the website's angle. This is an invaluable source of information, as it usually explains if the site is to be taken seriously, if it has a particular ideological angle, who the target audience is, and who writes for the site.

Bias
The majority of websites have a bias: a particular ideological view—be it political, religious, or economic. Sites that have a bias are more likely to be selective in what they cover, omit things that don't fit into their view, and tend more toward opinion than fact.

Who hosts the site?
".gov" sites are government websites and are officially approved information. ".edu" sites are usually from educational authorities, or opinion sites by students. ".org" sites are organizations, and every one is different. ".com" sites are usually commercial sites.

Reputation
Use a search engine to see what others have to say about a particular site and its writers. As anyone can put information online, checking on an author's credentials should establish if they are a recognized voice on a particular subject.

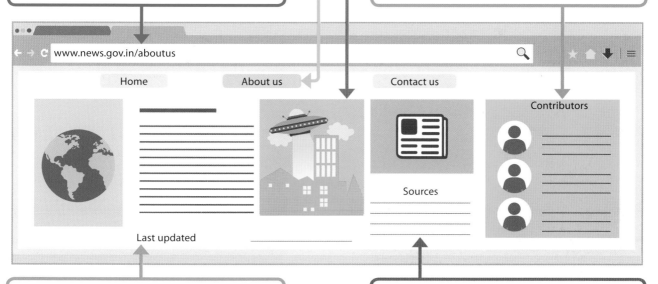

Up-to-date
Most sites show when a particular piece of information was uploaded. While this may not be as important for sites giving general information on something, it is crucial for news sites, where having out-of-date information is the same as having wrong information.

Sources
Sites that provide links to their sources—be they weblinks (sometimes included as hyperlinks in the body of the site) or lists of books or films—help to give the reader more context and show that the ideas on the site are the product of investigation and consideration.

Net neutrality

Net neutrality is the idea that Internet service providers (ISPs) should treat all data online in the same way and not block, discriminate, or charge users differently to access data.

SEE ALSO

❰ **150–151** The Internet and the World Wide Web

❰ **190–191** Hacking and privacy

Global development **216–217** ❱

What is net neutrality?

Net neutrality prevents telecom companies and ISPs from picking and choosing what content people can access. This includes blocking or censoring websites, as well as throttling (intentionally slowing) their service. Opponents of net neutrality claim that not all content is created equal. They feel that certain sites should be restricted, that people should pay more to access websites that are primarily concerned with entertainment, and that people should be able to pick what Internet services they want to pay for. Certain governments are already able to restrict access to large parts of the Internet.

▽ Two Internets
Many people believe that scrapping net neutrality would create a "poor Internet" with limited services and a "rich Internet" with full access to services. Access to content, resources, and education would depend on what a user can afford.

IN DEPTH

Preventing cybercrime

Many net neutrality laws include privacy protections, such as requiring customer consent before monitoring or sharing personal data. While generally a good thing, this also protects cybercriminals. If ISPs monitored networks, they could tell which customers were involved with criminal websites. However, critics argue that preventing crime isn't—and shouldn't be—the job of ISPs.

△ **Equal treatment**
Since its inception, the Internet has been mostly neutral. The majority of users can access the same data in the same way.

△ **Preferential treatment**
If net neutrality were abandoned, users who could not afford the expensive fast lane would be stuck with a slow or restricted service.

Why it's important

Some people argue that Internet access is now a human right. In many countries, the Internet plays an essential role in daily business and education. Restricting access would harm the poorest segments of the population the most. Net neutrality also plays a role in promoting free speech, encouraging competition, protecting privacy, and exposing corruption.

Minority groups

Social, ethnic, and religious minorities use the web to coordinate events and fight oppression within their country. Giving a government or an ISP the ability to stop their capacity to communicate effectively is essentially another form of oppression.

Freedom of speech

Net neutrality prevents companies, organizations, or governments from censoring opinions they don't like. Some governments around the world have already done away with net neutrality, to the detriment of their citizens' personal freedom.

Businesses

Without net neutrality, the Internet would favor big, established businesses with lots of money and make it harder for startups and entrepreneurs to gain a significant presence.

IN DEPTH

The counterargument

In 2014, Comcast deliberately slowed data for the entertainment site Netflix and forced the company to pay huge sums of money to fix it. Comcast argued that the bandwidth required for Netflix movies was a massive drain on resources. In other words, everyone's Internet was slower because so many people streamed content from Netflix. Getting rid of net neutrality would force resource-intensive content, such as Netflix, to pay for better infrastructure. It might also encourage ISPs to spread out into more rural areas. The Internet would be treated like regular commodities that respond to the market forces of supply and demand.

Net neutrality around the world

Since the early 2000s, countries around the world have been passing digital laws and trying to figure out how to regulate the Internet. Different places have different answers for questions, such as who should monitor content; who is responsible for cybercrime; and whether the Internet is owned by governments, ISPs, or people.

> **India: in favor of net neutrality**
> In 2016, the Telecom Regulatory Authority of India (TRAI) banned Facebook's Free Basics program on the grounds that it violated net neutrality. Free Basics allows users to access certain websites, chosen by Facebook, for free.

> **The United States: repealing net neutrality**
> In late 2017, the US government indicated it wanted to repeal net neutrality rules but sought to allay the fears of pro–net neutrality advocates by promising to deal with companies who exploit users.

> **Portugal: partial net neutrality**
> The Portuguese telecommunications company MEO offers users different packages of Internet access. For example, a user can pay for a messaging service only and pay more for video streaming or social media access.

> **Morocco: no net neutrality**
> The government has the right to block content that threatens the Moroccan monarchy, the Islamic faith, or public order. Transgressors face heavy fines or prison sentences. After recent crackdowns on online journalists, there is speculation about violations of human rights.

REAL WORLD

The Golden Shield Project

Nicknamed the Great Firewall of China, the Golden Shield Project is the Chinese government's project to restrict access to websites in the name of state security. Banned websites include Google, Facebook, and *The New York Times*. More than 2 million Internet police constantly monitor data being sent or received. State-approved Chinese companies such as the microblogging website Sina Weibo offer alternatives to the banned sites.

Digital divide

Not everybody has access to digital devices and the Internet, and the difference between those who do and those who do not is called the digital divide.

SEE ALSO	
‹ 212–213 Net neutrality	
Global development	216–217 ›
Equality and computer science	218–219 ›

Getting online

A great way to measure the digital divide is to look at access to the Internet. To use the Internet, a person needs some form of digital device, must understand how to use it, and has to be in a place where Internet access is possible and not extremely expensive. Generally speaking, people in the developed world have greater access to the Internet than those in the developing world. Even within countries, there is a digital divide between rich and poor citizens.

The **digital divide** is the difference between people **who have access** to digital devices and the Internet and those **who do not**.

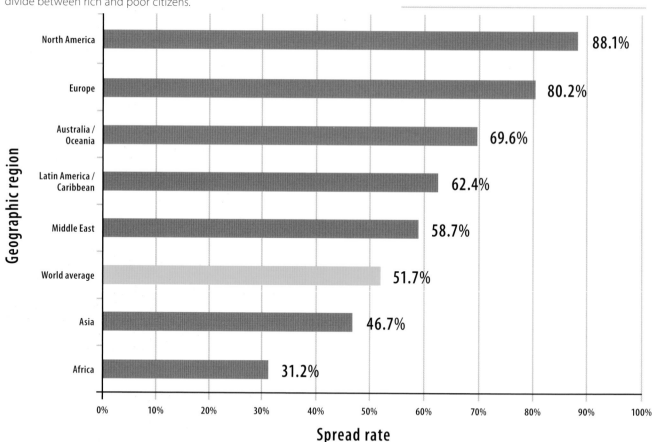

△ **Internet world spread rates by geographic regions**

Access to the Internet is not equally possible everywhere. Whereas North America, Europe, and Australia enjoy relatively high rates of online access, South America, most of Asia, and Africa do not. These figures vary from country to country: about 94 percent of people in Japan are online, but the average for Asia is less than half of that.

Source: Internet World Stats:
www.internetworldstats.com/stats.htm
Correct as of June 30, 2017.

Why it matters

The Internet is the greatest educational tool humans have created. The digital divide is really about the ability to access, understand, and use information. Those who lack at least one of these three abilities face the possibility of falling behind their peers, whether they live halfway across the world or on the same street.

Video conferencing software allows students to virtually attend lessons from wherever they are.

Email has become the standard way to apply for jobs.

Mail-in applications may not be accepted by some employers.

Mail sent

Mail box

△ **Teaching tool**
Educators are increasingly turning to the Internet to improve and organize their lessons. The Internet has also made it easier for students in isolated communities to receive the same standard of education as everyone else.

△ **In the workplace**
For most jobs, being able to use the Internet is a basic requirement, and an integral part of the job. Not being digitally literate is a bar to many jobs, and indeed, not being online means it's hard to even hear about job vacancies in the first place.

Who does the digital divide affect?

While generalizations can oversimplify, the fact remains that certain groups across the world tend to be on the wrong side of the digital divide. Usually a person might fall into two or more of these rough categories—for example, a woman living in a rural area.

△ **Lower-income people**
Those without access to some of life's basics may not be able to afford digital devices, the money required to run them, and the cost of a home Internet connection.

△ **Women**
In many parts of the world, women do not get the same educational opportunities as men. The digital divide mirrors wider pressures that women experience.

△ **Elderly people**
The Internet as we know it really took off in the mid-1990s. Those who were not part of the explosion in Internet usage may find digital devices hard to understand and use.

△ **People from rural areas**
People living in rural areas are more likely to have limited access to the Internet. Internet providers may feel bringing fast Internet to rural areas is not worth the expense.

REAL WORLD

Closing the gap

Across the world, governments, charities, and nongovernmental organizations (NGOs) are trying to close the digital divide on different fronts. Many governments have established schemes to bring fast broadband Internet to remote and rural areas while providing courses in digital literacy for older people. The nonprofit "One Laptop per Child" initiative has shipped millions of cost-effective laptops to kids all around the world.

Global development

Though digital technology has spread across the world, people in developing countries often experience significantly fewer benefits from it than those in developed countries.

SEE ALSO

❮ 48–49 What is hardware?
❮ 212–213 Net neutrality
❮ 214–215 Digital divide

A connected world

More than 2 billion people have access to the Internet, and 5 billion have cell phones. However, these people are not spread evenly across the globe. Most people in Europe have access to the Internet, while many in Africa do not. This situation is known as the global digital divide. This divide presents both challenges and opportunities as the world becomes ever more connected.

New technology helps countries catch up.

▷ **Shortcuts**
Developing countries are sometimes able to reduce the digital divide quicker by using the technology of the developed world. This effectively allows them to leapfrog over years of development and obsolete technology.

Potential for good

There is great potential for vastly improving people's lives across the world by using digital technologies. There are huge amounts of information available on the Internet, and wider access has the power to improve education worldwide. Additionally, the ability to gather a lot of data from people in a relatively short amount of time via smart devices and the Internet is crucial. This data can help governments and organizations react to problems and crises, from how best to help people after a natural disaster to understanding how to distribute crucial resources.

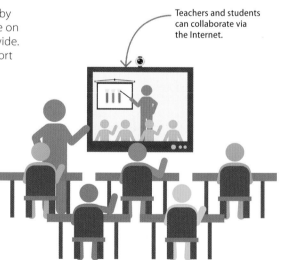

Teachers and students can collaborate via the Internet.

The Internet can help farmers increase crop yields.

△ **Ending hunger**
Hundreds of millions of people across the world are suffering from hunger. Digital technology opens up new possibilities for improving crop yields and coordinating distribution, potentially helping to lessen and even end this problem.

△ **Education for all**
Teachers, students, and parents can access online resources and libraries that wouldn't be available otherwise. They're able to connect with other educators and learners through communities and forums on the web.

Ethics

There are many ethical issues surrounding the digital divide. For example, installing up-to-date Internet communication cables in developing countries is likely to be time-consuming and costly, with the process potentially disadvantaging a country financially in the short and medium term. Some companies have provided Internet access to users in developing countries, but the only sites users could access without paying belonged to that company and the sites they approved of.

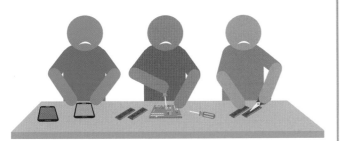

△ **Exploitation**
People in developing countries are often exploited by having to work long hours making technology for prosperous countries, with little or no chance of being able to afford what they make.

The environment

The effect of making digital devices on the environment is significant, and usually felt more in developing countries. Several of the components in smartphones are made from rare materials, such as gold and coltan. Sometimes the mining of these materials has both caused and funded serious conflict. The process of refining these metals also tends to produce toxic waste. Lastly, people tend not to dispose of their old digital technology properly, and this can produce toxic waste.

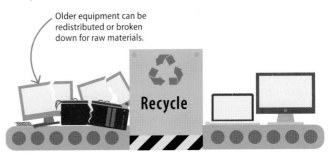

Older equipment can be redistributed or broken down for raw materials.

△ **Recycling computers**
Some organizations redistribute old but working computers to charities, including those in developing countries. Other companies recycle components of broken equipment into raw materials that can be used to make new devices.

"**Never before** in history has **innovation** offered promise of **so much** to so many in **so short** a time."
Bill Gates (b. 1955), American co-founder of Microsoft

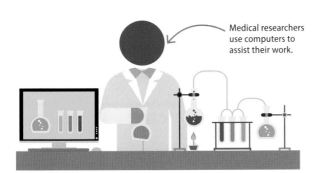

Medical researchers use computers to assist their work.

△ **Healthcare and well-being**
Digital technology means faster public health reporting and tracking, especially during epidemics. Researchers are also using digital technology to reduce the time taken to develop new treatments for illnesses.

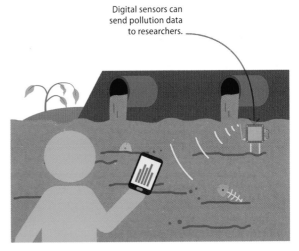

Digital sensors can send pollution data to researchers.

△ **Protecting the environment**
Various projects use digital technology and Internet connectivity to protect the environment. For example, underwater sensors can give researchers accurate real-time data about various pollutants.

Equality and computer science

SEE ALSO

‹ 28–29 Computer science

‹ 178–179 Online and digital identities

‹ 214–215 Digital divide

The majority of those studying and working in computer science are white, able-bodied males. What is the reason for this, and can computer science become more diverse?

Women and computing

The role women have played in the development of computer science has often been downplayed. In the early days of computer science, most programmers were women. Ada Lovelace, the first programmer, was a woman, and the team that coded the Electronic Numerical Integrator and Computer (ENIAC) in the 1940s was entirely female.

REAL WORLD

NASA and women

Women "computers" who did complex mathematical calculations by hand, along with female programmers, were heavily involved in the US space program in the 1960s. At NASA, they were part of the team that calculated flight paths for space probes and several Apollo rockets. American computer scientist Margaret Hamilton (b. 1936) led the team that programmed the on-board flight computer for the first Moon landing.

◁ **Less than a quarter**
In modern times, women occupy less than 25 percent of the worldwide jobs in the computer science industry. This is generally called the "gender gap."

Why is there a gender gap?

The number of women studying computer science or going into programming as a profession began to drop dramatically in the mid-1980s. One explanation for this is the decision of computer companies at the time to pitch computers as gaming devices and to target computers and games at males. This resulted in girls being given the impression that computing was "for boys." There are other possible reasons for the gender gap.

▷ **Perceptions**
Computer science is perceived as being a technical subject and, wrongly, one that naturally better suits males. Lack of encouragement makes it hard, particularly for teenage girls, to take part in an activity that is seen as unfeminine and in which they're outnumbered.

Why equality matters

Everybody has a limited understanding of the world and, especially, what the world is like for other people. Groups made up entirely of people with similar backgrounds tend to create products that will only really be of use to people from that background. By becoming more welcoming to and inclusive of women, minorities, and people from generally diverse backgrounds, companies can improve the ability of their products to appeal to a much wider section of users.

▽ **Diversity of perspectives**
Whether it's software or hardware, new products start with ideas. Including and considering many different kinds of ideas help technology work for more people.

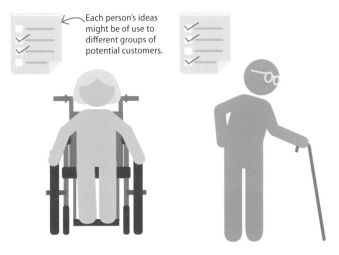

Each person's ideas might be of use to different groups of potential customers.

△ **Lack of role models**
If young women are only aware of male computer scientists, it may discourage them from considering it as a career. Introducing them to female role models can make computer science a viable option.

△ **Geek culture**
The popular image of a computer scientist is a male "geek," which puts off people who don't feel they fit this stereotype. In reality, many technology careers require teamwork, creativity, and different personalities.

Computer science and disabilities

SEE ALSO

❮ **36–37** Peripheral devices

❮ **62–63** Gaming consoles

Biological interfaces **234–235** ❯

Many people with disabilities rely on technology developed by computer scientists to help them with everything from reading and speaking to developing their own technology.

Independence

Computer science is used in a variety of technologies that help people with disabilities. Some of these technologies—such as hearing aids or screen readers—are specifically designed to assist people with disabilities. Others are developments that everyone uses regardless of ability level, such as online shopping sites and speech recognition. As a whole, these technologies allow people with disabilities to have more independence and also to take part fully in schools and workplaces.

▷ **Assistive technologies**

Assistive technologies help people overcome problems they face as a result of their disability. One example is an environmental control unit (ECU) that lets people with mobility problems control items in their house using a smartphone. Other examples help blind or deaf people communicate with those around them.

Speech recognition system / screen reader

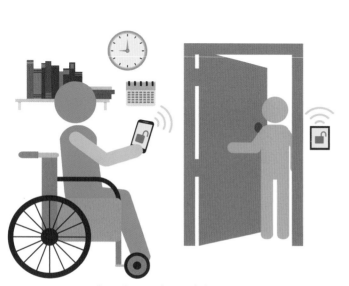

Smartphone app for smartlocks

Sign-language-to-speech program

Technology for learning

Technology has a powerful role to play in supporting the learning and social needs of people with a range of physical, sensory, communication, or cognitive disabilities. Some features are specially designed for people with disabilities, but many—such as spell-checkers used by people with dyslexia—are used by almost all computer users.

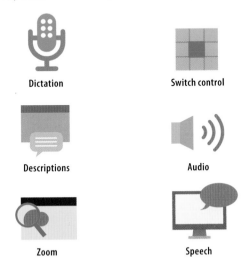

Dictation

Switch control

Descriptions

Audio

Zoom

Speech

△ **Accessibility options**
Mobile and desktop devices have built-in accessibility options such as magnification, color and contrast choices, page decluttering, and text-to-speech.

New technologies

New devices are emerging based on virtual reality that can help people who are newly disabled to adjust to navigating the world using, for example, a motorized wheelchair. Disabled people can also meet up and interact with others in "virtual world" applications.

▷ **Gesture control**
People with disabilities affecting their fine motor control can also interact with computers using devices that recognize gestures, such as the Leap Motion or Kinect controllers.

REAL WORLD

Charity-made apps

Several disability charities have created apps addressing the needs of the people they work with. These apps range from fundraising to helping people with disabilities in extreme situations, such as accessing life-saving relief in the aftermath of a natural disaster.

Computing and disabilities

Having a disability isn't a barrier to learning to code. Thanks to assistive technologies, people with a variety of abilities are able to learn coding skills and get jobs in the computer science industry. Many companies are happy for their programmers to work from home, which can be a helpful option for disabled coders.

BIOGRAPHY

Farida Bedwei

Born in 1979 in Nigeria, Bedwei was diagnosed with cerebral palsy at the age of 1. Despite her mobility and muscle coordination being affected, she has become an extremely successful software engineer and businesswoman.

◁ **Autism spectrum disorders**
Many people with autism spectrum disorders (ASD) have a natural attention to detail, which is extremely useful for coding.

The future of computers

Predicting the future

Technology is always changing. People have been trying to imagine the future of technology for hundreds of years. Some modern developments seem like they will have an impact on the future, but it is always hard to be certain.

SEE ALSO

❮ 54–55 Build your own computers
❮ 56–57 Wearable computers
❮ 88–89 Databases
The Internet of Things 226–227 ❯
Virtual reality 228–229 ❯
Cryptocurrencies 230–231 ❯

On the horizon

Inventions don't just pop out of nowhere: they're built on mountains of previous discoveries, designs, and failures. Specific predictions may be impossible, but it's broadly possible to see the big picture of where technology is heading, especially over the next few years. Some inventions, such as virtual reality, have been around for a while but have found a new lease of life with modern computing capabilities. Others, such as cryptocurrencies, are relatively new and are harder to be sure about.

IN DEPTH

Why predict?

Accurate predictions help industries decide where to focus their research efforts. If people know that nuclear-powered jetpacks are a bad idea, they won't pour time and money into inventing them. Predictions also help countries create new laws to deal with technology. Imagine how chaotic the world would be if traffic laws had never been created, or no one had bothered to standardize currents and voltages. Currently, many countries are struggling to define digital rights.

△ **Augmented reality (AR)**
Whether it's adding quirky filters to social media videos or superimposing information on eyeglasses, AR is making the world more customizable and interactive. Education, games, and even navigation are all changing.

△ **Virtual reality (VR)**
VR headsets are catapulting users into 360-degree virtual worlds. VR simulators have existed for years, and advances in hardware have finally made them more affordable.

△ **Robots**
Autonomous drones for surveillance, military combat, and search and rescue are now a reality. There are even cars that can drive themselves. While useful, it means more jobs are being lost to automation.

△ **Makerspaces**
These are work spaces where people can access high-tech tools such as 3D printers and Arduino boards. The maker mindset focuses on creativity, collaboration, and building things with new technologies.

△ **3D printing**
3D printers are becoming increasingly cheap and accessible. In addition to inspiring new trends, they are important in manufacturing and medicine and are used to create engine parts, jewelry, and even prosthetic hands.

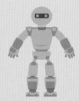

△ **Big data**
Everything from phones to watches has sensors nowadays. The same goes for industrial devices such as turbines and trains. These sensors create a huge amount of data that can be harvested for all kinds of uses.

Challenges

Before making predictions about the future, it's important to have a detailed understanding of current science. This limits the number of people who can make educated guesses. On top of that, the advancement of technology is a collaborative effort, where researchers, politicians, users, and businesses all have a part to play. It's almost impossible to see all the pieces at once.

△ **Timing**
Research often takes decades to generate results. The breakthrough could occur in 1 year, a few years, or not at all. No one knows for sure.

△ **Social behaviors**
Companies didn't expect smartphones to be used as flashlights. Even the most far-sighted developers can't predict how people will respond to a new technology.

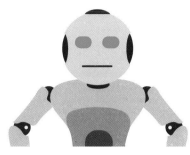

△ **Rise of interdisciplinary fields**
Fields like robotics or neuroscience, which draw from multiple fields, are extra tricky to predict because few people fully understand all their complexities in depth.

△ **Cell phones**
Phones can be used for everything from taking pictures to streaming music. This has created a feedback loop where industries create even more mobile content, which leads to people using their phones even more.

△ **Wearable tech**
Golf shoes that analyze your game, rings that can act as credit cards, fitness bracelets, and glasses with AR displays are already available to buy. These devices can link together and share information.

△ **Cryptocurrencies**
Cryptocurrencies are digital currencies that use cryptography to make financial transactions easier and more secure. The first, Bitcoin, was released in 2009. The value of a cryptocurrency can go up or down unpredictably.

△ **Digital assistants**
Advances in speech recognition and natural language processing (NLP) have allowed AI to be placed on devices as small as phones and watches. Navigating the digital world has now become easier than ever.

REAL WORLD

Failed predictions

New discoveries are exciting but often poorly understood. Whether it's electricity, artificial intelligence, or quantum computing, every big leap in science is accompanied by a flood of bad predictions. Other discoveries are way ahead of their time and require decades of research to develop the necessary supporting technology to get the product on the shelves. Below are some spectacular failed predictions.

Nuclear-powered vacuum cleaners (1955)

Missile-guided mail delivery (1959)

Vacations to the Moon (1969)

The Internet of Things

The Internet allows people to access data from millions of sources. The Internet of Things (IoT) is similar, but it connects devices instead of people.

SEE ALSO

❮ **56–57** Wearable computers
❮ **58–59** Connected appliances
❮ **88–89** Databases
❮ **198–199** Sharing content

What are the "things"?

To be part of the IoT, a device needs a sensor that collects data. It must also be able to communicate this data through Wi-Fi, Bluetooth, or phone networks. Not every smart device is part of the IoT. A Bluetooth speaker connects to devices but doesn't collect data. A fitness tracker may count your steps, but you can choose how that data is shared.

IN DEPTH

Why have IoT?

The logic behind the IoT is that more data means better decisions. Better decisions equal less work, which equals more free time. In a nutshell, increased connectivity is used to automate tasks. Imagine a bracelet that monitors your sleeping patterns and turns on the coffee maker when you awake, or a lock that can be activated from a phone when someone leaves the house. Both of these devices exist and can be configured for even more options.

▽ **Collecting and connecting**
More and more gadgets are getting smart makeovers. Smartphones have a variety of sensors from accelerometers to Global Positioning System (GPS) units. Self-learning thermostats use motion sensors to know when to switch on. It won't be long until refrigerators are able to work out what they have inside and whether or not it's fresh.

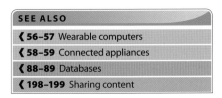

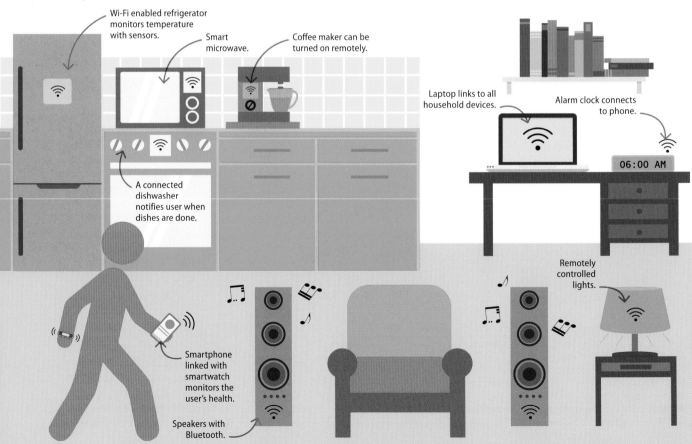

Wi-Fi enabled refrigerator monitors temperature with sensors.

Smart microwave.

Coffee maker can be turned on remotely.

Laptop links to all household devices.

Alarm clock connects to phone.

06:00 AM

A connected dishwasher notifies user when dishes are done.

Remotely controlled lights.

Smartphone linked with smartwatch monitors the user's health.

Speakers with Bluetooth.

Big data

The IoT has led to extremely large collections of information that are called "big data." As devices collect more and more information, the data produced can potentially be used to aid humans in real-world situations. Analyzing big data to find trends, patterns, and unexpected connections is done by extremely powerful computers.

▽ **Real-world applications**
If nearly every car, bus, and semi-truck took the same route, then a traffic jam is almost certain, even if another route is relatively free. Big data could potentially help navigation software to automatically direct traffic evenly across all available routes.

No traffic organization

The first route is jammed, but the other is relatively free.

With traffic organization

Traffic is directed evenly to both routes, which avoids a jam.

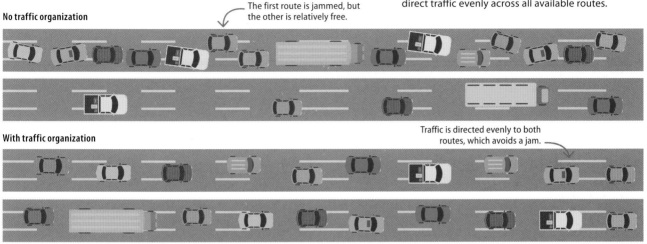

Privacy issues

While the IoT creates a lot of valuable data, it also creates a lot of data that people might prefer to keep private. Data collected by doctors can save lives, but in the wrong hands, it could be used to target consumer products at patients. Also, any digital system could potentially be hacked, which would make collected data insecure and vulnerable. Installing up-to-date security software, using strong passwords, and practicing safe browsing habits prevent most privacy breaches. It's also important to understand how and why data is collected.

> "**Everything** that **can be** automated **will** be **automated**."
> **Shoshana Zuboff (b. 1951), professor of business administration and writer**

△ **Collecting data**
First, it's important to know what data is being collected. Smart trackers, for example, can collect data on steps taken in a day, bouts of exercise, and even heart rate and sleep patterns. It's usually possible to request that certain data is not collected in a device's settings panel.

△ **Sharing data**
Second, it's good to know how the data collected is shared. Few people read the terms and conditions when installing apps. Some clauses allow data to be sold to unknown third parties. In the future, data from smart cars and fitness apps could be used to calculate insurance rates.

△ **Using data**
Finally, it's good to have an idea of how the shared data is used. While shared data from a thermostat or coffee maker might not seem like a big deal, the data can be used to learn a user's habits and create a profile.

Virtual reality

Virtual reality (VR) sounds like something that belongs in science fiction movies and television shows, but the idea has been around for many decades.

SEE ALSO

❮ **48–49** What is hardware?
❮ **224–225** Predicting the future
❮ **226–227** The Internet of Things

Augmented reality vs. virtual reality

Augmented reality (AR) is a virtual layer over real, physical things. One example is a social media image filter that adds whiskers or dog ears to a human face. Virtual reality, by contrast, creates an entirely new illusion of reality. It includes detailed sights and sounds that make the experience convincing.

▽ **Reality-virtuality spectrum**
Virtual reality can be seen as being the end point in a spectrum that starts as a real environment. Augmented reality adds specific virtual aspects, and augmented virtuality mixes interactive real-world aspects with a mostly virtual world.

The virtual image is projected onto a real space.

An illusion of reality.

Real environment

Augmented reality

Augmented virtuality

Virtual reality

How VR works

For a VR illusion to work, the user needs to feel like they're truly interacting with their environment. VR technology must respond to a user's actions in real time. Any glitch, lag, or gap breaks the illusion. VR requires powerful hardware and software that can predict a user's movements and prerender images.

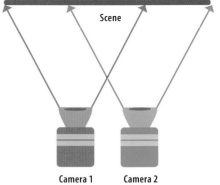

Scene

Camera 1   Camera 2

△ **Depth**
Since our eyes are several centimeters apart, each one captures a different view of the world. This must be recreated by VR for the illusion to work. Using 2D images to create 3D is called stereoscopic vision.

Motion-capture technology tracks movement to make virtual characters look fluid and real.

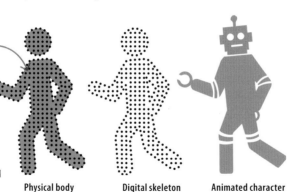

▷ **Modeling**
Everything in a virtual world must be created by coders. Moving characters are usually based on motion-tracking a human or animal and using the data to build a virtual character. This requires a lot of mathematical and computing power.

Physical body   **Digital skeleton**   **Animated character**

3D movies

In the 1890s, the first 3D movies were made using a technique called anaglyph 3D. Every scene was filmed with two cameras set a small distance apart. The two videos, one tinted blue and one tinted red, were combined digitally. Viewers wore glasses with one blue lens (to cancel out the red image) and one red lens (to cancel out the blue image). The result was a 3D-like effect.

Equipment

Rendering a visual display in a game or simulator requires a powerful computer to process thousands of numbers every second in order to decide what pixels to display. A graphics processing unit (GPU) is a specialized processor designed to handle high volumes of basic math operations. In other words, they work faster than a standard CPU, but they can only do certain types of work. If the GPU isn't powerful enough, the display will lag, creating a choppy, unrealistic experience.

△ **VR gear**
VR headsets cover the eyes. They render different images for each eye. Sensors inside the headset change the display in response to the user's head movements.

△ **Body suit**
These suits give tactile feedback through a mesh of sensors inside each suit's fabric. They can produce vibrations and simulate touching objects. Body suits offer users another layer of immersion into a virtual world.

The future of VR

For years, VR simulators have been used to train soldiers, policemen, and doctors as VR makes training safer, cheaper, and more effective. As the technology becomes cheaper and more accessible, high-quality simulators will be created for a wider range of jobs. Maybe someday VR will also include smells and physical sensations!

VR sickness

You've spent your entire life in the real world and are used to navigating it. Even the tiniest bit of lag on a headset display can cause a type of nausea known as virtual reality sickness. Another possible cause is related to motion sickness—where people experience nausea in response to movement—though people do not actually have to be moving to feel VR sickness.

△ **Playing games**
VR allows artists and game designers to take creativity to a new level. Instead of watching a screen, people can experience car chases and explore medieval castles in person.

△ **Education**
Virtual classrooms, where people can virtually experience training or a lesson, are possible with VR. The technology may also help with visualizing concepts in math and physics.

△ **Travel experience**
Some companies offer tours of famous places and monuments through VR technology. People can explore different corners of the world without leaving their seats.

Cryptocurrencies

At the intersection of the worlds of finance, the Internet, and cryptography are cryptocurrencies. These are digital currencies that have been causing a stir in since 2009.

SEE ALSO
❮ **94–95** Encryption
❮ **158–159** The deep web
❮ **224–225** Predicting the future

What are they?

A cryptocurrency is a fully digital form of currency. The first, bitcoin, was created in 2009, but there are currently more than 1,000 different ones. Cryptocurrencies are decentralized: they are not created or overseen by one government or bank. They make it possible to send money to others or pay for things from anywhere in the world without needing to convert money into local currency. Cryptocurrency transactions are made extremely secure with cryptography.

▷ **Bitcoin**
Bitcoin is the first and most valuable cryptocurrency. A satoshi—named after bitcoin's creator, Satoshi Nakamoto—is the smallest possible amount of bitcoin. There are 100,000,000 satoshis in 1 bitcoin.

BIOGRAPHY

Satoshi Nakamoto

The person who created bitcoin in 2009 gave his name as Satoshi Nakamoto and claimed to have been born in Japan in 1975. Aside from being active in the development of bitcoin until late 2010, not much else is known about Nakamoto. We don't know if he or she is a real person or a pseudonym. We don't know if he or she is even Japanese. What we do know is that the person who set up the system has roughly 1 million bitcoins.

How bitcoin works

Each cryptocurrency works in its own way, but many follow the lead of bitcoin. For a bitcoin transaction to work, both parties need to have a wallet (where currency can be stored) and an address (a string of letters and numbers that are used to send currency to and from).

Miners use complex cryptography to ensure the transaction is possible and receive a small amount of bitcoin in return.

Everybody can see the list of bitcoin transactions on the blockchain.

△ **Wallets and addresses**
Bitcoin is stored in a user's wallet. When making a transaction, users are encouraged to create a new address to maintain their anonymity.

△ **Bitcoin clients**
Users can then make a payment by using their computer or a handheld device. All they need is a bitcoin program, called a client.

△ **Miners**
The payment is then verified by miners. Miners are the people who maintain bitcoin. They check that someone spending bitcoins has enough for the transaction.

△ **The blockchain**
Once a transaction is made, it is added to the blockchain: the list of all confirmed bitcoin transactions.

What can they be used for?

People have used cryptocurrencies to buy many things, from coffee, to a house, and even to a seat reservation on a suborbital space flight. That said, the lack of understanding and the fluctuating value of cryptocurrencies mean that many businesses are reluctant to accept them.

▷ **Untraceable transaction**
Perhaps the most useful thing to use bitcoin for is to pay for things that either the seller or buyer (or both) want to keep untraceable.

Value

Bitcoins are worth what someone is prepared to offer for them, and for that reason, they fluctuate in value. Cryptocurrencies are still considered to be volatile, which means they are likely to experience big swings in value, as they are relatively new and nobody is sure what will happen to them in future.

> "[Bitcoin is] potentially the **greatest social network** of them all."
> **Tyler Winklevoss (b. 1981), American entrepreneur**

Just like a natural resource, bitcoin is mined, but it is digitally mined.

△ **Finite number**
Bitcoin's creators decided that, like a natural resource, there is a finite supply of bitcoin. Only 21 million bitcoins will ever be created—it's expected that the last batch will emerge in 2140. This will potentially increase its value over time.

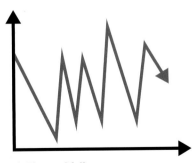

△ **Rise and fall**
Cryptocurrencies rely on people having confidence in being able to use them. They have no inherent value of their own. When a lot of people feel more confident about them, the value goes up, and it goes down when they don't.

△ **Robberies**
Though cryptocurrencies are designed to be anonymous, there has been an increasing number of robberies as they have become more valuable. These cause a drop in confidence of the currency, which results in fewer people wanting them.

REAL WORLD
Decentralization

Cryptocurrencies are decentralized, which means that no government oversees and regulates them. For a lot of cryptocurrency users, this is a positive thing, as they tend to feel that governmental interference has a negative impact on the value of money. At the same time, because no central power takes care of bitcoin, there is no authority to make sure it runs as planned and that if a massive crash happens users will not lose their money.

Global connectivity

The Internet has changed the way people connect, share, and learn. In many countries, it's an essential tool for schools and businesses. However, only half of the world's population is connected.

SEE ALSO

❮ **150–151** The Internet and the World Wide Web
❮ **196–197** Social media platforms
❮ **212–213** Net neutrality

A new human right

Mark Zuckerberg, the American founder of Facebook, argues that Internet access should be considered a basic human right, just like healthcare or clean water. Access to the Internet means access to knowledge. People in remote areas can find education, medical information, and weather data if they have a reliable Internet connection. Small businesses can increase their visibility and reach more customers online. Zuckerberg founded the nonprofit organization Internet.org to attempt to bring Internet connectivity to people in developing countries.

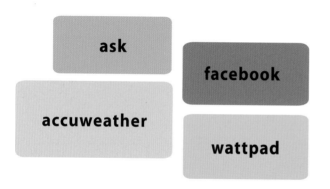

REAL WORLD

Project Aquila

Project Aquila is another Internet.org initiative. With a carbon-fiber body and a 111 ft (34 m) wingspan, Aquila is a solar-powered drone that acts as a moving cell tower located 11–17 miles (18–28 km) above ground. The goal is to create a network of drones in the stratosphere. The drones' mobility allows them to reach remote areas that don't have Wi-Fi access. Internet.org is also conducting research with high-energy lasers to increase transmission speeds.

◁ **Free Basics**
Free Basics is a partnership between Internet.org and phone companies within developing countries. The service allows users access to certain websites for free. This is great for users who can't afford a data plan, but some critics believe it affects net neutrality.

Laptops for all

Since 2006, the nonprofit initiative One Laptop Per Child (OLPC) has shipped its distinctive white and green XO laptops to kids all over the world. The XO is small and robust, can connect to the Internet, and is packed full of educational potential. OLPC hopes that the laptops will give children the tools to learn and unlock their own educational potential, and provide an extra reason to bring increased Internet connectivity to developing countries.

▷ **Educational benefits**
Communities with XO laptops report kids coming to school more often and staying in school longer. Students keep the laptops and can use them for homework and making school projects at night.

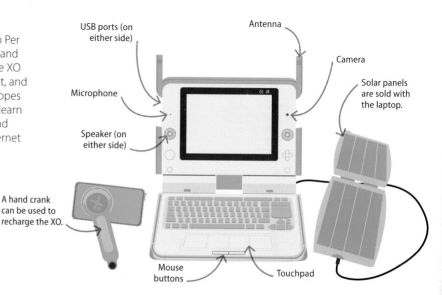

USB ports (on either side)

Antenna

Camera

Microphone

Solar panels are sold with the laptop.

Speaker (on either side)

A hand crank can be used to recharge the XO.

Mouse buttons

Touchpad

Project Loon

Project Loon is Google's version of cell phone towers in the stratosphere, with balloons instead of drones. At high altitudes, the balloons can avoid storms, birds, and aeroplane traffic. The winds are also a lot more predictable there. The balloons can be directed up or down to make use of air currents. In early tests, the balloons burst when they got too high. They also had problems with leaks. Now, however, the design has been improved, and balloons can stay airborne for more than 100 days.

Disaster relief ▽
The balloons are relatively cheap and quick to build. This is especially important for disaster relief projects, when local infrastructure may have been wiped out and people urgently need the ability to communicate.

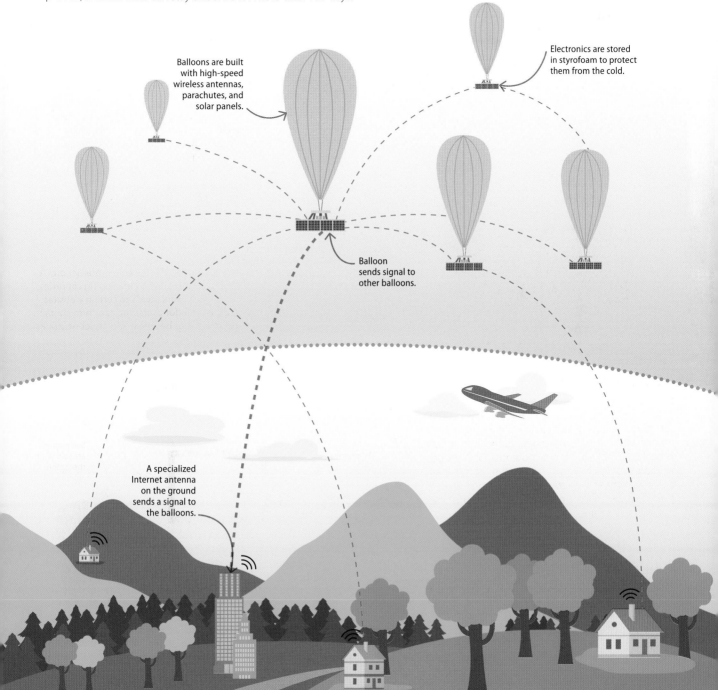

Balloons are built with high-speed wireless antennas, parachutes, and solar panels.

Electronics are stored in styrofoam to protect them from the cold.

Balloon sends signal to other balloons.

A specialized Internet antenna on the ground sends a signal to the balloons.

Biological interfaces

SEE ALSO
❮ **64–65** Hidden computers
❮ **220–221** Computer science and disabilities
❮ **224–225** Predicting the future

A biological interface is a technology that connects a biological system (such as a human's muscle) to a digital system (such as a computer). The interface is the point where the two meet.

How computers help

Digital systems are simple and straightforward. By contrast, biological systems have evolved over thousands of years by trial and error, and while they're very effective, they are not straightforward. When something in a human body breaks down, such as a weak heart or bad eyes, it can be extremely difficult to fix. Digital technologies aren't a perfect substitute, but they're relatively easy to produce and control. We can use them to tweak, correct, and enhance human organs. The biggest challenge is understanding the biological system well enough to interact with it.

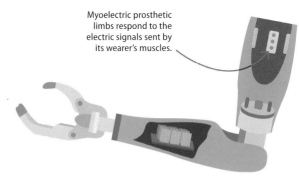

Myoelectric prosthetic limbs respond to the electric signals sent by its wearer's muscles.

△ **Prosthetics**
Prosthetics are used to replace lost arms, legs, and teeth, but can also be used to replace hearts. They range from motor-powered machines to metal rods with hinges. 3D printing technology has made it possible to build sophisticated, flexible, and affordable high-quality prosthetics. This is especially significant in developing countries.

Biometric passports

Biometric passports are passports that come embedded with a chip that stores the biological information of the holder. Sometimes this is simply the passport holder's name, details, signature, and picture. In other countries, the information includes fingerprints or eye maps. Some airports, such as those in Zurich, Switzerland, and Hong Kong, China, are testing new facial recognition software for check-ins and boarding gates, hoping to make the process safer and more efficient.

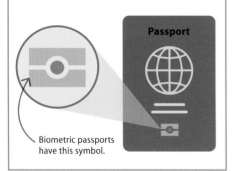

Biometric passports have this symbol.

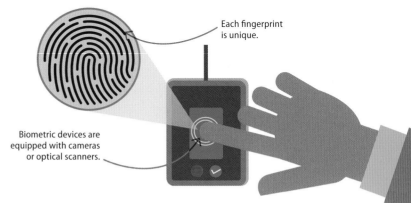

Each fingerprint is unique.

Biometric devices are equipped with cameras or optical scanners.

△ **Biometrics**
Biometrics are digital recordings of physical traits that can be used to identify a person. Examples include fingerprints, retina scans, voice recognition, and even a person's gait. Biometrics can be added to smartphones, ATMs, and locks. It's a more reliable system than keycards or passwords, but it raises the possibility of identity theft.

Implants

An implant is any device inserted inside the body. Some implants double as prosthetics, while others are enhancements, such as orthopedic pins or rods that support damaged bones. Other implants monitor bodily functions and automatically administer medicine based on its readings. While implant surgery is becoming safer and more common, there's always a risk that the body will reject the implant.

IN DEPTH

Going forward

It's impossible to tell where the future of biological interfaces is heading, but it's clear that they are becoming more common, and 3D printing is making them cheaper. There are many upcoming possibilities, from implanted chips used for identification to sensors that heighten our senses or give us new ones.

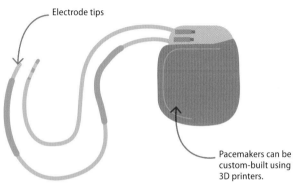

△ **Pacemaker**

A pacemaker consists of a battery, a generator, and wires with electrode tips implanted inside the chest cavity. It uses electric pulses to keep the heart beating in a regular rhythm. Certain pacemakers can also monitor a patient's vital signs, such as blood temperature, natural electrical activity, and breathing rate.

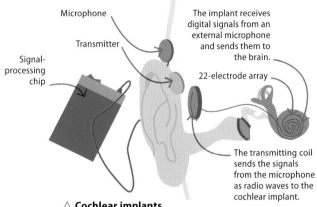

△ **Cochlear implants**

These implants are used for patients who are deaf or near-deaf. Unlike standard hearing aids, they require an implant attached to the cochlea, inside the ear canal. After surgery, it takes a few weeks of training for people with cochlear implants to interpret the new sounds they're hearing.

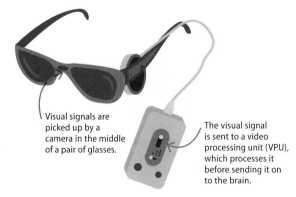

△ **Eye implants**

Companies are developing bionic eyes for people who are almost completely blind. Electrodes are implanted on and inside the eye in order to bypass natural photoreceptors and send electric signals directly to the brain. While still in the development stage, it's one of the most promising technologies for regaining sight.

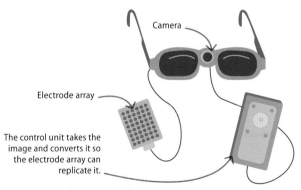

△ **Seeing with your tongue**

The BrainPort comes in two parts. The first is a pair of sunglasses with a digital camera. The second is a chip with 400 electrodes that sits on the user's tongue and translates the camera's video into electric signals. At first the data is meaningless, but with training, users can interpret visual images.

Artificial intelligence

SEE ALSO

❮ **32–33** Computing since the 1940s

❮ **224–225** Predicting the future

❮ **226–227** The Internet of Things

Artificial Intelligence (AI) is a family of algorithms that mimics the human behaviors of learning or reasoning. Most AIs are designed for analyzing data, pattern recognition, and simulations.

Playing with intelligence

One way the intelligence of an AI can be measured is by how it makes choices based on a set of rules, such as the rules of a game. Once the rules have been outlined, the AI simulates the outcomes of the various moves open to it and takes stock at each stage of the game to work out if it is going well.

A well-chosen heuristic gives the illusion of an intelligent opponent.

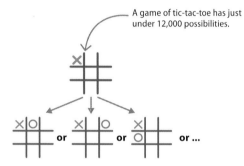

A game of tic-tac-toe has just under 12,000 possibilities.

△ **Likely outcomes**

The AI simulates a game move by move, working out how a particular move is likely to work out and how an opponent may choose to respond.

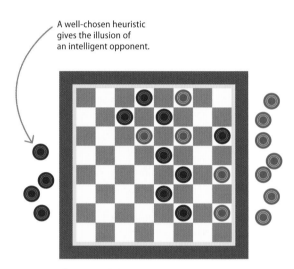

△ **Rules of thumb**

The AI uses heuristics (also known as "rules of thumb") to work out how the game is going. The heuristic might be how many pieces it has left in relation to the opponent.

Machine learning

Machine learning is the branch of computer science that gives a computer the ability to learn to do something with data, rather than explicitly programming it. A machine-learning algorithm learns by sifting through data bit by bit, and gradually building a model of which criteria are important and which are not for its chosen task. Eventually, it works out a way to do a task on its own based on what it knows and what it can do. Machine-learning algorithms can be used to play games, optimize transport schedules, or be the basis for robots to understand how to do work or recognize people.

▷ **Gradually becoming intelligent**

The more data that a machine-learning algorithm processes, the closer it gets to understanding and ultimately acting upon its task.

The Turing test

In 1950, English scientist Alan Turing invented a test of artificial intelligence. The test involves an evaluator who is able to ask a computer and a human questions by text, and they are able to reply. The evaluator doesn't know which of the responses are from the human and which are from the computer. If the evaluator cannot tell which is the machine more than 50 percent of the time, then the machine has passed the test and is said to be intelligent.

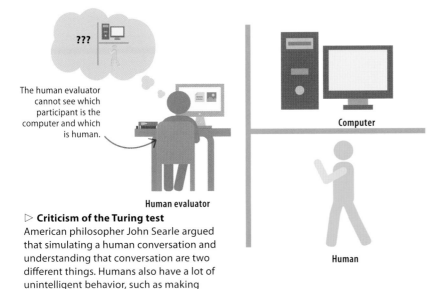

???

The human evaluator cannot see which participant is the computer and which is human.

Computer

Human evaluator

Human

▷ **Criticism of the Turing test**
American philosopher John Searle argued that simulating a human conversation and understanding that conversation are two different things. Humans also have a lot of unintelligent behavior, such as making spelling mistakes that might influence a human evaluator during the Turing test.

Issues

Allowing AI to make its own decisions might seem safe in a controlled environment, but if intelligent machines were to be used in a wider way, they could be involved in real-world life-and-death situations.

• **Ethical dilemmas:** A self-driving car hits a patch of ice and skids out of control. The car can either swerve into a wall and kill the passenger inside, or veer into a crowd, saving the passenger but potentially killing more people. Before, this decision rested with the human driver, but now it rests with the programmers of the self-driving car. The programmers also have another ethical dilemma in that their customers are unlikely to want to buy a car that will prioritize the safety of others over them—which may make the programmers lean toward saving the passenger at other people's expense.

• **Bad data:** If an AI is fed the wrong data, or if there are errors in the data or the way the AI is designed, it can make bad decisions. It can be difficult to identify and locate these problems.

General intelligence

Another goal of AI is to create a general intelligence capable of learning different types of information instead of one specific task. Logic AI, also known as classical AI, represents knowledge using symbols. It takes a top-down approach to intelligence by defining formulas that the computer can use to solve varied problems. A general intelligence AI will be able to figure out when something it already knows is relevant and useful to complete whatever task it is currently attempting.

"The **greatest danger** of artificial intelligence is that **people conclude too early** that **they understand** it."
Eliezer Yudkowsky (b. 1979), AI researcher and writer

▷ **Artificial neural networks (ANN)**
ANN algorithms are a kind of general intelligence and are loosely inspired by real brains. Layers of interconnected digital "neurons" manipulate numerical data using statistical equations.

Why now?

An increase in computing power has allowed increasingly sophisticated AI to be developed. Neural networks have been around since the 1970s, but until recently they took too much time to train. AI studies will affect the real world more and more as people continue to develop computer chips with ever-greater processing power.

Thinking outside the chip

SEE ALSO
❮ **76–77** Algorithms
❮ **104–105** Boolean logic
❮ **230–231** Cryptocurrencies

Computer science is more than learning languages or coding games. Since the middle of the 20th century, it has transformed the industries of the world.

Problem solving

Every advance in technology has been a response to a problem. Many early computers were created to help decode enemy communications in WWII. Bitcoin was invented to make digital transactions easier and to create a currency that wasn't tied to a particular country. To find a solution, it's important to first identify a problem.

▷ **Everything is connected**
The key to invention is identifying gaps. The world is full of problems just waiting for someone to come along with a solution. If an issue can be identified, classified, and discussed, then a solution can be dreamed up and potentially brought into reality.

STEM and STEAM

STEM is an acronym for science, technology, engineering, and math. It's an approach to learning that focuses on collaboration and hands-on problem solving. STEAM adds arts to the mix and encourages students to apply a creative and innovative approach to STEM projects. The goal is to create solutions to problems that take different perspectives and ideas into consideration. Computers are at the center of each of the STEAM disciplines.

△ **Science**
Science unlocks the secrets of the world around us. It teaches us how to plan, gather data, and critically evaluate our results.

△ **Technology**
Technology is everywhere. Understanding its strengths and weaknesses helps us become smarter, more responsible citizens.

Changing the world

Changing the world may seem like an impossible task, but all it takes is a special way of thinking. Innovation in the world of computer science requires looking beyond the details of algorithms, computer logic, and hardware and asking how computers can make the world a better place. Existing technology can then be improved to meet those needs.

"**Education** is the most **powerful weapon** which you can use to **change the world**."
Nelson Mandela (1918–2013), former president of South Africa

Ask questions
A good scientist doesn't accept facts at face value. Why must things work a certain way? Could they be better? Whether it's wondering if a highway could be more efficient or tackling the pollution problem, challenging the status quo is the first step to change.

Look for resources
It's important to understand a problem before it can be solved. Books, movies, podcasts, and experts in different fields can all help to give a complete picture of the issues being tackled. The best answers are often found in tiny details that are easy to overlook.

Try new things
The more things you're exposed to, the higher the odds that you'll make a new connection between two ideas. This leads to new technologies and new solutions. It also keeps people open-minded and humble, qualities that are essential in coming up with new ideas.

Ask other people's opinions
Many heads are better than one. People from different fields, ages, and ethnicities have different perspectives that can help shed light on a problem. The world is a big, complex place. It's unlikely that any one individual or group has the answers to everything.

△ **Engineering**
Engineering is a branch of applied science that's all about building and designing things, from prosthetic limbs, to computers, to skyscrapers.

△ **Art**
Arts is about lateral thinking: finding innovative solutions by approaching problems from new angles. It's creative, fun, and challenging.

△ **Mathematics**
Math is all about discovering patterns in the world around us. It's a key tool in fields such as finance, medicine, business, and of course science.

Careers

Computer science is one of the fastest-growing industries in the world. It contains a variety of jobs for different interests and skill sets, all centered around computing, data, and logic.

SEE ALSO	
❮ 28–29	Computer science
❮ 48–49	What is hardware?
❮ 62–63	Gaming consoles
❮ 172–173	Testing

Education

Getting a degree in computer science or a related field, which can take 4 to 5 years of study at a college or university, is the most straightforward entry into a career in computer science. These courses give students a complete understanding of the basics of computing, including application design, networking, databases, and security. Many programs also have the option of work placements. Some employers do not specifically require applicants to have a degree, however, and might be happy to hire people with fewer educational credentials and more experience in making things.

△ **Computer engineering**
A degree in computer engineering focuses on computing at the hardware level. Students are taught how to design circuits, processors, and sensors. Courses include physics and electrical engineering.

△ **Computer science**
The most general degree, a computer science degree teaches a little bit of everything and tends to have a more theoretical approach to the subject. It allows specializations like artificial intelligence (AI), networking, or cybersecurity.

△ **Projects**
When hiring, some companies pay more attention to personal projects than educational credentials. Projects demonstrate an applicant's ability to take initiative and are a good indicator of their skills. Examples of projects include games, mobile apps, or tailored algorithms made by a developer.

△ **Software engineering**
Software engineering emphasizes the software development process, including requirements analysis and testing. People who study software engineering tend to find it a very hands-on area, with plenty of practical work and fewer optional specializations.

△ **Online courses and certifications**
As the demand for computer science skills increases, online programming courses are becoming more popular. These courses tend to be more focused, more practical, and shorter than a full university degree.

Software developer

Software development is a great job for people who are meticulous, logical, and independent. It gives them the satisfaction of creating and improving programs. While coding is a solo activity, developers usually work in small teams, so collaboration is a crucial part of the job. It helps to study for a specialization, but it's often possible to get hired with a general computer science degree and learn the specifics on the job.

▽ **What they do**
Software developers write code for websites, desktop programs, and apps. They create everything from video games to specialized software for telecommunications, and from rockets to medical devices.

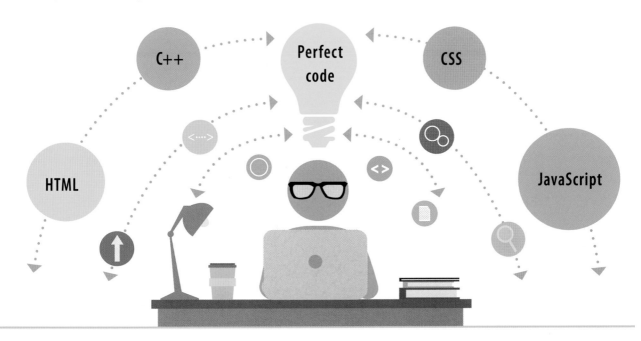

Hardware engineer

Hardware engineers design, test, and build components such as microchips and circuit boards. They also create programs to connect hardware to software. Hardware engineers face many of the same challenges as software developers but at the machine and physical hardware level. They tend to write short, specific code in languages such as C and C++ instead of developing massive applications. They have important roles in fields such as robotics and product design.

▷ **Making physical things**
Hardware engineers are detail-oriented and love challenges. They include people who like to tinker with physical things and want to create physical products.

System administrator

System administrators, also called sysadmins, make a company's technology work. They choose what systems their company should purchase, keep machines up-to-date, and fix bugs when they pop up. Sysadmins also make sure the various software running on a system meet the needs of the users. Sometimes they need to write quick scripts or tweak programs to fit with existing infrastructure. System administration is great for people who thrive on constant challenges and like doing a little bit of everything.

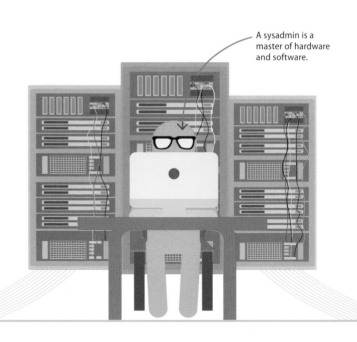

A sysadmin is a master of hardware and software.

▷ **Tech support**
Sysadmins also do tech support. In bigger companies, there are specific employees who run the help desk and are supervised by the sysadmin.

Research and development

Innovation is the key to a better world. Researchers look for problems and create solutions in the form of new algorithms, programs, and technology. They can work as professors at universities or be employed by public or private companies. Robotics, quantum computing, machine learning, and big data are just a few exciting trends that researchers are working on today.

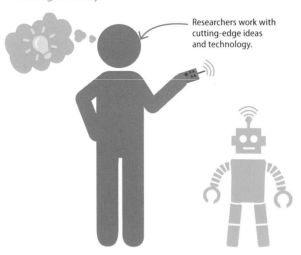

Researchers work with cutting-edge ideas and technology.

△ **Pushing the limits**
Depending on the project, research can be solitary or collaborative. People who enjoy pushing the limits of technology and using their creativity are well suited to this field.

Teacher

There are many opportunities to teach computer science at an elementary, high school, or college level. Teachers need both technical knowledge and social skills. They create lesson plans, give lectures, and check assignments. Museums and youth outreach groups often need educational content for kids in a tech-saturated world, and they need a tech-savvy person to write it.

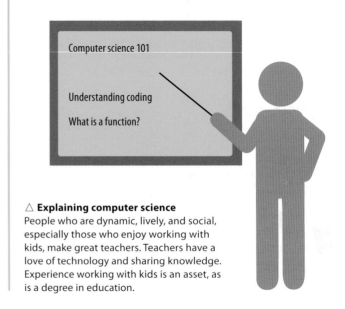

Computer science 101

Understanding coding

What is a function?

△ **Explaining computer science**
People who are dynamic, lively, and social, especially those who enjoy working with kids, make great teachers. Teachers have a love of technology and sharing knowledge. Experience working with kids is an asset, as is a degree in education.

Quality Assurance tester

Quality Assurance (QA) testers make sure that software is bug-free and ready to be shipped to customers. They design test cases, play around with software, and do their best to break programs—only to fix them afterward. Testing allows programmers to explore all the features of a product, as well as constantly learn new things. It's especially important in security fields.

▽ **Looking for flaws**
QA testers are people who are detail-oriented. A good tester has high standards, a good understanding of customers, and an eye for potential flaws.

Computer forensic analyst

Computer forensic analysts extract information from digital devices, such as flash drives or hard drives, in order to help solve crimes. With the growth of the Internet, combating cybercrime is more important than ever. Computer forensic analysts blend technical skills with detective work and often work for law enforcement agencies. Experience in studying psychology, sociology, and accounting all come in handy.

Solving problems ▽
Computer forensic analysts are people who like finding, analyzing, and piecing together digital evidence to solve crimes. Although some higher education programs exist, teaching is often done on the job through apprenticeships.

Technical writer

While many programmers are great at writing code, they're not always great at explaining it. Technical writers help fill this gap by writing documentation, instruction manuals, or computing guides for beginners and experts. They can also be employed by magazines and newspapers, covering stories about technology and science.

▷ **Writing whizzes**
Technical writers tend to be people who enjoy writing more than coding but have a love of technology. Good writers understand their audience and can express ideas in a simple and clear way.

Game developer

Game developers use their technical skills to bring video games to life. There are many specializations, including graphics, networking, and AI. A game developer might write code to render background textures or handle the physics of character movement. Experience with efficient, low-level languages such as C and C++ is handy, as well as knowledge of scripting languages.

▷ **Game design**
Some developers go on to become game designers. They're responsible for the overall vision and concept: the art, the story, and the gameplay.

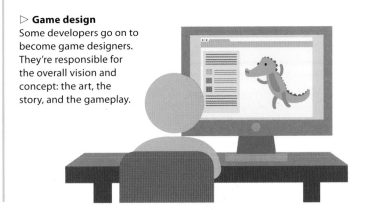

Useful links

There is a wealth of information online that covers the concepts mentioned in this book. Use a search engine to find out more.

Getting started

CS for All Teachers
A resource mainly for computer science educators, which contains projects, information, ideas for lessons, and age-specific guides.

Digital Unite: Guides
An array of resources that aim to help digital newcomers understand how to use computers and the Internet.

Wikibooks: Computers for Beginners
A complete guide for people with little or no prior computer skills.

TechRadar
Up-to-date articles and advice on buying and using technology.

Homeland Security: Cyber Security Division
Guidance, education and research, and threat reports from the official US Government website.

OpenLearn: Information on the Web
A free online course on how to use search engines to look for text and images, and advice on how to critically assess information online.

GCF Learn Free: Basic Troubleshooting Techniques
A free guide on some of the most common problems users face with computers and how to resolve them.

CSTeachers.org
Information for K–12 computer science educators worldwide.

What is computer science?

Intel: Making Silicon Chips
Information on how computer chips are made.

Computer History Museum
A museum dedicated to preserving and presenting the stories and artifacts of the information age.

Centre for Computing History Timeline
A timeline showing the progress of computational devices.

OpenLearn: Computers and Computer Systems
A free online course on computers, from hardware to how computers store and use data.

Hardware

Raspberry Pi
Resources on coding and physical computing for beginners.

Sonic Pi
An open-source programming environment for creating sounds and music with Raspberry Pi.

TeCoEd
A resource mainly for Raspberry Pi, but this website also contains game-based activities aimed at helping elementary school, middle school, and high school kids learn how to code.

Khan Academy: How Computers Work
Short YouTube lectures and reading material on how computers work, from what makes a computer to how hardware and software integrate.

Computational thinking

Khan Academy: Algorithms
Short YouTube lectures and reading material on algorithms, from types of algorithm, to sorting, to types of searches.

OpenLearn: Computational Thinking
Free online course on computational thinking from the Open University.

Data

Simon Singh, The Black Chamber
A comprehensive guide to encryption with interactive examples for beginners.

Unicode Consortium
Information on world scripts and emojis.

Lingojam Binary Translator
Translate English text into the binary representation used by a computer.

The Logic Lab
Explore logic gates by creating interactive circuits.

Studio.code.org: Binary Game
See how binary code works by playing this fun game.

OpenLearn: Analogue Universe, Digital Worlds
A free online course on the differences between analog and digital, and how analog information is represented by a computer in the form of numbers.

Khan Academy: Cryptography
Short YouTube lectures and reading material on cryptography, from ancient times to the modern day.

Programming techniques

Codecademy
Online interactive tutorials to learn programming languages such as Python, Java, HTML, and CSS.

Computerphile YouTube Channel
Beginner-friendly videos where experts explore the inner workings of computers. Includes computer history.

HackerRank
Fun coding challenges and global coding competitions.

Stack Overflow
The world's largest developer community, with extensive forums to answer questions and help troubleshoot problems.

TutorialsPoint
Simple, clear explanations on a variety of technical subjects.

Tynker
Online platform that introduces kids to programming through games and mods.

Programming languages

CoderDojo
A global network of free, volunteer-led, community-based programming clubs for young people.

EarSketch
A free educational programming environment that seeks to teach people how to code in Python and JavaScript through music composition and remixing.

W3 Schools
Tutorials on a wide range of programming languages used to create websites.

Code Club International
An international network of volunteers and educators who run free coding clubs for young people aged 9–13.

Code.org
Learn to code with fun tutorials or try out coding in an "Hour of Code."

Scratch
A drag-and-drop programming language ideal for kids and beginners, with a global community that shares projects.

Python.org
The online hub for the open-source programming language Python, with guides, third-party applications, and general information.

Cplusplus.com
Information, tutorials, and articles on the C++ programming language.

Javascript.com
Resources, news, and guides on the JavaScript programming language.

Kodu Game Lab
Create, share, and learn about the Kodu programming language.

Ruby
Downloads, documentation, libraries, and general information about the Ruby programming language.

Stack Overflow
Developers give advice to other programmers on coding issues.

Mother Tongues of Computer Languages
Diagram showing the evolution of programming languages.

Networks

ConnectSafely.org
Resources to help users understand and manage the risks of new technology.

FCC.gov
Official website of the Federal Communications Commission, containing consumer guides and telecommunications news.

Know Your Mobile
Reviews, user guides, and news about phones and wearable technology.

OpenLearn: Protocols in Multi-Service Networks
A free online course on how connected devices communicate with each other.

OpenLearn: Living with the Internet—Keeping it Safe
A free online course on malware, and advice on how to protect computers and networks from it.

Khan Academy: Internet 101
Short YouTube lectures and reading material on the Internet, from how it works to cybersecurity.

Safekids.com
Safety advice and browsing guidelines for both parents and children.

Website and app construction

Android Developers
Resources and technical documentation for Android app developers.

Apple Developer
Resources and technical documentation for Apple developers, including iOS and macOS platforms.

Get Coding Kids
This site contains coding missions that teach the basics of using HTML, CSS, and JavaScript and make it possible for kids to make a website, app, and game.

GitHub Community Forum
Global community of developers collaborating on projects and sharing ideas.

World Wide Web Consortium (W3C)
Organization that creates and manages standards for the web.

Digital behaviors

Cybersmile
Advice on how to deal with online bullying.

PBS Cyberbullying
Resources for parents and young people about online bullying.

Parenting for a Digital Future
Blog about bringing up kids in the digital age.

Social media

Internet Matters
Information, advice from experts, and tips on social media—from what it is, to what children use it for, and how to keep them safe.

Common Sense Media: Social Media
An independent, nonprofit website dedicated to helping young people by providing unbiased information, trusted advice, and innovative tools to help them cope in the digital world.

NSPCC: Net Aware
A UK-based guide for parents on social media platforms, with a searchable database, statistics on why kids use specific social media sites, and information from other parents on how robust things such as the privacy and reporting settings are.

Digital issues

SWGfL: Digital Literacy
Free materials designed to help people to think critically, behave safely, and participate responsibly in the digital world, divided by Key Stage or Year Group.

Internetworldstats: Digital Divide
Statistics and information on the digital divide, with an overview of the topic.

Center for Global Development: Data and Technology
Information on how data and technology are helping the quest to reduce poverty and inequality in developing countries.

Computerscience.org: Women in Computer Science
An overview of the current status of women in computer science, with statistics and career and support resources.

Girl Develop It
Girl Develop It is a nonprofit organization that exists to provide affordable and judgment-free opportunities for women interested in learning web and software development.

Girls In Tech
A nonprofit organization focused on the engagement, education, and empowerment of women in the technology industry, with chapters all over the world.

Association for Women in Science
An organization that promotes equality, research, and the advancement of women working across a broad range of scientific industries.

Black Girls Code
A nonprofit organization aimed at providing technology education for young and preteen African-American girls.

TED Talks
Online lecture series with prestigious speakers. Topics include technology, entertainment, and design.

Wired Magazine
Monthly magazine focusing on the global impact of new technology.

The future of computers

IEEE Spectrum
Magazine edited by the Institute of Electrical and Electronics Engineers with articles, blogs, and videos about cutting-edge technology.

Maker Share
Online community of makers documenting projects and organizing workshops.

OpenLearn: Machines, Minds and Computers
A free online course on what intelligence is and how computers may become intelligent in the future.

OpenLearn: The Internet of Everything
A free online course on the Internet of Things, from the technologies that underpin it to what the data produced can be used for.

STEMCenterUSA.com
Resources to help bring STEM into the classroom.

Glossary

abstraction
The process of filtering out unnecessary information when solving a problem.

algorithm
A series of steps taken to solve a problem or carry out a task.

analog
Relating to or using signals or information represented by a continuously variable physical quality, such as weight, length, or voltage.

application (app)
A piece of software designed to achieve a particular purpose.

application programming interface (API)
An API is a set of functions that accesses the features of data of an operating system, application, or other service.

array
A collection of similar elements with a specific order.

artificial intelligence (AI)
A type of intelligence that is demonstrated by computers.

ASCII
Short for American Standard Code for Information Interchange. ASCII is a character-encoding standard for electronic communication.

assembler
A program that translates assembly language (a low-level programming language) into machine code.

augmented reality
A view of a physical, real-world environment that has been enhanced with virtual elements.

augmented virtuality
A view of a mostly virtual environment that has been enhanced with real-world elements.

bandwidth
The amount of data that can flow into a network.

big data
A huge amount of data, such as that collected by Internet-connected smart devices.

binary system
A coding system that uses 0s and 1s to represent information in a computer.

biological interface
A technology that connects a biological system (such as a human's muscle) to a digital system (such as a computer). The interface is the point where the two meet.

biometric data
Any biological information—such as a person's height or weight.

bit
The basic unit of information in the binary system, a bit is a single 0 or 1. Eight bits make up 1 byte.

Boolean logic
A branch of mathematics that has two values: 0 and 1. Also called Boolean algebra.

bug
A software error in code.

Cascading Style Sheets (CSS)
A programming language that describes how to display HTML elements in a web browser.

central processing unit (CPU)
The part of a computer that controls most of its operations. It consists of the control unit (CU), which carries out instructions, and the arithmetic logic unit (ALU), which performs calculations. The CPU is also known as the microprocessor.

cloud
A term used for specialized computers that provide services through the Internet, such as storing files.

code
Instructions written in a programming language that tell a computer to do something.

compiler
A program that converts an entire program into an OS-specific file in one go.

compression
Reducing the size of a file in order to make it easier to share or store. Lossless compression keeps the original information intact; lossy compression results in some loss of information.

computational thinking
The thought process in figuring out problems and finding solutions in ways that can be understood by a computer, a human, or both.

computer
An electronic device that manipulates data.

computer chip
A set of electronic circuits on a small piece of semiconducting material, usually silicon. Also known as an integrated circuit.

computer science
The study of the use of computers: how they work and what they can be used for.

constant
A quantity that can't change when a program is running, if ever—for example, the value of Pi.

cookie
A packet of data sent by a website to a user's computer that is used to identify the user and track their browsing.

cryptocurrency
A wholly digital form of currency that operates without a central bank.

cybersecurity
The protection of computers and data from attacks by malicious people online.

dark web
The most restricted part of the Internet, viewable only by using a special web browser.

data
Information that is processed or stored by a computer.

database
A program that lets people store and search data effectively.

debugging
The process of finding and fixing bugs (errors) in programs.

decomposition
The process of breaking a problem down into smaller subproblems.

decryption
The process of using a cipher and a key to reveal the meaning of encrypted text.

deep web
The part of the Internet that is not listed on search engines.

digital
Involving the use of computer technology or the use or storage of data as digital signals. Digital signals are expressed in 0s and 1s.

digital divide
The difference between people who have access to digital devices and the Internet and those who do not.

digital identity
The set of identifiers used by organizations to authenticate who a user is so the user can access the organization's services.

digital literacy
The ability to be able to find, use, and share accurate information online.

encoding
The process of turning information—such as images, sounds, or text—into a format a computer can understand.

encryption
The process of making a message unreadable to everyone except the person or people it was intended for.

file
A resource for storing information on a computer.

firmware
A type of program that is embedded into a device's CPU and controls how the device works.

function
A mathematical formula that takes input data and acts upon it to produce output data. Functions are made up of variables, constants, and arrays.

functional language
A programming language that defines a program as a series of mathematical functions.

geek
An informal term for someone who is obsessive about a certain topic or group of related topics.

gender gap
The difference in status, opportunities, and attitudes between men and women.

hacking
Any act that makes a piece of technology do something it wasn't intended to do. Hackers can be grouped into white, gray, and black hat hackers, depending on their intentions.

hardware
The physical parts of a computer that exist as objects in the real world.

heuristic
Any approach to problem-solving or learning that uses a quick and simple approach, as opposed to a thorough one. A "rule of thumb" is an example of a heuristic.

hub
The central part of a network, through which information flows into and out of the network.

Hypertext Markup Language (HTML)
A programming language for creating webpages and web applications. HTML is divided into elements called tags, semantics, and attributes that each hold a specific type of information.

Hypertext Transfer Protocol (HTTP)
The data transfer protocol used on the World Wide Web.

imperative language
A programming language that operates as a series of commands that are executed one by one.

input
Any information that is put in, taken in, or operated on by a process or system.

Internet
A massive global network created from connections between billions of computers.

Internet of Things
The name given to the network of interconnected devices with embedded computers.

interpreter
A program that translates and executes the source code of another computer program one line at a time.

key
In cryptography, any additional information that is used to encrypt or decrypt a message.

keylogger
A computer malware program that tracks what keyboard keys are pressed in order to gain access to passwords and other information.

logic gate
A device that carries out computer calculations with binary numbers.

machine code
Instructions that a computer can understand and uses to send instructions to the computer's hardware.

machine learning
The branch of computer science that gives a computer the ability to learn to do something with data, rather than explicitly programming it.

malware
Malicious software that gains illegal access to a computer or system. Malware includes worms, viruses, spyware, trojans, rootkits, ransomware, backdoors, and hybrid threats.

microprocessor
Another name for the central processing unit (CPU).

motherboard
The main circuit board of a computer, which holds the CPU, memory, and connectors for the hard drive and optical drives, among other connections. The motherboard allows hardware components of a computer to communicate with each other.

net neutrality
The principle that governments or ISPs should not block, discriminate, or charge users differently to access the Internet.

network
A group of connected devices that can share resources and data. Networks can be classified by size or topology (layout).

node
Any device that sends or receives data through a network.

object-oriented language
A programming language that includes the concept of objects that model real-world things. An object usually has fields (containing data) and methods (containing code) that represent behaviors.

online identity
The self or selves that a user presents to the online world.

operating system (OS)
Software that manages a computer's hardware and software resources and makes it easier for them to be used. Common examples are Linux, macOS, and Windows.

output
Something that is produced by a person or machine, or the place where information leaves a system.

pattern recognition
The process of seeing repetition in a predictable manner. Pattern recognition is an important part of computational thinking.

peripheral
Any piece of hardware that allows users to interact with a computer.

photoresist
A substance that is used in the manufacture of computer chips that protects parts of a chip in development from being eroded by the manufacturing process.

pixel
Short for picture element. A tiny area of illumination on a computer display screen, one of many from which an image is composed.

program
A collection of instructions that performs a specific task when executed by a computer.

programming
The process of giving instructions to a computer.

programming language
A formalized set of words and symbols that allows a person to give instructions to a computer. High-level languages are closer to human language. Low-level languages are closer to binary code.

protocol
A set of rules that governs the transmission of data between devices—for example, Hypertext Transfer Protocol, which is used for visiting websites.

random-access memory (RAM)
A computer system's short-term memory, used to store calculation data.

read-only memory (ROM)
A place where data that is needed for the computer to function, such as firmware and start-up instructions, is usually stored.

register
A place in a CPU where data currently being used can be stored temporarily.

relational database
The most common type of database, where information is stored in tables. The tables are made up of rows, called records, and columns, called fields.

resolution
A measure of the amount of information in a computer file, such as an image.

routing
The process of finding the shortest path between two devices across the Internet.

search engine
A program that looks through the World Wide Web for webpages containing particular words or phrases inputted by the user.

server
A computer program or device that responds to requests across a computer network to provide a network or data service.

social media bubble
The phenomenon of a user seeing only things they like on social media. Users in a social media bubble may be isolated from the ideas and opinions of anyone not in the bubble.

social media platform
A type of website or application that allows users to connect to each other and create and share content.

software
The operating system, programs, and firmware that allow a user to access a computer's hardware.

STEAM
An acronym for science, technology, engineering, arts, and mathematics.

streaming
The process of allowing a user to access information not stored on their computer over the Internet. Streaming is popular for watching films or listening to music online.

syntax
The structure of statements in a computer language.

transistor
A tiny device that is used to amplify or switch electric current.

translation
The process of converting one programming language into another. Translation usually refers to breaking a high-level language down into a low-level language.

Transmission Control Protocol / Internet Protocol (TCP/IP)
A set of rules that governs the connection of computer systems to the Internet.

troubleshooting
The process of fixing common problems that arise when using computer hardware or software.

truth tables
A diagram of inputs and outputs of a logic gate or circuit. In a truth table, the binary value 1 equals the logical value TRUE, and the binary value 0 equals FALSE.

Turing test
A test outlined by English mathematician Alan Turing that centers on the ability of an evaluator to assess whether any particular machine can be said to be intelligent.

Unicode
The single worldwide standard for encoding characters used in electronic communication. Unicode is much larger than ASCII.

Uniform Resource Locator (URL)
Also known a web address, URL is a standardized system for locating and identifying content on the World Wide Web.

universal serial bus (USB)
A standard developed to define cables, connectors, and their protocols for connection, communication, and power supply between computers and peripheral devices.

update
New code that is released by a programmer or company that fixes bugs or adds new features to a website, application, software, or program.

upgrade
Completely new software that is designed to replace an older website, application, software, or program.

variables
1 The nonessential details that alter how a model can behave or appeal.
2 Storage items that can take on more than one value during the course of a program.

virtual reality
A computer-generated 3D image or environment that can be interacted with in a seemingly real way.

viruses
Tiny pieces of code that attach themselves to pre-existing files before replicating themselves. Viruses corrupt data and slow down operating systems.

visual language
A programming language that is based on blocks of code instructions that the programmer fits together. Visual languages are ideal for children or people new to programming.

visualization
The process of turning information—such as a coordinates or a big dataset—into a model, graphs, or images.

webpage
A single destination on the World Wide Web.

website
A collection of webpages.

Wi-Fi
A facility allowing computers to connect to the Internet or communicate with each other wirelessly in a particular area.

World Wide Web
An information system that runs on the Internet that allows webpages to be connected to other webpages by hypertext links.

Index

3D movies 228
3D printing 224

A

A/S/L (age/sex/location) 178
abacuses 30
abstraction 68, 72–3, 124
accelerometers 53
accessibility options 221
activity trackers 57
adapters 144, 171
advertising, targeted 191, 207
Agile development style
    169, 175
AJAX (Asynchronous JavaScript
    And XML) 135
al-Jazari, Ismail 31
al-Khwārizmī, Abu Abdullah
    Muhammad ibn Mūsā 31, 77
Al-Kindi 31
algorithms 31, 69, 76–7, 118, 206
    ANN 237
    applying 102–3
    machine-learning 236
Allen, Paul 33, 55
Amazon 127
analog computers 100, 101
analog programming 100–1
analog signals 144
Analytical Engine 99
anonymous browsers 159
Antikythera mechanism 30
antivirus software 23
Apollo missions 81, 218
Apple App Store 200
Apple Computers 33
application programming
    interface (API) 124–5
applications 44, 45
apps 16, 19, 41, 53, 64
    app-based appliances 59
    charity-made 221
    social media 200–1
    updates 175
Arduino 54, 55
arithmetic logic unit (ALU) 42
ARPANET 150, 151
arrays 106, 107, 109
artificial intelligence (AI) 95,
    119, 236–7

artificial neural networks
    (ANN) 237
arts 239
ASCII 84–5
assemblers 112
assembly language 122
assistive technologies 220, 221
attributes 163
audio encoding 92
augmented reality (AR) 224, 228
autism spectrum disorders 221
automatons 60
avatars 178

B

Babbage, Charles 98, 99
backdoors 157
backing up 15
bandwidth 154, 155
BASIC 122, 123
Bedwel, Farida 221
Berners-Lee, Tim 150, 198
bias 211
big data 89, 224, 227
bigoted material 186
binary adders 87
binary code 30, 40, 80, 82–3,
    118, 119
binary searches 76
Bing 151
biochemical circuits 141
biological interfaces 234–5
biometrics 234
bitcoin 159, 230–1
bitmaps 90
bits 80
black hat hackers 22
blocks 137
blogs 18, 185
"Blue Screen of Death" 24
Bluetooth 64, 226
body movements 53, 62, 137
body suits, VR 229
Boole, George 104, 105
Boolean logic 86, 88, 104–5, 108
botnets 157, 159
boundaries, setting 180
Braille 83
branching 108, 169
breakpoints 115

browser extensions, fake 190
browsing habits 191
bubble sort 77
bubbles, social media 206–7
buffering 154
bugs 114–15, 173, 175
bus topology 147
buses 43
business 213
bytecode 128
bytes 80

C

C programming language
    118, 126
C++ programming language 127
calculating devices 30–1
calendars, online 18
cameras
    digital 48, 90–1
    see also webcams
careers 240–3
Carrier-Sense Multiple Access
    (CSMA) 149
Cascading Style Sheets (CSS)
    135, 162, 163, 164–5, 166
castle water clock 31
censorship 212–13
central processing unit (CPU)
    34, 42–3
chaining 132
chatrooms 178
chips 33, 35, 38–9, 42, 48, 80
    manufacturing 38–9
ciphertext 94, 95
circuit design 104, 105
class blueprints 107
classes 129, 165
client-server networks 145
clock-speed 43
closed networks 207
cloud APIs 125
cloud computing 151, 152–3
COBOL 119, 122
cochlear implants 235
codecs 93
coding communities 69
color 90
Colossus 32
communication protocols
    144, 148

communications, online 184–5
comparison websites 21
compatibility problems 167
compilers 82, 113
compression 19, 91
computational thinking
    66–77, 139
computer engineering 240
computer science 28–9, 240
confirmation bias 206
connected appliances 58–9
connection speeds 81
connections 148–9
connectivity, global 232–3
connectors 144
consoles 62–3
constants 106, 109
contactless payment 64
control unit (CU) 42
controllers, game 62, 137
cookies 157, 167, 191
Creative Commons 183, 199
criminal behavior 75
criminal websites 159
cross-site scripting (XSS) 167
crowdsourcing 185
cryptocurrencies 225, 230–1
cryptography 31, 32, 103
Curiosity rover 119
cyberbullying 188–9
cybercrime 212
cybersecurity 22–3

D

dark web 158, 159, 186
data 78–95
    clearing 191
    collection 63
    digital vs. analog 100
    displaying 40
    packets 149
    privacy 65, 190–1, 227
    retrieving 106–7
    storage 15, 81, 106–7, 152–3
    theft 22, 23, 65
    transferring 15
    what is data? 80
data processing 76–7
data protection 65
data usage 25
databases 88–9, 105

dating, online 196
DDoS (Distributed Denial of Service) attacks 157
debugging 115
decentralization 231
decimal system 82
declaration blocks 165
decomposition 68, 70–1
deep web 158–9
design patterns 170, 171
desktop computers 50, 51
developing countries 214, 216, 217, 232
Difference Engine 98
digital assistants 58, 225
digital citizens 182–3
digital data 100
digital divide 214–15, 216, 217
digital footprints 202
digital formats 144
digital identities 178–9
digital literacy 210–11
digital property 183
digital toys 60–1
digital world 28–9, 182
digitization 80–1, 83
Dijkstra, Edsger 103
disabled people 37, 53, 57, 220–1
disaster relief 216, 221, 233
discussion forums 196
Distributed Denial of Service (DDoS) 22
do-it-yourself (DIY) computers 54–5
DO-WHILE loops 109
documentation 174
Domain Name System (DNS) 148
domain-specific languages 140
dots per inch (DPI) 91
drawing 75
Dropbox 15
drugs 159, 186

E

EDSAC 32
education 229, 232, 239, 240, 242
  Internet and 215, 216
Eich, Brendan 166
the elderly 215
electronic tagging 57
elements 165
email 16, 17, 148, 156, 184
embedded systems 119
emoji 85

encryption 94–5, 149, 157, 158
End-User License Agreements (EULA) 179
engineering 239
ENIAC 32, 218
Enigma code 32, 95
environment 217
environments, programming 169
equality 218–19
Ethernet cables 37
ethics 65, 217, 237
expansion slots 35
extended ASCII 84–5
external hard drives 49
external hardware 48
eye implants 235

F

fabs 38
Facebook 19, 127, 146, 167, 179, 197, 200
Facetime 184
facial recognition 65
fake news 181, 207
fake profiles/accounts 187
feedback, integrated user 171
fiber optic cables 144, 151
Fibonacci 31
fields 88
File Transfer Protocol (FTP) 148
files
  ASCII 84
  compression 19
  deleting 15
  looking for 15
  opening 15
filtered reality 207
firewall software 23
fitness trackers 65, 225, 226
flowcharts 77
FOR loops 109
forensic analysts, computer 243
Fortran 119, 122
frame rate 93
Free Basics 232
freedom of speech 213
freezing 24, 115
frequency analysis 94
friends, online 199, 202
functional languages 121
functional tests 172
functions 109
future computers 222–43
  predicting 224–5

G

game developers 243
game programming 135, 138
gaming 33, 62–3, 229
  genres 63
  networks 205
  and social networks 204–5
  systems 155
  terms 205
Gates, Bill 33, 34, 55, 194, 217
Gauss, Karl 102
"geeks" 219
gems, Ruby 133
gender gap 218–19
general intelligence 237
gesture control 221
Git 169
glitches 24–5
global development 216–17, 239
Go 140
goals, gaming 204
Golden Shield Project 213
"gone viral" 195
Google 41, 127, 146, 151, 167, 233
Google Drive 15
Google Glass 57
Google Play 200
Gosling, James 128
GPS (Global Positioning System) 28, 103, 226
graphical user interfaces (GUIs) 173
graphics 43
graphics cards 63
graphics processing units (GPU) 49
gray hat hackers 22
gyroscopes 53

H

hackers 22–3, 103, 149, 157, 175, 185, 186, 190–1, 227
half-adders 87
Hamilton, Margaret 218
hard drives 35, 37, 44, 49
hardware 14, 41, 46–65
  capacity 81
  devices 48–9
  engineers 241
  specialized 153
  upgrading 49
Haskell 140
Hastings, Reed 154

hate, online 205
Hawking, Stephen 37
headphones 25, 36
headsets, VR 49, 229
healthcare 57, 65, 217, 234, 235
"Hello, World!" program 121
heuristics 236
hexadecimal system 40
hidden computers 64–5
high-level languages 110, 119, 122
Hollerith, Herman 99
home computers 123
home networks 145
home security systems 58
Hopper, Grace 114, 122
hosts, site 211
household devices 14
HTML (Hypertext Markup Language) 135, 162–3, 164, 166
HTTP (Hypertext Transfer Protocol) 124, 144, 148, 149, 198
HTTPS (Hypertext Transfer Protocol Secure) 95, 144, 149
hunger 216
hybrid cloud storage 152
hybrid computers 101
hybrid threats 157
hyperlinks 150, 151

I

IBM
  punch card 99
  RAMAC 350 91
icons 16, 138
IDE (integrated development environment) 126
identities 178–9, 187, 197
IDLE 131
Ids, unique 165
IF-THEN-ELSE control structure 108
illegal content 181
images
  ASCII 84
  computer screen 40
  encoding 90–1
imperative style of programming 120
implants 235
information, evaluating 211
inline styling 165
input data 109

input devices 42, 48, 53
input validation 171
Instagram 19
instant messaging 184
instructions, precise 69
integrated circuits 38, 39
integration testing 172
interaction, online 183
interest-based networks 197
internal hardware 48
Internet 144, 150–1, 194, 196
  digital divide 214–15
  and global development
    216–17
  net neutrality 212–13
Internet Protocol (IP) address
  148, 149, 191
Internet Service Provider (ISP)
  148, 212, 213
Internet of Things (IoT) 89, 125,
  129, 226–7
Internet.org 232
interpreters 82, 112, 132, 133
issue tracking software 173, 175

J

Java 128–9, 134
Java Virtual Machine (JVM)
  128, 140
JavaScript 134–5, 162, 166–7
Jobs, Steve 33, 123, 152
Johnson, Katherine 32

K

Kemeny, John G 123
keyboards 37, 41, 44, 48, 62, 210
keyloggers 22, 23, 156, 190
keywords 21, 105
Kilby, Jack 38, 39
Kodu 138–9
Kurtz, Thomas E. 123

L

LAN (local area network) 146
laptops 50, 51, 232
law, breaking the 182
LED 54, 55
Leibniz, Gottfried 82
lexing 113
libraries 113, 124, 129, 130, 135
light 90
LilyPad microcontrollers 54
linear searches 76

linkers 113
Lisp 119
location tracking 201
logging in, difficulty with 24
logic errors 114–15
logic expressions 105
logic gates 86–7
loops 109
Lovelace, Ada 31, 99, 218
low-level languages 110, 119
LSB (least significant bit) 82
lurkers 197

M

machine code 110, 111, 113,
  118, 122
machine learning 236
machine learning languages 141
Macs 51
magnetic tape 81
maintenance, software 175
maker movement 55
makerspaces 224
malware 23, 156–7, 159
MAN (metropolitan area
  network) 146
manuals 174
markup languages 163
mathematics 77, 95, 100,
  104, 239
Matsumoto, Yukihiro 132
Maya animation tool 127
media sharing 195
  networks 197
memory 43
merge sort 77
mesh topology 147
micro:bit 54, 55
microblogging 185
microphones 25, 92
Microsoft 33, 55, 146
  Kinect controller 62, 137, 139
  MS-DOS 33
  Store 200
  Windows 51
  Xbox 360 138
microtransactions 204
Minecraft 129
minority groups 213
model-view-controller design
  patterns 171
models 73
modular code 70
monitors 37, 44, 48
Moore, Gordon 39

motherboards 34–5, 48
motion-capture technology 228
mouse 37, 41, 44, 210
MSB (most significant bit) 82
Multicast 154
multiple data centers 153
music 92, 133, 154, 155
muting 202
Muzak 155

N

Nakamoto, Satoshi 230
Napier, John 31
NASA 41, 45, 131, 218
natural language 121
net neutrality 212–13
Netflix 213
networks 142–59
  closed and open 206–7
  hidden 73
  types of 146–7
  what is a network? 144–5
neural networks 237
news, and social networks 203
newsfeeds 195, 197
noise 101
NoiseSocket 148
nonfunctional tests 172
NoSQL databases 88

O

object-oriented programming
  (OOP) 107, 120, 128–9, 133,
  134, 138
objects 107, 133
One Laptop Per Child (OLPC) 232
onion router 158–9
online identities 178–9, 182
opcodes 111
open networks 207
operands 111
operating systems (OS) 16,
  44–5, 51
operators, Boolean 104, 105
optical discs 81
optimization 113
output data 109
output devices 36, 42, 49, 53
oversharing 199

P

pacemakers 235
packets 149

pareidolia 74
parental advice 191
parsing 113
passports, biometric 234
password grabbing 190
password managers 23
passwords 22, 23, 24
patterns
  altering 75
  recognizing 68, 74, 75
  using 74
peer-to-peer (P2P) networks 145
peripheral devices 36–7
personal computers 33
personal information, sharing
  186
phishing 22, 190
photo editing applications 17
photo sharing 185
physical computing 55
physics 138
PIN numbers 23
pixels 40, 90, 91
plant monitors, smart 59
PlayStation Network 205
plugboards 100
plug-ins 167
pop-ups 134
pornography 186
ports 34
power units 35
presentation software 18
printers 25, 36, 44, 49
privacy 65, 190–1, 227
  settings 187, 191
private-key cryptography 95
problem solving 68, 238
processing devices 48
profiles 178–9, 195, 202
program structures 108–9
programming 29
  early methods 98–9
  techniques 96–115
programming languages 29, 73,
  116–41
  breakthroughs 122–3
  function of 118–19
  future 140–1
  translation 110–11
  types of 120–1
Project Aquila 232
Project Loon 233
prosthetics 57, 234, 235
protocols 144, 148, 149
proxy servers 191
pseudocode 77

public-key cryptography 95
public/private chat 203
publishing, on social networks 203
punch cards 81, 98, 99, 122
Python 118, 130–1

Q

Quality Assurance (QA) testers 243
Quantum Computing Language (QCL) 141
qubits 141

R

R 140
railway maps 72
RAM (random-access memory) 34, 43, 49, 63, 81
ransomware 157
Raspberry Pi 54, 55, 123
rasterization 90
Real-time Streaming Protocol (RTSP) 148
Real-time Transport Protocol (RTP) 148
recycling 49, 164, 217
regression tests 173
remixing 69
removable hard drives 37
REPL (Read-Evaluate-Print Loop) 133
representational state transfer (REST) 125
research and development 242
resolution 91
resource sharing 145, 153
reviews, online 196
"Right to be Forgotten" law 199
ring topology 147
Ritchie, Dennis 110, 126
robots 41, 224
    home 59
    toys 61
ROM (read-only memory) 43
rootkits 156
routers 37, 151
routing 144, 149
RTOS (real-time operating systems) 45
Ruby 118, 132–3
runtime errors 115
Rust 140

S

satellites 29, 144, 151
saving work 15
scaling 170
scams 159
scanners 48
Schickard, William 31
Schrems, Max 179
science 238
Scratch 119, 136–7
ScratchJr 136
screen breaks 180
scripting languages 133
scripts 134, 137, 166
SD memory cards 15
search engines 20–1, 151, 211
    setting a default 20
search terms 21, 105
searching, effective 21
Searle, John 237
Secure Sockets Layer (SSL) 95
security
    APIs 125
    cloud storage 153
    cyber 22–3
    cyberbullying 188–9
    data packets 149
    hacking and privacy 190–1
    JavaScript 167
    malware 156–7
    networks 145
    online 185, 186–7
selectors 165
self-driving cars 102
self-harm 186
selfies 195
semantics 163
sensors 57, 61, 64, 65, 224, 226
servers 145
Shannon, Claude 86
sharing 198–9
shopping 64
Simple Mail Transfer Protocol (SMTP) 148
Skype 184
sleep patterns 180, 226
slide rules 100
slideshows 18
smart devices 58–9, 129
smartphones 19, 52–3, 58, 151, 180, 184, 200, 225, 226
smartwatches 56, 57
social engineering 22, 190
social media 29, 73, 89, 180, 182, 194–5

apps 200–1
    bubbles 206–7
    hackers 23
    platforms 196–7
    safety 187
    shared content 198–9
social networks 19, 73, 194, 197
    gaming and 204–5
    using 202–3
social publishing platforms 196
software 14, 41
    application 16–17
    developing and designing 168–9, 241
    errors 114-15
    maintenance and support 174–5
    planning ahead 170–1
    rental 153
    system 16
    testing 172–3
Software Development Life Cycle (SDLC) 168, 169
software engineering 240
solid-state drives (SSDs) 81
solutions, multiple 69
Sonic Pi 133
sound 25, 40
sound waves 92
source code 111
sources 211
space probes 45, 218
spaghetti code 170
spam 156
speakers 49
spell-checkers 221
spreadsheets 17
sprints 169
spying devices 65
spyware 156
SQL (Standard Query Language) 88, 140
star topology 147
steam 205
STEAM 238
steganography 90
STEM 238
stereoscopic vision 228
storage
    cloud 152–3
    devices 49
stored program computers 32
strategy design pattern 171
streaming 154–5
strong ties 206, 207
Stroustrup, Bjarne 127

stylesheets 164
subproblems 70, 71
substitution ciphers 94
supercomputers 33
support desks 174
switches 80, 83
switching pages (Kodu) 139
syntax 166
    errors 114
system administrators 242

T

tablets 52–3, 180, 200
Tabulating Machine 99
tags 163
TCP 154
technical writers 243
technology 238
televisions 28
testing, software 168, 172–3
text, display 40
texting 184
thinking skills 69
tongue, seeing with 235
topology 147
Tor network 158–9
Torpedo Data Computer (TDC) 100
touchscreen 52–3, 210
toys, digital 60–1
traffic control 64, 227
transgender people 219
transistors 38, 80, 83
translation 110–11, 118
Transmission Control Protocol (TCP) 149
transposition ciphers 94
trees 140
trending tools 89
trojans 156, 157
trolling 187, 205
truth tables 86, 87
tubes 83
Turing, Alan 95, 237
Turing test 237
tutorials 174
Twitter 19, 125, 207
two-factor authentication (2FA) 191, 201
TypeScript 140

U

UDP 154
unfriending 202

Unicast 154
Unicode 85
unit tests 172
universal language 141
updates 175
upgrades 175
Upton, Eben 123
URL (Uniform Resource Locator) 148
USB (universal serial bus) 15, 34
user acceptance testing 173
user guides 174
user stories 175
user-generated content 194
utilities 45

V

values, fixed 106
variables 73, 106, 107, 109
vectors 90
Venn diagrams 104, 108
Verilog 140
video
  applications 17
  calls 18, 61

cameras 64
cards 43
chatting 184
encoding 92, 93
sharing 185
streaming 154, 155
virtual reality (VR) 49, 221, 224, 228–9
virus protection 186
viruses 22, 156, 159
visual aids 18
visual programming languages 138–9
visual style of programming 120
visualization 89
voice commands 53
von Neumann architecture 42
von Neumann, John 42
VR sickness 229

W

WAN (wide area network) 146
Waterfall development style 169
Wayne, Ronald 33
weak ties 206, 207

wearable tech 54, 56–7, 61, 225
web apps 135
webcams 25, 36, 93, 137, 184, 186
webpages 151, 158, 162–3
websites 124, 151
  construction 18, 133, 134, 135
  deep web 158–9
  updates 175
WhatsApp 148
WHILE loops 109
white hat hackers 22
Wi-Fi connections 25, 37, 52, 226, 232
Wi-Fi mirroring devices 23
Windows PC 51
wireless networks 144
women 215, 218–19
word processors 17
workplace, Internet in 215
World War II 32
World Wide Web 150–1, 162, 198
World Wide Web Consortium (WC3) 162
worms 156, 157
Wozniak, Steve 33

X–Z

Xbox Live 205
Yahoo! 151
zero, concept of 30
zero-day vulnerabilities 175
zip programs 19
Zuckerberg, Mark 197, 232

Acknowledgments

DORLING KINDERSLEY would like to thank: Charvi Arora, Bharti Bedi, and Emma Grundy Haigh for editorial assistance; Revati Anand for design assistance; Surya Sarangi for picture research assistance; Victoria Pyke for proofreading; and Helen Peters for the index.

The publisher would like to thank the following for their kind permission to reproduce their photographs:

(Key: a-above; b-below/bottom; c-center; f-far; l-left; r-right; t-top)

31 Getty Images: Science & Society Picture Library / SSPL (br). **32 NASA:** (bc). **37 Alamy Stock Photo:** JEP Celebrity Photos (tr). **38 Getty Images:** Andrew Burton / Getty Images News (bl). **40 123RF.com:** Kornilov14 (cr). **42 Alamy Stock Photo:** Photo Researchers / Science History Images (bl). **45 NASA:** JHUAPL / SwRI (cr/New Horizons spacecraft, fcr). **55 Getty Images:** Jamie McCarthy / Getty Images Entertainment (cr). **57 Alamy Stock Photo:** DPA Picture Alliance (br). **60 akg-images:** Fototeca Gilardi (br). **69 123RF.com:** Wavebreak Media Ltd (tl). **71 NASA:** (bc). **73 123RF.com:** Rawpixel (bl); Balint Sebestyen (bc). **74 Alamy Stock Photo:** Paul Weston (cr). **77 Getty Images:** SVF2 / Universal Images Group (tr). **81 NASA:** (cr). **83 123RF.com:** Rangizzz (cra). **84 Dreamstime.com:** Artaniss8 (br). **86 Getty Images:** Alfred Eisenstaedt / The LIFE Picture Collection (cra). **91 Alamy Stock Photo:** Interfoto (br). **92 Dreamstime.com:** Choneschones (cr). **95 Alamy Stock Photo:** Fine Art Images / Heritage Image Partnership Ltd (cr). **101 123RF.com:** Andrija Markovic (br). **102 Getty Images:** Noah Berger / AFP (br). **105 Getty Images:** Photo 12 / Universal Images Group (cr). **114 Naval History and Heritage Command:** (cra). **119 NASA:** (bc). **122 Getty Images:** Bettmann (crb). **123 Alamy Stock Photo:** Keith Morris (br). **125 123RF.com:** Balein (cr). **129 Alamy Stock Photo:** Veryan Dale (br). **140 123RF.com:** Alexmit (crb). **141 123RF.com:** Ximagination (cra). **155 Dreamstime.com:** Thiradech (tr). **166 Getty Images:** Bloomberg (c). **179 Getty Images:** Joe Klamar / AFP (br). **195 123RF.com:** Ferli (cra). **197 123RF.com:** Panom Bounak (cla). **198 123RF.com:** Drserg (cra). **201 123RF.com:** Hkeita (br). **204 123RF.com:** Macrovector (cl). **215 Alamy Stock Photo:** Joerg Boethling (crb). **218 Alamy Stock Photo:** NASA Image Collection (cr). **221 Image courtesy Farida Bedwei:** (crb). **229 123RF.com:** Victor Zastolskiy (tl)

All other images © Dorling Kindersley
For further information see: **www.dkimages.com**